For Dad

"Our Bums"

"Our Bums"

The Brooklyn Dodgers in History, Memory and Popular Culture

DAVID KRELL

Foreword by Branch Rickey III

McFarland & Company, Inc., Publishers
Jefferson, North Carolina

LIBRARY OF CONGRESS CATALOGUING-IN-PUBLICATION DATA

Krell, David, 1967–
    "Our bums" : the Brooklyn Dodgers in history, memory and
popular culture / David Krell ; foreword by Branch Rickey III.
        p.   cm.
    Includes bibliographical references and index.

    ISBN 978-0-7864-7799-9 (softcover : acid free paper) ∞
    ISBN 978-1-4766-1973-6 (ebook)

    1. Brooklyn Dodgers (Baseball team)—History.   2. Baseball—
Social aspects—United States.   3. Baseball—United States—
History.   I. Title.

    GV875.B7K74 2015
    796.357'640974723—dc23   2015028978

BRITISH LIBRARY CATALOGUING DATA ARE AVAILABLE

Printed in the United States of America

McFarland & Company, Inc., Publishers
  Box 611, Jefferson, North Carolina 28640
  www.mcfarlandpub.com

Table of Contents

Acknowledgments

Writing a book is a solitary endeavor, but not one that truly isolates. On this journey of authorship, I benefited from the insight, enthusiasm, and experience of a special group of people whose contributions, both tangible and intangible, proved invaluable.

Family support was plentiful. My mother and my sister, Sheila Krell and Staci Krell, offered compliments, encouragement, and excitement before even one word was written. I am eternally grateful.

Jim Gates, Tim Wiles, Freddy Berowski, Cassidy Lent, and Matt Rothenberg at the National Baseball Hall of Fame and Museum performed a yeoman's job in helping me gather research on the Brooklyn Dodgers. With unparalleled patience, they guided me in my quest to enhance Brooklyn Dodgers scholarship. These guardians of baseball's legacy answered numerous questions about arcane areas of Dodgers history, allowed access to the Hall of Fame's files, and encouraged the pursuit of adding another book to the already burgeoning Dodgers library.

Branch Barrett Rickey, more commonly known in the media as Branch Rickey III, kindly accepted my invitation to write the Foreword. He was truly gracious about my approach to researching, studying, and documenting the team's history.

Ryan Fischer-Harbage is a literary agent proven to be a gentleman and a scholar in the publishing industry. Ryan's non-fiction book proposal class at Media Bistro provided a platform for this book's genesis. No author had a better mentor in navigating the complexities of the writing process from proposal to publication.

Megan Purcell gave me the gift of eagerness. With unbridled fervor at every juncture in this book's evolution, she advocated for the book's completion when naysayers appeared to multiply. I am humbled by her generosity.

Roger Kahn, the *éminence grise* of Dodgers historians, graciously hosted me at his home on a December afternoon and regaled me with stories about the impact that the Dodgers made on Brooklyn.

Carl Erskine brought the Brooklyn Dodgers of the Jackie Robinson era to life in our conversations about his playing days, Dodgers teammates, and the enduring mystique of the team.

Brian Biegel and Joshua Prager, chroniclers of the famous "Shot Heard Round the World," deconstructed the culture of the Dodgers-Giants rivalry and how it culminated on October 3, 1951, with Bobby Thomson's home run.

Giovanna Drpic, Vanessa Marmot, Kimberly Rae Miller, April Salazar Froncek, and Melanie Schutt offered editorial insight that broadened the book's perspective. Chelsea Choppy thoughtfully helped expand my collection of books about the Brooklyn Dodgers. I found useful research fodder in my interviews with Harold Friedman, Sol Gabay, Joel Hecker, and Fred Wilpon for my *Entertainment, Arts and Sports Law Journal* article referenced in the Preface.

Benjamin Gocker and Ivy Marvel were my liaisons at the Brooklyn Public Library. They walked me through the important process of securing rights to the library's photographs. John Horne and Connie Robinson performed the same vital function at the National Baseball Hall of Fame and Museum.

Elizabeth Fuller supplied priceless information about Marianne Moore's papers at the Rosenbach Museum and Library.

Dennis Northcott helped me find key documents concerning Branch Rickey in the George Howard Williams collection at the Missouri History Museum.

Mark Moore at the Cleveland Public Library offered the Martin Stone Files, which contained useful information about Jackie Robinson.

Jennifer Brathovde, Jeffrey Flannery, Patrick Kerwin, Bruce Kirby, Joseph Jackson, and Lewis Wyman at the Library of Congress aided my excavation of the Jackie Robinson Papers, Branch Rickey Papers, and Arthur Mann Papers.

A journalist's role model with a career spanning nearly 50 years as a reporter, columnist, and best-selling author, Bob Greene shared his views about the reach of the Brooklyn Dodgers across the country. On a personal level, he offered treasured words of encouragement during the home stretch of the book's completion.

Writing and speaking opportunities helped me hone my examination of baseball's place in society. It is a continual process, indeed. Special thanks to:

Marc Appelman, Jeff Schatzki, Deborah Jayne, and Jacob Pomrenke at the Society for American Baseball Research (SABR) for keeping the flames of baseball history alive through journals, conferences, and biographies;

Leslie Heaphy, Dick Clark and Larry Lester at SABR's Jerry Malloy Negro League Conference;

Peter Mancuso at SABR's Frederick Ivor-Campbell 19th Century Conference and NYC 19th Century Interdisciplinary Symposium;

Scott Fischthal and Neal Traven at SABR's 44th Annual Conference;

Lyle Spatz and Jan Finkel at SABR's Baseball Biography Project;

Cecilia Tan at SABR's *The Baseball Research Journal*; Stu Shea at SABR's *The National Pastime*;

Elissa Hecker at the New York State Bar Association's *Entertainment, Arts and Sports Law Journal*;

Craig Muder at the National Baseball Hall of Fame and Museum's *Memories and Dreams* magazine;

Bill Simons at the Cooperstown Symposium on Baseball and American Culture;

Richard Puerzer, Paula Uruburu, Natalie Datlof, and Deborah Lom at Hofstra University's 50th Anniversary of the New York Mets conference;

Shannon Stark, Keith Blacknick, and Dan Twohig at the Queens Baseball Convention;

Spencer Shangkuan, Mike Carlucci, and Joe Diglio at the website thesportspost.com; and

Martin Grams at the Mid-Atlantic Nostalgia Convention.

Finally, a highly significant part of this book rests on interviews with people willing to share memories. I am indebted to those who helped arrange the interviews and to those who participated: Linda Adler, Marty Adler, Dawna Amino, Scott Andes, Hildy Angius, Marty Appel, Dan Beck, Anne Berlin, Ronald Bittel, Woody Burgener, Mark Cane, Mela Cassvan, Lara Wiskin Cohen, Greg DiGiovanna, Sheldon Epps, Robert Garfinkel, Stan Goldberg, Mark Goldman, Bob Greene, Darlene Greene, Jill Greenwald, Stuart Greenwald, Ted Hollembeak, Ralph Hunter, Hugo Keesing, Ron Klein, Arnie Korfine, Jason Korfine, Nick Kostis, Connie Mack III, Ken Mailender, Howard McCormack, Lonette McKee, Paul Parker, David Povich, Maury Povich, Joshua Prager, Kenneth Prager, Arthur Ritz, Samuel Roberts, Kenneth Roth, Sari Roth, Eddie Seckler, Edward Schmidt, Ronald Schweiger, Debra Sifen, Louis Silverman, Gerald Stern, Walter Vail, John Willey, Jerry Wiskin.

Foreword
by Branch Rickey III

What legend it has become, a lore that still lingers even though more than 50 years have passed since Brooklyn was home to its beloved Dodgers.

The city was left behind in that move to the West Coast, but the "magic" and legend of that attachment lingers, and vibrantly so in many cases. Mr. Krell sets forth a compelling array of anecdotes, quotes, reflections, first-hand accounts, and well-researched history. He illuminates a subject often referred to conversationally in our era but not elaborated on much in writing. His telling of that all-encompassing web which was fan loyalty to the Brooklyn club can't fail to capture your imagination.

As Brooklynites of the 40s and 50s and their offspring have since spread out across our great country, there is hardly any hidden corner of our nation where one cannot or does not encounter that special someone still zealous to dwell on their personal history of family sense of loss and readily anxious to recall vividly that irrevocable dispossession when their treasured team was taken from them.

While it has taken this many decades for the bitterness to subside, the hollowness hasn't. Loyalists still cling, now having become stalwart in their convictions, and can surely be matched against those of any other affiliation in any sport. So many fans in other places who've also lost a team, faced with the indisputable finality firmly against their cause, have slipped into disappointed resignation. Instead, the Brooklyn allegiance seems to remain inflexible.

"*Our Bums*" is more than just a sports story, it is a reflective appraisal that shares with anyone willing to wonder why all the fuss about addiction of the most wonderful and tragic kind. A kind of Shakespearean roadmap for the modern sports fan to better understand what is passion when it owns you over anything your brain can try to impede.

As a grandson, I cannot in good conscience omit mention in this foreword of my grandfather, Branch Rickey, who had his own life so inextricably woven into that web, my father's, too, and really all three generations of our family at the time. That the family name will go down in history in attachment to Jackie Robinson is a legacy of profound honor—but my grandfather immediately recognized it would be wrong to claim recognition for that deed [signing Jackie to the Dodgers] since it had only reversed an ancient and odious injustice. "It would shame a man to take credit for that."

He was coming from a prodigious trail of success with the St. Louis Cardinals, a baseball team renowned for having built "the Gas House Gang" and in far fewer years had now assembled Snider, Hodges, Reese, Furillo, Reiser, Roe, and Erskine, only to add Robinson, Campanella, and Newcombe. The nucleus of what could soon be built into a dynasty of its own was where my grandfather's real ego was invested. The fabric of his working career was woven around developing championship teams and the Dodgers were becoming his signature achievement. The Rickey family's official connection to the Brooklyn club was unexpectedly severed along the way, much as would be that of the fans years later. And, similar to the fans, that fondness for an underdog, for players with shining personas and for the environment where Ebbets Field was the core of the essence of life, our family has never relinquished its dreams of what could have been.

So, here's to Mr. Krell. I commend him for putting in words the fairy tale and tragedy tied into one. In an era when our modern reality seems almost void of unblemished heroes or any glimmer of concepts like chivalry, *"Our Bums"* finds that Brooklyn was baseball's Camelot.

Branch Rickey III—*also known as Branch Barrett Rickey—is the president of the Pacific Coast League, a position he has held since 1998. Previously the president of the American Association, he also worked in scouting and as the director of player development for the Pittsburgh Pirates and the Cincinnati Reds.*

Preface

There are few things more emotionally powerful than a memory. My earliest baseball memory is playing with my paternal grandmother, Rebecca Krell, using a plastic ball and a plastic bat in the backyard of my family's home in Springfield, New Jersey. I don't know the exact date, but my best guess places it circa 1971, when I was four years old. She documented the event in a letter indicating my newfound passion. One section stands out: "When we were playing baseball, you said, 'I love this game,' and you didn't want to stop. I don't blame you—it is a good game. Not like football, where so many get broken bones! Of course, you will get better and better if you practice."

A few years later, my Little League career began. Practice, I did. Improve, I didn't. Hardly stellar, I had one moment of glory. It occurred at the Springfield Community Pool's baseball field, the crown jewel in Springfield's baseball system for one simple reason—it has lights. Every Little League team played at least one night game there. In the distance, you could see the illuminated tower of the Springfield Presbyterian Church. Built in the mid–18th century, it was—and still is—a town landmark. Further lighting the suburban backdrop was the neon sign for the Springfield branch of The Money Store, an alternative lending institution made famous by Phil Rizzuto's ubiquitous television commercials in the New York City metropolitan area during the 1970s and 1980s.

A night game at the pool's baseball field was an event, indeed.

Possessing a modicum of athletic talent with an average right arm, I played second base because I could easily make the throw to first base. One night, a batter smacked the ball in my direction. Instinct overcame fear; I took a few steps to my left, stuck out my glove, and the ball stayed in the webbing. I don't think anyone was more surprised than me. My self-esteem skyrocketed thanks to praise from teammates, cheers from the crowd, and an inner sense of satisfaction. It was, however, a short-lived experience. When the umpire stuck out his hand, I shook it. He said, "I want the ball."

Mickey Mantle greeted by Yogi Berra (left), Joe Collins (15), and Hank Bauer (9) after driving them home with a grand slam against the Brooklyn Dodgers in the 1953 World Series (National Baseball Hall of Fame Library, Cooperstown, New York).

And so, I learned that baseball glory is fleeting.

Playing baseball was just one part of enjoying the sport. Where other kids were content to simply play the game, I needed more to sate my appetite for baseball knowledge. John M. Rosenburg solved my problem with *The Story of Baseball*, an oversized, hardcover book for children, first published by Random House in 1962 and updated in several versions until 1977. Rosenburg traced the history of baseball from the sport's genesis to the present with brief but informative chapters. Photographs occupied space on nearly every page. A records section detailed the greatest players and their statistics.

And I devoured it all.

I read *The Story of Baseball* after Little League games, on rainy Sunday afternoons, and during cold winter months as I waited for the ritual of baseball's renewal, beginning with spring training. I shepherded it to the apartment of my maternal grandmother, Rose Scherer, to keep me occupied when I slept over. *The Story of Baseball* had a dual purpose—a literary companion functioning as a passport to the touchstones, lore, and history of baseball. It's where I discovered the 1919 Black Sox scandal, Carl Hubbell striking out five consecutive batters in the 1934 All-Star Game, and Jackie Robinson breaking the color line with the Brooklyn Dodgers.

My quest for baseball history didn't stop with Rosenburg's opus, though.

A few days each year, our elementary school received the Arrow Book Club catalog boasting an abundance of literature for children. We selected our books for purchase, then waited a few weeks for their arrival. Naturally, I selected books from the sports genre, for example, *Great Baseball Pitchers*, *Heroes of the Major Leagues*, and *Unsung Heroes of the Major Leagues*. They remain in my collection. Now I can add my own book to it.

Our Bums was born from a 2011 article that I wrote for the New York State Bar Association's "Entertainment, Arts and Sports Law Journal" about an early 1990s case involving the Brooklyn Dodgers name—*Stealing Home: Major League Baseball Properties, Inc. v. Sed Non Olet Denarius, Ltd. and the Glory, Heartbreak, and Nostalgia of the Brooklyn Dodgers*. Restaurant entrepreneurs started The Brooklyn Dodger Sports Bar and Restaurant, an enterprise that caught the attention of the Los Angeles Dodgers and Major League Baseball. Represented by the powerhouse firm of Willkie Farr & Gallagher, they sued on the basis of infringement. The small firm of Fischetti & Russo represented the restaurant owners.

David beat Goliath.

In its ruling for the restaurant owners, the Second Circuit Court of Appeals relied partially on the Dodgers' abandonment of Brooklyn after the 1957 season and consequent minimal use of the Brooklyn Dodgers trademark.

To pursue the challenge of writing a book about the Brooklyn Dodgers, I entered a writing workshop at Media Bistro, a continuing education school with an ampleness of programs for writers. My journey of research took me to the National Baseball Hall of Fame and Museum, where the A. Bartlett Giamatti Research Center contains thousands of files, including letters, articles, and biographical files on every baseball player who has played in the major leagues. I also researched the collections of Branch Rickey, Jackie Robinson, and Rickey confidante Arthur Mann housed at the Library of Congress. My methodology was simple—turn over every page. Laborious, to be sure, research has its rewards—adrenaline raced through my veins when I held Jackie Robinson's handwritten letter to Branch Rickey after Rickey left the Dodgers.

I tracked down every book related to the Dodgers that I could find through Willis Monie Books in Cooperstown and Amazon.com. The Pro-Quest database provided a gateway to digitized versions of newspapers, including the *New York Times* and the *Los Angeles Times*. The New York Public Library's microfilm collection of newspapers was an invaluable resource, including one newspaper that is vital to any researcher involved in Brooklyn Dodgers scholarship—the *Brooklyn Daily Eagle*. Documentaries, movies, novels, songs, poems, and television shows featuring the Dodgers helped me address the popular culture angle.

If the heart of this book is comprised of stories unearthed from archival newspaper articles, out-of-print books, and popular culture offerings, then the book's soul is comprised of the memories of Brooklyn Dodgers fans. By using the phrase "Brooklyn Dodgers" in Google searches and Google Alerts, I found fans willing to share their experiences about living in Brooklyn during the team's heyday between 1947 and 1957.

Their tales of living in Brooklyn, going to Ebbets Field, and rooting for the Dodgers deserved to be chronicled. Each person told a different story in the same way—with an affection that went beyond recounting a memory. During several interviews, fans who are septuagenarians and octogenarians told me that talking about the Brooklyn Dodgers made them feel like they were kids again. It was not unusual to hear a choked-up voice.

My father, though he is no longer here, cast a huge presence as I wrote this book. His story is chronicled in the Prologue and the Epilogue.

Taking on the challenge of authoring a nonfiction book requires emotional, mental, and physical stamina. Passion for research and writing can overcome these challenges, no matter how fearsome they appear. But what ignites that passion? It's different for everyone. The first research paper that I ever wrote was in sixth grade for Ms. Remus at Florence M. Gaudineer Junior High School. My topic: William Shakespeare. I dove into every area of Shakespeare's life—birth, death, family, plays, the Globe Theatre, London. Immediately, I embraced the challenge of delving into a topic to uncover nuggets of information, organize them, and create a narrative. It felt natural.

With a precise outline and a narrative of Shakespeare's life captured through my best penmanship, I handed in the paper right before Thanksgiving. About a month later, right before Winter Break, Ms. Remus returned our papers. I got a 4.0, which is equivalent to an A+. Ms. Remus wrote, "You really exhausted the topic!" I floated on air the whole way home.

Coincidentally, I am writing this preface and completing the final draft of the manuscript exactly 36 years to the day that I finished and dated my sixth grade Shakespeare report. What I learned about the rewards of research, persistence, and curiosity in a junior high school classroom remain with me.

Some things never change. The best things never do.

Prologue:
"He sure hit the hell out of that one"

Morgues were louder.

When Mickey Mantle crushed a Russ Meyer pitch for a grand slam in Game 5 of the 1953 World Series between the Brooklyn Dodgers and the New York Yankees, he muted 36,775 people in a ballpark now considered a baseball cathedral, then considered Brooklyn's second home. Ebbets Field. Not everyone in attendance on that October afternoon was a Dodgers fan. But the silence of Brooklynites drowned any outbursts from the opposition. Once again, those pinstriped Adonises of the Bronx eclipsed the Dodgers.

"The sun still shone brilliantly for the fifth game of the 1953 world series [*sic*] at Ebbets Field yesterday. But for Brooklyn everything went black in mid-afternoon," wrote John Drebinger of the *New York Times*.[1] With his legendary eloquence, Red Smith of the *New York Herald Tribune* wrote, "At 3 o'clock he walked to the mound and threw one to Roy Campanella. It didn't get there."[2]

Campanella was more succinct, but no less poetic for baseball fans. "He sure hit the hell out of that one," Campanella said.[3] Respect laced his mourning.

Mantle's stroke echoed a moment from the 1920 World Series, when Elmer Smith of the Cleveland Indians hit a grand slam at Cleveland's League Park. In the same game, Indians second baseman Bill Wambsganss made an unassisted triple play against the Brooklyn team, then known as the Robins. When Mantle hit his grand slam, he extended the Yankees' lead in Game 5 from 2–1 to 6–1. The Yankees eventually won the game, 11–7. And they won the 1953 World Series in six games.

"When you throw your best pitch and a guy hits it like that Mantle did, then there's just nothing you can do about it," said Meyer, a 15–5 pitcher during the regular season.[4] Meyer had sought counsel from fellow Dodgers pitcher Carl Erskine, who succeeded against Mantle in Game 4. "I struck out Mickey Mantle four straight times the day before he hit the grand slam," explains Erskine. "Russ Meyer asked me what pitches I used to strike out Mantle. I said that he'd chase the curveball in the dirt. Meyer got the call for Game Four and Mantle pounded his overhand curveball. Russ had a big curveball, but it wasn't a sharp curve."[5]

Mantle nearly didn't make the Yankees lineup for Game 5. Rud Rennie of the *New York Herald Tribune* added a touch of sarcasm when he reported the incident that threatened to sideline the slugger from Oklahoma:

> Casey Stengel, the Yankee manager, almost did not play Mantle. The center-fielder, eager to take another turn at bat in practice, came around the batting cage to get to the plate just as Irv Noren sliced a line drive in his direction. The ball struck Mantle hard on the left hand and left leg and, for a while, it was doubtful whether he would be able to play. Gus Mauch, the Yankee trainer, froze the hand and the leg as an emergency treatment to make it possible for him to get into the game.
>
> With his hand unfrozen, Mantle had struck out seven times. Maybe it would be good if Mauch kept Mantle frozen for the remainder of the series.[6]

Mantle's thawed hand allowed him to take Meyer's first pitch over the fence after Dodgers manager Charlie Dressen sent rookie pitcher Johnny Podres to the showers. Another Dodgers rookie played in his first World Series in 1953—James William "Junior" Gilliam. In a year of other beginnings—Lucy Ricardo giving birth to Little Ricky on *I Love Lucy*, Chevrolet debuting its Corvette, and Ian Fleming introducing James Bond in the novel *Casino Royale*—Gilliam excelled, winning the National League Rookie of the Year Award. He led the National League with 17 triples, led the Dodgers with 125 runs scored, and batted .278. In the field, he succeeded Dodgers favorite Jackie Robinson at second base as Robinson moved to third base and the outfield.

Earlier that October 4 morning, while the Dodgers and Yankees prepared for their latest battle, a ringing telephone pierced the Sunday morning quiet of 72 Mapes Avenue in the Weequahic section of Newark, New Jersey. Weequahic, a middle-class Jewish area, was a little more than a decade away from the launch of an exodus leading Newarkers to the surrounding suburbs—Springfield, Cranford, Westfield, and dozens of others. In its mid–20th century heyday, Weequahic thrived with merchants on Bergen Street and Chancellor Avenue, fraternities and sororities for teenagers, and 17 synagogues.[7]

A 17-year-old boy, just a few years younger than Podres, answered the phone. That boy later became my father, Carl Krell.

The caller was Joe Sirotkin, a cousin who had business in his blood. Joe was a Depression Era kid who started companies in his 20s, building them into arenas of allegiances for his employees—some stayed with Joe for more than 50 years, till he passed away at the age of 90 in 2013. He rewarded loyalty with loyalty. It was a trait my father not only admired, but also espoused.

Joe used prime seats at New York City sporting events as coinage of appreciation for clients. But on this day, he had an extra ticket for Game 5. Joe offered it to my father, who began his odyssey to Ebbets Field at Pennsylvania Station in Newark. He rode the Hudson and Manhattan Railroad train, traveling through the Uptown Hudson Tubes under the Hudson River to the 33rd Street stop in Manhattan's Greeley Square, a stone's throw from Herald Square and Macy's on the corner of 34th Street and 7th Avenue. Then he took the subway to Brooklyn's Prospect Park station for the final leg of the journey to baseball nirvana. Crowned with wavy black hair, his head swiveled with the slightness of a pendulum whose clock needed winding. Telescoping the crowd approaching Ebbets Field, his blue eyes searched for openings amongst the throngs of Dodgers worshippers anticipating a victory to break the 2–2 tie in the Series.

Navigating through the stadium's rotunda, he looked up at the iconic baseball-shaped chandelier with white baseballs and crossed bats while conversation enveloped him. It was everywhere, welcoming anyone caring to join. Chatter at Ebbets Field vocalized a passion for baseball enhanced by a Brooklynite's confidence in dissecting the game. It was part of the Ebbets Field culture with no requirement for entry. In a five-part series entitled *Assorted Metropolitan Crowds* for the *New York World-Telegram* in 1932, Joseph Lilly explained:

"Who'll he pitch—Vance or Clark?"

A momentous question in Flatbush. Stand in the rotunda of Ebbets Field any day the Brooklyn Dodgers are playing at home and you'll hear nothing else but such questions—and the answers to them—as the fans go into the stands.

And not only the answers, but the rejoinders:—"Why, he'll pitch Vance because"—"Why, he won't be dumb enough to pitch Vance, and I'll tell you why"—

The arguments start the minute the crowd begins to arrive, and they do not stop until the last man is out in the ninth.[8]

As my father reached his seat, suited gentlemen looked askance at him. Their arched eyebrows indicated curiosity, not contempt, as they regarded the young interloper while pondering his reasons for intruding the inner sanctum of prized seats reserved for the wealthy business class. This section belonged to men, after all, not boys. They looked at one another for an answer, but found equal puzzlement. Their curiosity subsided with Podres' first pitch as the teenager displayed an intellect, appreciation, and understanding of the game's nuances, players, and history seldom paralleled by even a diehard baseball fan.

By the end of the 1960s, long after the Dodgers left—some say abandoned—Brooklyn for Los Angeles, my father evolved into a man with aspirations for a quiet, successful life. He obtained a B.S. in Economics and an M.B.A. in Finance from NYU, married a legal secretary—my mother, Sheila Scherer—from the Weequahic neighborhood, lived in a garden apartment on Vine Street in Elizabeth for eight years, started a career in real estate appraising with a specialty in tax appeals for industrial and commercial real estate, and moved with his wife and two children to a house in the northern New Jersey suburb of Springfield, where he lived for 29 years till he passed away at 63 in 1999.

Twenty-five years after the Mantle grand slam, history repeated itself as a successful friend of the family offered World Series tickets to my father. It was another Dodgers-Yankees matchup. This time, I was there. Only after writing this book did I fully comprehend the importance of these bookend events concerning baseball, the Brooklyn Dodgers, and fathers and sons.

By the end of this story, so will you.

1st Inning:
One Borough Under Blue

"It was Brooklyn against the world. They were not only complete fanatics, but they knew baseball like the fans of no other city. It was exciting to play there. It was a treat. I walked into that crummy, flyblown park as Brooklyn manager for nine years, and every time I entered, my pulse quickened and my spirits soared."[1]—Leo Durocher

To be a Brooklyn Dodgers fan in the 1950s was to experience magic.

A Dodgers home game at Ebbets Field was neither a pastime nor an exercise in leisure. It was a way of life in the borough initially named Breucklen by the Dutch. Brooklynites believed the Dodgers' continued existence to be a certainty, like the Sun rising in the East, fireworks on July 4, and gravity. "There was an intimacy about Ebbets Field that you don't forget," said Don Drysdale. "If you are a starting pitcher, you warmed up in front of the dugout before the game, not in the bullpen. You felt as though the fans were right on top of you, because they almost were. It was a carnival atmosphere, small and always jumping."[2]

Kids met their Dodgers heroes on WOR's *Happy Felton's Knothole Gang*, a live television show revolving around a competition at Ebbets Field before Dodgers home games. Dodgers judged the baseball skills of three Little Leaguers, ultimately choosing one as the best player. During the games, music filled the Ebbets Field air, thanks to the Dodgers Symphony band, Hilda Chester and her cowbell, and organist Gladys Gooding. An umpire's call favoring the opposition triggered a rendition of "Three Blind Mice."

A blue script font for the "Dodgers" name affixed to the team's jerseys provided a hint of elegance for a fan base steeped in Brooklynese, a dialect that shatters pronunciations.

English: "I hurt myself slipping on an oil slick."

Brooklynese: "I hoyt myself slippin' on an earl slick."

The Brooklyn Dodgers were more than players; they were sentinels patrolling the verdant kingdom at 55 Sullivan Place, an address no longer on Brooklyn's post office rolls. Bats, their weapons. Gloves, their shields. Jackie Robinson broke racial boundaries, Roy Campanella overpowered National League pitching, and Carl Furillo mastered baseball caroms off Ebbets Field's idiosyncratic right field wall. "Ballplayers liked to play in Brooklyn because Brooklyn fans knew baseball better than any other fans in the league," explained Sandy Koufax, a born and bred Brooklynite, in Koufax's 1966 eponymous autobiography cowritten with Ed Linn. "Hard as they rooted for the Dodgers, they appreciated a great play or a great player no matter where he came from."[3]

Nicholas Kostis emigrated from Brooklyn to Cleveland decades ago, but time spent in the glow of Indians lore has not dimmed Kostis' affection for the Dodgers. Owner of Cleveland's Pickwick & Frolic Restaurant and Club, Kostis also saw Game 5 of the 1953 World Series from a vantage point far removed from my father's. Very far removed.

Kostis was a student at P.S. 9 on Vanderbilt Avenue and Sterling Avenue, within shouting distance of Grand Army Plaza, when his exploits at Game 5 achieved notice by a photographer for the *New York Times*:

The Dodgers team was not just a bunch of guys that played baseball. They touched our hearts. Brooklyn was a special place in those days and nothing contributed to it more than the Dodgers' presence. There was always optimism in the air. When the Dodgers were in the World Series, sometimes the school schedule would be abbreviated to allow us to listen to the ball game on the radio.

For Game 5, we either cut school or were off school. The atmosphere was one of excitement about being in the series and Game 5 was an important game. I lived at 376 St. John's Place, an apartment building between Washington Avenue and Underhill Avenue, about five or six blocks from Ebbets Field. We were close to the Brooklyn Museum and Eastern Parkway.

My family was on the second floor in a railroad apartment. Eileen Bannon lived on the first floor. Her father was the building's superintendent. John McNamara lived four buildings down from us. Don Curristan lived three buildings down.

We were friends, but Don, Eileen, and John went to school at St. Teresa's while I went to P.S. 9. We rode our bikes down Bedford Avenue to get to Ebbets Field. We wished and hoped for some way to get into the stands, but we didn't quite know how we would do it. Anyway, we knew about big swing doors that opened for the groundskeepers to access the field. The doors were 20–30 feet high. And there was a crack where the doors met in the middle. We could see Duke Snider through the crack!

A photographer saw us and asked us to hold our pose so he could take our picture. He asked what we were looking at and he took the photo. When I got home, I told my mom because my dad was at work. He had a place on Furman Street on the docks where he ran a vending coin operated manufacturing and remanufacturing business. So, I told my mother about the photographer. She didn't think much of it. Actually, she probably thought I either made up the scenario or exaggerated it.

The next day, I went to the newsstand and flipped open the *New York Times*. There we were! I ran home and showed my mother. Boy, did her tune change! She bought all the papers at the newsstand!

Being at the World Series for us kids was sourced in our wanting to be close to the excitement and be among the believers that day. We'll never have that kind of closeness again.[4]

To be a Brooklyn Dodgers fan in the 1950s was to bathe in glory's warmth and prostrate oneself from heartbreak's chill.

When the Dodgers lost the 1950 National League pennant to the Philadelphia Phillies, they did it on the last day of the season. Pitching ace Robin Roberts, he of the pinpoint fastball, led the Phillies to victory. But the Dodgers' achievements in 1950 earmarked the Brooklyn ball club as a powerhouse. Duke Snider hit three home runs in a Memorial Day game as did Roy Campanella on August 26. Five days after Campanella's display of power, Gil Hodges smacked four home runs in a night game at Ebbets Field against the Boston Braves, each home run off a different pitcher—Warren Spahn, Norman Roy, Bob Hall, and Johnny Antonelli. Two lefties, two righties.

These were not isolated instances of excellence. Consistency flowed through the 1950 Dodgers lineup, culminating in a National League roster awash in Dodger blue for the All-Star Game: Roy Campanella, Gil Hodges, Don Newcombe, Pee Wee Reese, Jackie Robinson, Preacher Roe, and Duke Snider.

The Dodgers pounced on the opposition in 1951 like a panther devouring a gazelle. By the middle of August, the Dodgers held a lead of 13½ games over their cross-town archrivals, the New York Giants. As the humid days of August submitted to the cool breezes of September, the Giants ascended the National League standings. Both teams ended the season with matching win-loss records. To determine which team would represent the National League in the 1951 World Series, a three-game play-off commenced.

The Giants and the Dodgers split the first two games. And then, the Dodgers' grand collapse concluded with a final slice through the prism of hope. Russ Hodges' repeated five-word proclamation on a radio broadcast summarized the finish: "The Giants win the pennant!" There was no salve for this wound created in storybook fashion on an overcast October day at the Polo Grounds.

It happened in the bottom of the ninth inning of Game Three, thanks to a Bobby Thomson home run that immortalized Thomson and Dodgers pitcher Ralph Branca.

Prompted by the furor ignited by his 2001 article in *The Wall Street Journal* revealing a sign-stealing scheme at the Polo Grounds,[5] Joshua Prager excavated the 1951 season in his 2008 book *The Echoing Green*, establishing evidence that the Giants knew the opposing team's pitches—an envoy in the Center Field offices of the Polo Grounds used a spyglass to determine the catcher's signs, then he relayed them through a codified electrical system to a buzzer in the bullpen, where another Giant communicated the sign to the batter, for example, by tossing a ball in the air.

Thomson admitted to Prager that he knew Giants coach Herman Franks was in the bullpen informing batters on October 3, 1951. Whether Thomson knew the sign, though, remained in doubt. "I'd have to say more no than yes," said Thomson, explaining that his preoccupation with teammate Don Mueller's injury, among other events during the game, may have diverted his attention.[6] Thomson confirmed to *USA Today* that he knew signs because of the spyglass scheme, but doubled down on his affirmation of being in the dark regarding the fatal pitch. "We did steal signs and I did take some, and I don't feel good about it. But I didn't get the sign on that pitch. Ralph says I did, and if that eases the burden of what he's carried around all these years, I'm glad for that."[7]

When Thomson hit the home run, it generated a feeling of *déjà vu*. Hope, once again, teased Dodger fans like a Homecoming Queen who flirts with the male student body but brings the quarterback from a rival school to the Homecoming Dance.

Brooklyn Dodgers fans in the 1950s represented a kaleidoscope of ethnicity. Jews. Poles. Italians. Irish. Germans. Hispanic. Black. Asian.

Diversity mirrors Brooklyn's official motto inspired by the original Dutch settlers—"In Unity There Is Strength"—and it continues into the 21st century. Nowhere was the borough more unified than within Ebbets Field. Marty Adler, founder of the Brooklyn Dodgers Hall of Fame, believed that Brooklyn's populace used baseball as a portal to the American experience:

> You can't talk about the Brooklyn Dodgers unless you talk about the makeup of the people. Many people in Brooklyn during the mid–20th century were relatively new citizens of the United States. Baseball is part of our country's DNA.

What better way for people to become ingrained in the national spirit than joining in the cheering and rooting for a baseball team? All of these groups of immigrants spoke different languages, ate different foods, and worshipped in different religions. They came together to root for the one dynamic and the one constant in the borough.[8]

Fred Wilpon, owner of the New York Mets and a Brooklyn native, shares the view that the Dodgers served as a gateway to assimilation:

> I'm a kid who grew up in Brooklyn. I was steeped in being a very avid Dodger fan. I have great memories of going to a dozen or more ball games with my dad. That was joyous. I remember being ten years old and my dad holding my hand as we walked into Ebbets Field after we got hot dogs on Sullivan Street.
>
> As a sandlot player, I followed the Dodgers. Everyone I knew was a Dodger fan or a Yankee fan. The era of the 1930s and 1940s was a time of cultural change. My family came from Europe, settled in America, and wanted education. Baseball became a passionate focus for that era. We were passionate about this lovable team that was bumbling. And then, they evolved into a very good team.[9]

Baseball provided a common language as the Dodgers united the borough from high society millionaires in Brooklyn Heights to working class families in Greenpoint, from beachgoers at Coney Island to Italian and Jewish immigrants settling in Bensonhurst. Brooklynites fused behind the Dodgers, building a collective identity through the emperors of Ebbets Field.

One nation under God. One borough under blue.

To be a Brooklyn Dodgers fan in the 1950s was to know epic loss.

After the 1957 season, Dodgers owner Walter O'Malley left Brooklyn in his wake when he guided the borough's flagship sports team to the beachhead of Los Angeles. His maneuver lacerated the hearts of Dodgers fans. Consequently, they formed a cohesive hatred for their traitorous enemy equal to—maybe even greater than—their zeal for the team.

O'Malley's villainous status endures, rightly or wrongly, as a malevolent counterweight to nostalgic joy—he robbed the fans' identity cornerstone when he countenanced a move to bring Major League Baseball to the West Coast in the form of the Dodgers. An often-told joke remains in circulation: "A guy says to his friend, 'If you were in a room with Hitler, Stalin, and Walter O'Malley and you had a gun with two bullets, what would you do?' The friend says, 'Shoot O'Malley twice.'"

Their spirit amputated, Dodgers fans mourned the loss represented by the soulless void of a silent Ebbets Field. Obsolete, decaying, and vacant as a once gloried dominion of baseball excellence, Ebbets Field no longer served a valuable function. It began as the innovative brainchild of then-owner Charles Ebbets in 1913, symbolized a nucleic fixture for Brooklyn, and aged into an archaic edifice balancing on the precipice of ignominy. Its storied life ended in 1960 with demolition that placed an arctic exclamation point at the end of an already frosty sentence—The Brooklyn Dodgers are no more!

If fans run their fingers over the memories, they feel scars that never fully healed.

O'Malley's decision to move the Dodgers a continent away from Brooklyn after the 1957 season was anchored by a sweetheart deal with the power brokers of Los Angeles—they gave him the real estate of Chavez Ravine gratis for the new Dodger Stadium. Not since Peter Minuit purchased Manhattan Island for 60 guilders on behalf of the Dutch had a land deal bared such incomparable value for the land's new settlers.

The Dodgers began their southern California tenure in the Los Angeles Memorial Coliseum while sprawl, sunshine, and suburbs replaced streets, stoops, and subways as the backdrops for the team's exploits. Full of ardor for its adopted sons, Los Angeles had sudden custody of a baseball heritage that began in the 1880s with an urban fan base significantly comprised of immigrants. "As for the attitude and knowledge of Dodger fans in the Coliseum, it was unfair to compare them with the fans in Brooklyn for one very simple reason. It was unfair to compare *any* fans anywhere with those fans in Brooklyn,"[10] said Don Drysdale.

The Los Angeles Dodgers emblemized a city expanding to become a metropolitan force in commerce, population, and industry. The Brooklyn Dodgers, on the other hand, formed a communal thread throughout Brooklyn. During the Dodgers' last season in Brooklyn, radio announcer Vin Scully seamlessly wove community outreach into his broadcast of the Dodgers-Cubs game on WMGM 1050 AM on June 4, 1957.

> In the Dodger bullpen and gee, it could be quite a night. Joe Pignatano is a Brooklyn boy. He has not caught a pitch in the major leagues and he's very close to it. He appeared as a pinch runner but he's never been behind the plate. Wouldn't it be a great thing to have the boy in the game tonight, if the Dodgers, with this comfortable lead of six-nothing might very well decide now to give him a chance.
>
> The oh-and-one pitch to Don Zimmer. Curveball hit slowly to third. Banks up with it. Goes back to Morgan. They get one. On to first. In time for the double play. And down to third goes Carl Erskine. So, the double play, five to four to three.

18

Say, I tell you what. You might know the Pignatanos. If you do, maybe his wife [is] taking care of the baby. Not watching or listening to the ball game. Give her a call. Looks like Joe's gonna break into the major leagues tonight!"[11]

Community. That's the Brooklyn way.

Pignatano got one hit in two at bats, the Dodgers won, 7–5, and Koufax struck out 12, an early indication of his future phenom status. Scully's request reflects an era when you could walk down any street in Brooklyn and not miss a pitch. Every storefront, every car, and every open window had a radio tuned to the Dodgers game with the voice of Scully, Red Barber, or Connie Desmond serving as a Greek chorus broadcasting the exploits of the boys of summer. It was magical, soon to be ephemeral because of Walter O'Malley.

O'Malley wasn't the first team owner to relocate—the Braves left Boston for Milwaukee in 1953 and the rival Yankees began their lives in 1901 as the Baltimore Orioles. Sports teams are not public trusts, though that is irrelevant for fans of the Brooklyn Dodgers, as is scholarship supporting a pro–O'Malley thesis—O'Malley reluctantly left Brooklyn after battling with New York City's pre-eminent power broker, Robert Moses, to keep the team in the borough. Moses, chairman of New York City's Triborough Bridge Authority, indicated indifference regarding O'Malley's desires to keep the Dodgers in Brooklyn. Resting his decision on legal principles, he refused to condemn land for O'Malley to construct a new stadium.

Moses' exercise of power—or refusal to exercise it—does not, however, absolve O'Malley of treason on the streets of Brooklyn. Moreover, the burden on Brooklyn's soul increases from the absence of Ebbets Field and the presence of the words "Los Angeles" in dialogue, reports, or paraphernalia concerning the Dodgers. The phrase "Los Angeles Dodgers" is intellectually illogical, further exposing the wound of abandonment for fans of the Brooklyn Dodgers. The name "Dodgers" proclaims a Brooklyn legacy of trolleys that dominated mass transportation in the borough more than a century ago. Pedestrians had to "dodge" them to avoid injury. Or worse. Once called the "Trolley Dodgers," the team's moniker shortened to "Dodgers."

Illogicality regarding team names is not limited to Brooklyn, certainly. When the aptly named New Orleans Jazz moved from the rum-soaked environs of Bourbon Street to Utah's mountainous land of sister wives, Mormons, and the Osmonds, the team's name remained. Gillespie, Coltrane, and Davis don't exactly inspire visions of Salt Lake City, though.

The Colts, named for the noble equine gods governing the Preakness Stakes, reflected geographic pride as Baltimore's gridiron emblem. Less so in Indianapolis, a Midwestern metropolis recognized not as an equestrian center, but as an auto-racing mecca with devotees that pledge allegiance to a checkered flag.

Debuting in 2009, Citi Field—the home stadium for the New York Mets—venerates Ebbets Field with a design mirroring the Brooklyn ballpark. The stadium's Jackie Robinson Rotunda welcomes fans with pictures, videos, and quotes testifying to Mr. Robinson's courage. Wilpon says:

> This was a team that people sort of wrapped their arms around. Ebbets Field was small. You felt close to the event. The players lived in Bay Ridge and Flatbush. Brooklyn people are very passionate and they're passionate about their teams. Because I was part of the emotion of the Brooklyn Dodgers, I thought that we could possibly keep that feeling alive with the new stadium's design.
>
> I have fond memories of the Brooklyn Dodgers in the Jackie Robinson era. If you couple that with my feeling of Jackie Robinson's importance irrespective of his status as a Dodger, Citi Field's Jackie Robinson Rotunda honors him properly. He is an American icon who defined integrity.
>
> I know Mrs. Robinson very well since my teenage years. I also knew Jackie Robinson. I deeply felt that this man's contribution to baseball and society demanded more than a plaque or statue. We received some objections that the rotunda was too focused on the Dodgers. But we're trying to keep the unique heritage of the Dodgers alive through the stadium's architecture and the rotunda.[12]

Brooklyn Dodgers fans in the 1950s were a part of a family at Ebbets Field and another family at home. Throughout Brooklyn, families two or three generations deep lived in the same neighborhood, building, or apartment. Arnie Korfine grew up on Ocean Parkway in a two-family house where the Dodgers commanded attention, even from those who did not speak English:

> My grandmother came here in 1905 from Russia. She didn't speak three words of English, but she listened to the game broadcasts on a huge RCA Victor console radio in the dining room. I would lie on the floor while she darned socks. Every eight or ten minutes, she remarked in Yiddish, "What a fine man!" My grandmother was talking about Red Barber. Just the romance of his voice with that lyrical, southern accent transcended language. When Vin Scully took over, he garnered the same respect. During the Dodgers' early years in Los Angeles, you saw photographs of fans at Dodger Stadium listening to Scully's broadcasts on transistor radios.
>
> The years between 1947 and 1956 were special. It was a different world, one that was safe to grow up in. Following the Brooklyn Dodgers was our lifeblood.

If just one other kid was outside, you could play stoop ball or box ball or have a catch. If there were two other kids, you could have a game of running bases. With four kids, triangle baseball consisting of home plate, first base, and second base. We would replay last night's game. We would replay all-star games. It was just an amazing period. You felt like everyone in Brooklyn was your friend.[13]

Ebbets Field was heaven on earth for Brooklynites who dreamed of nothing more in their philosophy than the activities taking place within the stadium's confines formed by Bedford Avenue, McKeever Place, Sullivan Place, and Montgomery Street. Apologies to Hamlet. Then again, Hamlet and his buddy Horatio never went to a baseball game at Ebbets Field. They would probably have been fans of the Giants, anyway. Or worse, the Yankees.

Arthur Ritz, a graduate of Brooklyn Technical High School who lived on Maple Street between Troy Avenue and Albany Avenue in East Flatbush and later became a civil engineer, wore a Harry M. Stevens vendor uniform at Ebbets Field through his high school and college years:

> My wife wears a ring on her 4th finger. I paid for it from the commission for 100,000 bags of peanuts. A penny a bag was the commission—10 percent for 10 cents a bag. Beer was 25 cents a bottle. Soda was 10 cents.
>
> Harry M. Stevens Inc. had the franchises for Yankee Stadium, Ebbets Field, the Polo Grounds, Roosevelt Stadium, and the local racetracks. My first year working for them was 1945. Working for Stevens was a great adventure. I learned a bunch of new words that you can't find in the dictionary. It was a tough place to work, but you had the added attraction of the ball games. We were there at eight in the morning for an afternoon ball game, but we got paid nothing for the extra setup, which was hours of work. Stevens only paid commission. There was no pay if the game was canceled.
>
> As a Stevens employee, we weren't supposed to collect autographs from the players but I was able to get a few autographed baseballs anyway. Once, I handed a ball to Dixie Walker. He looked at me in my Stevens uniform and told me I'm not supposed to have it. Then, he took it.[14]

Sol Gabay, a Brooklynite who moved to New Jersey, lived next door to my family for more than 40 years. He and my father frequently reminisced about the Dodgers, trading stories about experiences at Ebbets Field.

When the Dodgers left Brooklyn, I stopped looking at baseball games. It was a sad feeling when they left. The team was a part of life in Brooklyn. We left the house at 8:00 a.m. to go to Ebbets Field and be the first people through the gate. They usually opened the gate at 11:00 a.m. The biggest thrill was going to a doubleheader. When the Mets won the World Series in 1969, I took up baseball again. Some Dodgers fans became Mets fans right away when the Mets debuted in 1962. But the Brooklyn Dodgers and Ebbets Field never leave you. They've never really gone away. You still have it in your bones. If you weren't there, you couldn't understand the feeling of being a fan of the Brooklyn Dodgers.[15]

To be a Brooklyn Dodgers fan in the 1950s was to scour the sports pages on the day after a game for headlines, box scores, and the inside story from the Dodgers' beat reporters on slumps, streaks, and injuries. In *The Boys of Summer*, a 1972 memoir-biography about the 1952–1953 Brooklyn Dodgers, Roger Kahn described his memories of covering the Dodgers for the *New York Herald Tribune*: "Plus, Ebbets Field was an intimate place where I could pick a friend of mine out of the stands. There was physical proximity between the players and the fans. The players lived mostly in Bay Ridge. There was a likelihood that you went to the same supermarket as a Dodger player or took your kids to the same pediatrician."[16]

Brooklyn had an underlying sense of identity, and still does, because of its geopolitical pedigree indicating past glory as a city until its incorporation by New York City in 1898. Today, Brooklyn would be the fourth-largest American city with a population bigger than the combined populations of Boston, Seattle, Baltimore, and Denver. Since 2002, Ron Schweiger has fulfilled a mission of pride by monitoring Dodgers heritage as Brooklyn's borough historian:

> What is it that ignites passion, loyalty, and wistfulness decades after the Brooklyn Dodgers' departure for Los Angeles? What justifies hundreds of books about Dodgers scholarship? There is no answer, sociological or otherwise, to explain the magical grip that the Dodgers maintain on their fans and succeeding generations captivated by the nearly mythic stories of Ebbets Field and the players who wore Dodgers uniforms, not merely as a geographical signifier, but as a boast. Brooklyn, with its magnificent bridge, hosted the Dodgers as a communal treasure known to visitors and natives alike as a surety. Its permanence was taken for granted, as often happens in relationships between fans and teams. Heartbreak, certainly, may be part of the bittersweet brew filling a Brooklynite with a yearning for yesteryear. Thoughts of the girl that got away, for example, occupy the same amount of bandwidth as those of a blossomed romance, only to be open on rare occasions with *compadres* owning the same emotional territory. Ask a comedian to talk about any performance and it's a good bet that he or she will fully detail a gig in Cincinnati when nobody laughed, the time a heckler in Atlanta wouldn't shut up, or the club owner in Denver who refused to pay an agreed upon fee. It's part of the human journey, explicit where the Dodgers of Brooklyn are concerned.[17]

In his 1981 novel *The Man Who Brought the Dodgers Back to Brooklyn*, David Ritz constructed a fantasy of the Dodgers once again playing in the borough. Ritz's tale revolves around childhood friends Bobby Hanes and

Squat Malone. Bobby is a rich kid who grows up to be a combination of Donald Trump, Ted Turner, and Bill Veeck. Squat is a working-class kid with major league potential who, as a young adult, loses a leg in a car accident. Both are diehard fans of the Brooklyn Dodgers.

Bobby buys the Dodgers, moves them back to Brooklyn, and plans to rebuild Ebbets Field exactly as it once stood. No easy tasks, these. In real life and in Ritz's Dodgerverse, Ebbets Field's successor was Ebbets Field Apartments, an urban housing development. Bobby offers to move the tenants, temporarily, to an "unoccupied city project in Bensonhurst" before moving them to a Bay Ridge complex that the Dodgers will build with bigger apartments and the same rent. Furious, the tenants resent having to move for a rich guy who bought a baseball team because of ambition mixed with nostalgia. At the meeting where Bobby reveals his vision, the tenants ignite bedlam by pelting him with eggs.[18]

Refusing to succumb, Bobby has another meeting with an added incentive for the tenants—executive suites that will be available only for the tenants, free of charge. "Your seats, your food will be free; you will be kings and queens in your own palace," explains Bobby.[19] A lifetime pass plus a cash settlement for each tenant sweetens the pot. Once again, Ebbets Field will be a part of Brooklyn.

Bobby is a devilish sort, one who gets in trouble but moderates the consequences through charisma. He redeems himself by bringing the Dodgers home, rebuilding Ebbets Field, and filling the manager position with Squat, a venerable baseball man who ultimately forgives Bobby's peccadilloes while acknowledging their cemented bond—the Brooklyn Dodgers. A dual love interest develops—Bobby romances reporter Oran Ellis while Squat falls for his star pitcher, Ruthie Smelkinson, the first woman to play in the major leagues.

Ritz's whimsical tale coincided with a political maneuver to reset the Dodgers' provenance to Brooklyn. In 1981, New York state senator Tom Bartosiewicz introduced legislation to create the Brooklyn Sports Authority with a $200,000 budget for assessing opportunities to construct a baseball stadium. Bartosiewicz's plan was imaginative, if not fanciful. Ultimately, though, it was all wind and no sail. Bartosiewicz struck out, but New York governor George Pataki and Brooklyn borough president Howard Golden saw possibility in the idea. Together, they appointed a committee in 1997 to restore the gloried name "Brooklyn Dodgers" as a reality, not a phrase evoking the past.

The Dodgers stayed in Los Angeles.

In the deep rivers of a Brooklynite's heart, however, where eddies of emotions bounce off currents of realities, the Dodgers belong to Brooklyn. Not Los Angeles. Brooklyn.

The Brooklyn Dodgers fan in the 1950s was a caretaker of a baseball birthright. As baseball crawled out of its crib toward its first wobbly steps of organization in the mid–19th century, Brooklyn's baseball genesis began with amateur teams—Atlantics, Excelsiors, Putnams, Eckfords. The Atlantics played in the National Association of Base Ball Players (NABBP), an amateur society that began in 1857. They won championships in 1864 and 1866. The National Association of Professional Base Ball Players (NAPBP) debuted in 1871, but Brooklyn did not have a team in that league. The NABBP and the NAPBP disbanded in 1875; the National League succeeded them in 1876.

A listing of Brooklyn's baseball firsts appeared in a 1955 book published by *Sport* magazine offering biographies of the National League teams, each team handled by a different writer. Dan Parker handled the Dodgers[20]:

- First ball game to which admission was charged was played at the Fashion Race Course on Long Island with a Brooklyn club as the host
- Brooklyn Excelsiors made the first road trip in baseball history
- Brooklyn's Capitoline Grounds was the first enclosed ball park; it was built during the Civil War
- Al Reach became the first professional baseball player when he accepted a salary to leave the Brooklyn Eckfords for the Philadelphia Athletics in 1864
- William "Candy" Cummings threw the first recorded curve ball when he pitched for the Brooklyn Stars against the Atlantics
- Eddie Cuthbert invented stealing second base when he played for the Philadelphia Keystones playing in Brooklyn one day in 1865
- Dickey Pearce of the Brooklyn Atlantics invented the bunt in 1866
- Henry Chadwick, an adopted Englander who became a Brooklynite, invented the box score, wrote the first rule book in 1858, and chaired the first rules committee that had a national scope

"If you gather from all this that Brooklyn is a borough steeped in baseball tradition," wrote Parker, "you have grasped the pernt, as they say at Bedford Avenue and Sullivan Place, crossroads of the Dodger fans' uni-voise."[21]

Brooklyn's professional baseball auspices began when the Hartford Dark Blues of the National League moved to Brooklyn in 1877 to become the Hartfords of Brooklyn. Disbanding after the 1877 season, the Hartfords left a professional baseball abyss in the borough. Another team filled it in 1883—the year that the Brooklyn Bridge debuted, connecting Brooklyn and Manhattan. Brooklyn would never be the same.

And neither would baseball.

2nd Inning:
"No grander name
on earth than Brooklyn"

"The field was even greener than my boy's mind had pictured it. In later years, friends of ours visited Ireland and said the grass there was plenty green all right, but that not even the Emerald Isle itself was as green as the grass that grew in Ebbets Field."[1]—Duke Snider

Without George Taylor, the Brooklyn Dodgers might never have happened.

A city editor pushing 30 at the *New York Herald*, Taylor embraced baseball as an alternative profession to journalism. And a potentially lucrative one, given Brooklyn's passion for amateur baseball. But Taylor's bank account lacked the heft required to launch a baseball venture, necessitating assistance. A backer later balked at the cost of building a stadium and hiring players. "The trouble with the 'angel' was his wings were not well developed, and he soon came back to earth,"[2] wrote future Dodgers owner Charles Ebbets in *History of Baseball in Brooklyn*, a series of articles for the *Brooklyn Daily Eagle* in 1913.

Taylor kept the lease on the land he eyed for the ballpark—a tract with boundaries of Third Street, Fifth Street, Fourth Avenue, and Fifth Avenue. It dropped him into a financial quagmire. Taylor appealed to John Brice, an attorney, hoping that Brice could play matchmaker in finding a white knight to rescue the dream of professional baseball in Brooklyn. Brice didn't have to look far; he found a prospect renting a desk in his office on Liberty Street in Manhattan: Charley Byrne.[3]

Byrne indulged in New York's cultural life accessed by wealth amassed in New York City real estate dealings. "As a real estate investor, he knew that Brooklyn was on the rise,"[4] wrote Ronald G. Shafer in the 2011 book *When the Dodgers Were Bridegrooms*. A population trending upward provided a highly significant lure for a baseball team seeking to establish a fan base.

Members of the 1890 Brooklyn Bridegrooms (Brooklyn Public Library—Brooklyn Collection).

27

But Byrne, while wealthy, could not meet Taylor's requirements. Or he didn't want to assume the risk, solely. So he brought his brother-in-law into the ownership structure—Joseph J. Doyle, a 45-year-old casino owner. "Fat Joe, however, began sweating when the costs of just the initial grading and preparations for the ballpark exceeded $12,000,"[5] wrote Shafer. Doyle persuaded fellow casino owner Ferdinand "Gus" Abell to join the venture. Byrne commanded the team's operations as team president while Doyle and Abell enjoyed silent partnerships.

Brooklyn's new baseball venture honored history with its ballpark named Washington Park—General George Washington led the colonial rebels in the Battle of Long Island on the ballpark site. Pockets full of capital and heart full of baseball, Taylor saw his dream evolving into a reality.

With no opening in the National League or the American Association—baseball's two major leagues at the time—Byrne applied to the American Association's minor league, the Interstate Baseball Association. Brooklyn's new team commenced its professional life in an ISBA double-header against the Wilmington, Delaware, team on May 1, 1883. The teams split the games—Wilmington won the first game, 9–6, Brooklyn won the second game, 8–2.

On May 9, about 1,000 fans watched Brooklyn's first home game, a 7–1 victory against Harrisburg. Because Washington Park was not ready, Brooklyn used Prospect Park rather than forfeit the game. Unnamed, the teams received reportage in the *New York Times* as the Brooklyn Inter-State Club and the Harrisburg Club. Taylor managed the Brooklyn team, its first home game marred by Harrisburg's behavior. "The visitors were beaten by the Brooklynites, and disgusted the Brooklyn players as well as the onlookers by their continual growling at the decisions made by the umpire," reported the *New York Times*.[6]

The coverage in the *Brooklyn Daily Eagle* mirrored the *Times* account. "There have been some pretty rough nines seen on the park grounds in its history, but a worse lot of 'kickers,' or a more undisciplined and badly managed professional nine has never played in Brooklyn than the mixed lot of professional roughs who opposed the Brooklyn team in this match."[7]

The *Eagle* also warned the Harrisburg team about the consequences of conduct. "The Harrisburg club had better see to it that their team is placed in more competent hands when traveling, or they will find themselves expelled from the association which their team now discredits."[8]

Washington Park debuted on May 12; by a score of 13–6, Brooklyn beat Trenton, a team with better sportsmen than its predecessor. "The visiting team behaved throughout like gentlemen, not a word being heard in disputing the decisions of the umpire during the entire game, and the same credit is due the home team," reported the *Eagle*. "Indeed the Trentons presented a most favorable contrast to the rough behavior of the Harrisburg team last Thursday at Prospect Park."[9]

On the same day that Byrne unveiled Washington Park, he hired Charles Ebbets, a 23-year-old office factotum. Ebbets excelled, no matter the size, import, or value of the task. "He sold tickets, hawked score cards through the stands, attended to all the little drudgeries in the business office that the other employees were glad to shirk, and made friends for the club by his good humor and his patience,"[10] wrote Frank Graham in the 1945 book *The Brooklyn Dodgers*.

Ebbets chose baseball as his path after compiling a curriculum vitae boasting architecture and publishing. His architecture experience included working on the plans for the Metropolitan Hotel and the second incarnation of Niblo's Garden, both downtown Manhattan structures. Ebbets' entrepreneurial streak surfaced in his publishing aspirations.[11] "He had gone into the publishing business on a small scale, printing cheap editions of novels and textbooks, and when his salesmen had been slow to get rid of them, he had sold them from door to door himself,"[12] explained Graham.

Brooklyn ended its first year with a flourish, winning the 1883 Interstate Baseball Association championship by beating Harrisburg 11–6 on September 29, the last day of the season. Harrisburg joined the Eastern League in 1884, only to dissolve on July 4 with a record of 16–25.[13] After the 1883 season, Brooklyn jumped to the major leagues when it joined the American Association.

Byrne schemed to strengthen the ball club's roster by acquiring the New York Metropolitans from Erastus Wiman, a businessman eager to jettison the "Mets" from his portfolio, which included the Staten Island Cricket Club and the Staten Island Ferry. The Mets also belonged to the AA.[14] It seemed simple enough. Wiman wanted out. Byrne wanted in. But so did John Day, the Mets' original owner; Day had sold the Mets to Wiman's group of investors while keeping his ownership of the National League's New York Gothams. Byrne, needing to act quickly to prevent Day from getting control, consulted Abell and Doyle on possible actions. Byrne purchased the Metropolitans on October 1, 1887, for $25,000.[15]

Byrne's purpose was not to own the Mets. Rather, he wanted to strip its roster, keep the best players, and sell the remainder. He got first base-man Dave Orr, outfielder Darby O'Brien, and pitcher Al Mays in the deal.[16] The Kansas City Cowboys, a new franchise in the American Association, bought the leftover players.[17] Byrne continued amplifying the Brooklyn team by purchasing Al Bushong from the St. Louis Browns along with pitchers Bob Caruthers and Dave Foutz.

The Mets, though non-existent as a team, still existed as an entity. On March 7, 1888, the stockholders of the American Association teams decided to maintain the status quo. The *New York Times* reported, "It was agreed that the Mets should remain just as they are, and if at any time it was found convenient to place a club in this city it would be done."[18]

Day had other plans, however. He wanted exclusivity in the New York City market for the Gothams. If the American Association patched together a squad for another incarnation of the Mets or advocated an expansion team with the Mets name, Day would have unwanted competition. He countered by threatening to compete in American Association markets if the league expanded with another team in New York City. "The Metro-politan Club today is a thing of the past, and the American Association has virtually forfeited its franchise in New-York City [*sic*]. If another club were placed in this city it could only be done by breaking a clause in the national agreement," said Day.[19]

Threats were moot. The 19th-century Mets, though technically exist-ing, never played after the 1887 season.

Charles Ebbets, meanwhile, with his mop of thick, curly brown hair and bushy mustache, was on a path of destiny in the Washington Park office. Even if his job consisted of menial tasks—unglamorous at best and boring at worst—Ebbets loved baseball, learning not only where the t's were crossed and the i's dotted, but how, when, and why.

In the wake of the "Blizzard of 1888" devastating the Northeast, Ebbets looked forward to the warm embrace of spring—baseball's annual renais-sance. He likely scoured the New York City newspapers for information about baseball. With newspaper ink faintly coloring his hands as he turned the pages of the *Eagle*, he saw the genesis of a branding change for the Brooklyn team resulting from marital bliss overwhelming its players dur-ing the winter of 1888. The *Eagle* remarked, "Eleven of the Brooklyn team are blessed with charming wives, and they have something to work for beside their own individual pleasure. Most of these Benedicts are yearling bridegrooms. The other five are unlucky bachelors who are likely to be caught out by some Brooklyn belles this season."[20]

On April 11, 1888, the same day that future automobile mogul Henry Ford married Clara Bryant, *Sporting Life* popped a marital-related question buttressing the logical label for the Brooklyn squad: "Now isn't this a 'bridegroom' team?"[21]

Brooklyn Bridegrooms. It was not the only nickname enjoyed by the team before "Dodgers" became the permanent label.

After winning the American Association championship against the St. Louis Browns in 1889, the Bridegrooms lost the World Series to the National League's New York Giants. The following year, the Bridegrooms moved to the National League, won the 1890 championship, and played to a draw in the World Series against the AA's Louisville Colonels—the modern-day World Series began in 1903, though championships were labeled "World Series" in the 19th century. Louisville and Brooklyn each won three games and played one game that ended in a tie.

In 1890, Brooklyn had three major league teams—the Gladiators of the American Association, the Bridegrooms of the National League, and the Wonders of the Players' League. A buccaneering operation pilfering teams from the duopoly of the AA and the NL, the Players' League launched what became known as the "Brotherhood War."

The Jolly Roger should have been the league's official flag.

Every war has its casualties—the National League survived, the Players' League folded after one season, and the American Association limped through 1891, the league's last season.

Byrne merged the Bridegrooms with the Brooklyn team from the Players' League, the Wonders. He moved the team to the Wonders' home field in Eastern Park, located in Brooklyn's East New York section. It was an easy destination for mass transit users at the turn of the 20th century because several trolley and streetcar lines converged near the site. This inspired the Trolley Dodgers team name, based on the custom of dodging Brooklyn's trolleys to avoid injury or death. Fluidity abounded regarding team names.

The 1890s saw the team change nicknames from Ward's Wonders to Foutz's Fillies to Hanlon's Superbas. John Montgomery Ward and Dave Foutz managed the Brooklyn team from 1891 to 1892 and 1893 to 1896, respectively. Ned Hanlon managed from 1899 to 1905. Consequently, the "Superbas" name paid homage to a vaudeville troupe—Hanlon's Superbas.

As the Brotherhood War's devastation subsided, George Chauncey noticed value in the Brooklyn franchise. A former Players' League investor, Chauncey knew baseball from his playing days with the Brooklyn Excelsiors, found success as a real estate investor, and combined his passions as an investor in the Brooklyn Wonders. Chauncey later became the president of the Mechanics' Bank in Brooklyn.

It would not be the last association between a bank and the Dodgers.

Chauncey's involvement went beyond strengthening the financial ledgers of the team. He inspired the Eastern Park move and spearheaded the firing of the team's manager, Bill McGunnigle, despite the team's success.[22] Incorporating under the name "Brooklyn Baseball Club," the new ownership group issued stock—"[T]he stock of 100 shares capitalized at $250,000 with the Byrne-Doyle-Abell group taking just over 50 percent (Taylor had sold his interest in 1885) and the Chauncey group, with associates E. F. Linton and H. J. Robinson, taking the balance," noted Bob McGee in *The Greatest Ball Park Ever: Ebbets Field and the Story of the Brooklyn Dodgers*.[23] Structurally sound, the team—and the borough—shed an ocean of tears when Charley Byrne died in 1898. More than a businessman, Byrne's leadership inspired Brooklyn with hope, integrity, and fairness. The *Brooklyn Daily Eagle* eulogized:

> The national game was under many obligations to him. No man took greater pride in it and no man has done more to keep it clean. He saw nothing incompatible between good ball playing and good behavior on the field. He set his face against anything in the nature of rowdyism and never averted it. There were times when this was more or less detrimental to the immediate prospects of the club and when a resort to methods he would not tolerate might have saved a game, but with bullies he had no sympathy and his interest in base ball as a profession and pastime was as great as his concern for the welfare of the local club.[24]

Chauncey eyed Ebbets to fill the team's presidential void. He sweetened the opportunity by offering a financial stake that would also secure Ebbets' long-term plans in Brooklyn. Ebbets liked the idea, buying 22½ percent of the Brooklyn Baseball Club stock from Chauncey. Another opportunity arose when Ferdinand Abell wanted to sell his stock, but Ebbets couldn't raise the necessary capital.[25]

Ebbets moved the club from Eastern Park to the second incarnation of Washington Park. Located in south Brooklyn between the parallels of First Street and Third Street and the corresponding parallels of Third Avenue and Fourth Avenue, the new Washington Park was on a northwesterly diagonal from its progenitor.[26]

As Ebbets settled into his new executive role, Brooklynites became acclimated to a new status for their collective home—annexation to New

York City. The journey of annexation forfeiting Brooklyn's independence was neither quick nor smooth. Ebbets' patron, George Chauncey, endorsed consolidation as a real estate play. "This appeal will be made, and when Brooklyn is wedded to New York it will be shown that her people have decided wisely,"[27] wrote Chauncey.

Sourced with power from Chapter 331, Laws of 1890, the New York State Legislature created a Commission of Municipal Consolidation Inquiry "to inquire into the expedience of the proposed consolidation and to submit a report with recommendations."[28] The 11-member commission with offices at 214 Broadway in Manhattan considered expanding New York City by joining "Brooklyn and several smaller contiguous cities and towns."[29]

The Commission presented a bill to the 1893 legislature concerning a vote on the consolidation issue by "the people of the district affected"[30]; the bill had more than 10,000 names. Although the Legislature adjourned before a vote could take place, the bill enjoyed another introduction in 1894. It passed, and Governor Levi P. Morton signed it into law—Chapter 64, Laws of 1894—which allowed "merely for a public vote and for an official certification of that vote to the Secretary of State."[31] On October 15, 1894, the commission clarified, "Your vote is only a simple expression of opinion. Actual consolidation does not come until the legislature acts.[32]

On November 6, 1894, the election took place.[33]

District	For Consolidation	Against Consolidation
New York	96,938	59,959
Kings	64,744	64,467
Queens	7,712	4,741
Richmond	5,531	1,506
Mt. Vernon	873	1,603
Eastchester	374	260
Westchester	620	621
Pelham	261	153

Brooklynites voted for consolidation by a margin of 277—or .002 percent; the tally differed when excluding the county towns that Brooklyn annexed five months before the election. In this paradigm, Brooklynites voted against consolidation by 1,034, or .008 percent.[34]

The state assembly passed the bill, 91–56. The state senate passed the bill, 38–8. On May 11, 1896, Governor Morton signed the bill authorizing annexation.[35]

Brooklyn, once a city thriving on independence, prosperity, and metropolitan pride, became a borough. Loyalists opposed the change, regarding annexation as a sacrifice of heritage for the sake of power, politics, and money. It was, in their eyes, a crime of the heart. Similar feelings arose 60 years hence, when Walter O'Malley uprooted the Dodgers. Brooklyn had unclean hands regarding annexation, however—its legacy included absorbing Williamsburg, Greenpoint, Bushwick, Flatbush, New Utrectht, Gravesend, and Flatlands.

A new dawn for Brooklyn's political status meant a possible name change. New York East, for example, was under consideration as a new moniker. On May 22, 1897, the *Brooklyn Daily Eagle* featured comments of dozens of Brooklynites on both sides of the naming issue[36]:

Since we have voted for annexation our address should be New York.—William M. M. Hyde of 717 Greene Avenue

There is no Brooklyn. The new charter makes one great city; so let it be one; waive all sentiment and let us have a great commonwealth, recognized the world over as such and have the divisions New York East, New York West, New York North, New York South. As Mr. Seth Low [Brooklyn's mayor from 1881 to 1885] says: 'The several boroughs must bury their former individuality. We must forget that we were Brooklynites and know only that we are genuine New Yorkers, alive to all her interests and always loyal.—James Wright of 144 Seventeenth Street

To be known as New York East is to secure the advantage to be derived by consolidation. Reason, pecuniary considerations and patriotism demand we take the name and work for the prosperity, fame and glory of the New York of the present and future.—H. H. Dunwoody, 217 Carlton Avenue

But why call it New York East, which sounds like East New York? Would not New York S. E. be sufficient? And surely Brooklyn is more southeast than east of New York. We will always have the Brooklyn Eagle as a daily reminder of the name we are so proud of and sentimental people can have their letters directed to Brooklyn, New York, if the name should be changed, without danger of an hour's delay in delivery. Let the borough of Brooklyn be called New York. S. E.—J. G. Wall, 328A President Street

Any Brooklynite who has traveled beyond the confines of his town knows the prestige and glory that go with the name of New York. Let us cease being provincial. It is time we were done with the foolish Brooklyn bred, Brooklyn born and Brooklyn till I die business. Law, reason and natural trend of events, helped by propinquity, has made us New York, let us be to the world what we are, viz., New York and not some Lonesomehurst hanging upon the skirts of the metropolis.—"Young Brooklynite"

To wipe out the name of Brooklyn entirely from the map and be known only as New York East, seems to me an outrage and would result in changing the name of many corporations who have taken the name of Brooklyn.

There are hundreds of them which have taken the name of Brooklyn. How would New York East Academy of Music, New York East Library, New York East Savings bank or New York East Eagle sound?—George M. Eddy

We are progressive, and let whatever further progress we make be in the noble name of Brooklyn; and to her, under a favoring providence, be all honor and praise. I am a woman, and really thank God that I am an American woman— a Brooklyn woman—and that somewhere in my composition burns a spark of loyalty and patriotism. Perhaps the sentiments of many will be expressed in the following lines:

> Boast not to me of this Greater New York, sir!
> Remember some hearts are still loyal and true.
> Our city's the scene of life's battles well fought, sir!
> O many are they who can say this to you!
> Kindled within us, this fire's unquenchable—
> Love of our city, our schools and our homes.
> You're taking all from us, and—what! Change our name, sir!
> Never! no, never! the firm answer comes!
> —Ida W. Derby, 115 Vernon Avenue

The name Brooklyn is very dear to me. It has always been my home. No grander name on earth than Brooklyn.—Miss M. E. Gavens of 508 Lexington Avenue

The *Brooklyn Daily Eagle* sided with the loyalists in an editorial on October 19, 1897: "We shall lose an ancient and honorable name from the map, but for a century we who live here will know no other."[37] Fifty years prior, another editorial in the paper called annexation "absurd" when the idea was raised. It was as unthinkable in 1845 as the Dodgers leaving Brooklyn in the 1950s. The editorial compared Brooklyn's growth in population, commerce, and land to those of New York.

The annexation of BROOKLYN to *New York!* How amusingly absurd!—the chances are, a thousand to one, that New York will solicit annexation with us. The census will show that in growth we have distanced her altogether, and it is our intention to go on in the same, or even greater ratio, increasing our population and enlarging our borders, until, as Manhattan Island is now all New York, so Long Island will be all Brooklyn—or such other name as we shall assume more worthy of our magnificent dimensions.[38]

As revelers welcomed the new year on January 1, 1898, Brooklyn said goodbye to its past of independence, but maintained its name. The *Eagle* reported, "There was no trace of boisterousness, as there was no trace of sadness. The occasion was one of importance, one not soon to be forgotten, and all realized that every detail of the observance must be carried out decently and in order."[39] During the waning days of the 19th century, the United States did some annexing as well. After the U.S.S. *Maine* exploded in Havana's harbor, the United States went to war with Spain. Because Spain governed Cuba, the U.S. held it responsible for the Maine bombing; the Spanish-American War led to the U.S. annihilating the Spanish naval fleet based in Santiago harbor and annexing the Philippines, Guam, and Puerto Rico.

The war lasted 100 days.

As the fin de siècle approached, Charles Ebbets involved the team in a plan that looked clever on paper. Brilliant, even. To complete it, he looked southward to Baltimore, the city that gave us the B & O Railroad, *The Star-Spangled Banner*, and Babe Ruth.

It almost destroyed baseball in Brooklyn.

Ebbets' scheme began with Harry Von der Horst, who floated through life like a balloon at the wind's mercy. At least his father thought so.

With seed money from his family's Eagle Brewery and Malt Works on Belair Avenue in Baltimore, Harry formed a baseball team in 1882 branded by an appropriate geographical sobriquet—Orioles, named after Maryland's state bird. A fanciful investment, perhaps, but a profitable one if Harry could make it work—team ownership provided an automatic outlet for the family's beer product. Despite a potential financial boost, John Von der Horst looked askance at his son's baseball investment. Orioles historian Burt Solomon says that Harry's lifestyle contrasted with his family's business acumen, leading to subpar performance on the team's balance sheet. "Unfortunately for the Eagle Brewery, Harry did not have his father's mind. He was smart and energetic enough when he tried. That was the problem. He was too fond of living to keep his mind on hard, unpleasant things. That was how Harry thought of it. The old man saw it differently, as wasting time and money on nonsense."[40]

It's a common tale of the *jeunesse dorée* class benefiting from wealth built by previous generations through persistence, cunning, and gravity—and risking it on leisure, frivolity, and investments based on instinct rather than practicality.

No micromanager, Von der Horst opened his checkbook cushioned by beer revenue, hired Ned Hanlon to manage the Orioles, and brought first-class baseball to Baltimore—the Orioles won three consecutive championships from 1894 to 1896. Still, the Orioles could not attract a fan base with enough lucre to keep the team in Baltimore. So, Harry changed his focus from the environs of Chesapeake Bay to the hinterland of Brooklyn, striking a deal with the Brooklyn team allowing him to own stock in both clubs. For the 1899 season, Hanlon moved to Brooklyn to manage the team now featuring former Baltimore players Wee Willie Keeler, Hughie Jennings, and Joe Kelley. Hanlon also owned team stock as part of the deal.

Bringing Hanlon to Brooklyn proved to be a valuable tactic—Brooklyn won the pennant in Hanlon's first year at the helm and repeated in 1900 when Iron Joe McGinnity and Jimmy Sheckard moved from Baltimore to Brooklyn. Meanwhile, the 1899 season was moot for the Orioles; after the season, the National League abolished the team. A new Baltimore Orioles franchise in the American League lasted two seasons—1901 and 1902—before moving to New York City in 1903 and becoming the Highlanders, later the Yankees.

Within four years, two Baltimore franchises evaporated, leading the jewel of Chesapeake Bay to wonder about its future in professional baseball. Brooklyn, less so. The waters seemed calm and the sky clear for the S.S. Brooklyn Base Ball Club. But a potential tsunami lurked beneath the surface. Its name was Ned Hanlon. Benedict Arnold by way of Absalom.

A carefree approach to life caught up to Harry Von der Horst when stock market losses carved a crater in his financial portfolio. Consequently, Hanlon saw an opportunity to realize his quest for ownership, authority, and a move from Brooklyn to Baltimore. But Hanlon didn't count on Charles Ebbets.

Needing funds to keep the team under his aegis, Ebbets strategized for Von der Horst to sell his ownership stake to furniture mogul Henry Medicus, an Ebbets ally with deep pockets.[41] Hanlon countered with a legal technicality. On November 12, 1906, at the annual stockholders meeting for the Brooklyn Baseball Club, Hanlon claimed that the director positions held by Ebbets, Medicus, Albert C. Wall, and Charles H. Ebbets, Jr., were illegally obtained because of a failure to comply with the Corporation Act of New Jersey. He offered a written copy of the statute.

> Pointing to Section 13, he showed them that the law of the state, under which the Brooklyn Baseball Club was incorporated, expressly provides that every corporation shall file with the secretary of state a report, authenticated by the officers of the annual meeting of the corporation, containing the names of the persons elected to the directorate and the executive offices, within thirty days after the holding of the meeting.[42]

Hanlon's argument rested on the 1905 annual meeting report's filing date of October 17, 1906, well past the 30-day window. Section 43 of the act sanctioned removal as the penalty for non-compliance.[43] Hanlon's *coup d'etat*, if successful, would install Hanlon, Abell, Howard C. Griffiths, and Robert Wright as the only directors. Ebbets et al. would be ineligible to serve on the board because they held office during the default period.

Hanlon had 8½ percent of the Brooklyn's club stock, Ferdinand Abell as an ally, and fire in his eyes. Ebbets had 51 percent of the club's stock, Medicus' infusion of cash, and an inviolable commitment to Brooklyn. Loyalty personified, he refused to buckle. "We intend to keep the team in Brooklyn, whereas the minority interests want to take it to Baltimore, according to their own statements in the press. Their policy is to pull the club apart, ours is to hold it together in Brooklyn,"[44] declared Ebbets.

Hanlon filed three lawsuits. One sourced in a $30,000 loan that Hanlon had made to the Brooklyn club during the wake of the Brotherhood War. To finance the loan, Hanlon used the money he received from the National League as payment to dissolve the Baltimore team and now he wanted it back.[45]

Ebbets could have resolved the dispute by selling Brooklyn players Tim Jordan and Harry Lumley to the New York Giants for the funds needed to settle with Hanlon. Even if Ebbets fought Hanlon rather than settle, the money generated from a sale could serve as a financial cushion if Hanlon won his case. Despite the practical appeal of selling Jordan and Lumley, Ebbets declined the Giants' offer. "I felt that if I had sold those two star players at that time the fans would run me out of Brooklyn," said Ebbets. "To my way of thinking, it was my duty to Brooklyn fans to keep those players in spite of the fact that we needed money worse than we did players at that time. It wouldn't have been fair to our patrons to sell those players."[46]

Fairness. That's the Brooklyn way.

Ebbets strengthened his ownership in the Brooklyn baseball team by buying out Ferdinand Abell. When Hanlon abandoned his quest after losing in court, he sold his stock to Ebbets and left for Cincinnati to manage the Reds.[47] Ebbets amplified his ownership further when Von der Horst died—the beer scion crafted his will to allow Ebbets the option to purchase his stock. Again, Ebbets needed a white knight as George Taylor did during the embryonic stage of the team. Chauncey worked his influence to secure loans for Ebbets, who "continued to buy stock here and there from small holders" to consolidate his ownership. "By 1909 he owned the club right down to the last turnstile,"[48] stated the *New York Herald Tribune* in Ebbets' 1925 obituary.

Charles Ebbets was the sole owner of the Brooklyn team, whatever name the fans and the press chose for it. He pursued his vision of a modern stadium with expanded capacity in Flatbush. Where detractors saw a fetid site appropriately named Pigtown—pigs fed on the garbage—with odors that could make a sewer worker convulse, Ebbets envisioned fragrances of freshly cut grass filling the air in a grand arena to replace the aging Washington Park.

A new stadium emerged because of the love affair between Brooklyn and its Dodgers. The *New York Times* extolled this relationship dynamic in 1912, a year before Ebbets completed his vision:

> Through many seasons of losses and disappointments he has carried the Trolley Dodgers, losing money year after year, when those about him lost faith in the game as a paying proposition. But the confidence of Mr. Ebbets has never been shaken. He believed years ago, as he does to-day, that Brooklyn is a major league city and that it would support a good ball team.[49]

With the Dodgers' Washington Park outdated and undersized for a growing fan base, Ebbets' Pigtown investment would be practical—a brick-and-mortar stanchion for a fan base aching for leisure lined with fervor. Ebbets' vision was concrete, in the literal sense, exemplifying the shift from the quaint but dangerous standard of wooden stadia—a 1911 fire destroyed much of the third incarnation of the Giants' home stadium, the Polo Grounds—to grander, bigger, and safer arenas. Money was secondary to Ebbets, who placed a premium on the fans' enjoyment. "I believe the fan should be taken care of. A club should provide a suitable home for its patrons. This home should be in a location that is healthy, it should be safe, and it should be convenient,"[50] stated Ebbets.

In *Leslie's Weekly*, Ebbets reinforced the Brooklyn fan base as the reason for building a new stadium: "We must give our patrons what they express an evident desire for, and in progressive baseball to-day this means comfort, safety and faster play than ever before."[51] No small task, Ebbets consolidated the disparate parcels on the Pigtown site. He kept the process secret, buying the parcels through a dummy corporation. And he had every piece necessary, save one. It was 20 feet by 50 feet.

Tracking the parcel's owner was a worldwide affair—California, Berlin, Paris. Finally, Ebbets located him in Montclair, New Jersey, and bought the land for $500.[52] When Dodgers owner Walter O'Malley revealed plans to build a successor to Ebbets Field in the 1950s, Arthur Daley recounted the Ebbets story in his *Sports of the Times* column in the *New York Times*. "No one ever received five hundred bucks faster,"[53] said Daley.

Alfred Steers got the reaction he hoped for, though it wasn't surprising given the aura of excitement orbiting the crowd of more than 500 people congregated for the next chapter in Brooklyn's baseball history—groundbreaking for the new ballpark on March 5, 1912.

Speechmaking came with the territory for Steers, the Brooklyn borough president. Perched on a platform adorned with flags and bunting, he verbally hugged the crowd with his reminiscences about the borough's baseball legacy. And they hugged back, cheering throughout his remarks. "I tell you what I want to see, and I know you all want to see it, too, and that is for Brooklyn to proudly take her place at the top of the baseball world, as she did in the old days when I was a boy and used to peek through the holes in the fence," said Steers. "And I think Mr. Ebbets will give us the best team in the country, and it will play right here in this park."[54]

To initiate the groundbreaking, Ebbets wrapped his hands around the ebony handle of a shovel—a gift from the Castle Brothers contractors working on the site—then plunged the solid silver spade into the ground.

From left to right: Charles Ebbets, Wilbert Robinson, Steve McKeever, Ed McKeever (National Baseball Hall of Fame Library, Cooperstown, New York).

Ebbets' ballpark had no moniker, though. Would it be the third Washington Park? Brooklyn Stadium? How about Dodger Field? Ebbets had acceded to the traditional Washington Park label at the groundbreaking ceremony until Len Wooster, sports editor of the *Brooklyn Times*, suggested, "Washington Park, my eye! It's Ebbets Field. You put yourself in hock to build it and it's your monument."[55]

Ebbets rode a wave of adoration consummated by more glad-handing, back-slapping, and cheers at a VIP luncheon that he hosted at the Consumers' Park Restaurant. Steers, Ebbets Field Architect Clarence R. Van Buskirk, and journalists were among the guests.[56]

Because he could not finance the stadium on his own, Ebbets submerged his ownership interest to assure Brooklyn of a world-class, state-of-the-art sports palace. He made a deal with Steve and Ed McKeever, the contractors who owned the construction company building the ballpark, to finance the park's completion by selling them 50 percent of his stock.

If the Dodgers organization ever creates a coat of arms to reflect its remarkable legacy, Charles Ebbets' name will undoubtedly enjoy a prominent place in the escutcheon. With a new stadium on the horizon, Brooklyn's baseball future seemed brighter than Coney Island sunshine on a clear July day. For Ebbets, though, a cloud hovered.

He was no longer the team's sole owner.

3rd Inning: Red, White, and Dodger Blue

Brooklyn is loyal to baseball because baseball has been loyal to Brooklyn.[1]—Advertisement

Chaos would have been an improvement.

On Opening Day 1912, a month after the Ebbets Field groundbreaking, more than 25,000 people squeezed into Washington Park to see the Giants play Brooklyn. The crowd exceeded the ballpark's capacity by about 8,000. Because Brooklyn's ticket office stopped selling tickets well after the crowd entered the stadium, Washington Park bordered on a full-scale riot. The *New York Times* reported, "Hoodlums raided the boxes and took all the chairs vacated by disgusted occupants and carried them out close to the base lines and stood up, forming a bank of humanity that hid the playing field from those behind. The police were not able to clear the whole playing field."[2]

Players became sentinels defending their fortress. New York City's mayor William Gaynor—grandfather-in-law of actor Fred Gwynne, portrayer of Herman Munster, who would secure a place in Dodgers popular culture five decades later when Leo Durocher scouted him on *The Munsters*—ordered the police reserves to come to the park and restore order. Those looking for egress from the mob found the exits overcrowded.

The game began at 4:30 p.m., a half-hour after its scheduled starting time. With darkness overtaking daylight, Umpire Bill Klem called the game after an hour and 45 minutes; the Giants led 18–3 after six innings. With a seating capacity exceeding 30,000, Ebbets Field would not have the overcrowding problem of Washington Park.

Ebbets Field opened a year later, on April 5, 1913. Brooklyn fans saw the Dodgers win an exhibition game against the Yankees by a score of 3–2, helped by an inside-the-park home run smashed by Dodgers rookie outfielder Casey Stengel. But when Charles Ebbets surveyed his stadium namesake after its debut season, he saw a monument to mediocrity. Victory eluded Brooklyn. And it had been that way for quite some time.[3]

Year	Manager	Wins	Losses	Pct.	Place	Games Behind
1905	Ned Hanlon	48	104	.316	8th	56½
1906	Patsy Donovan	66	86	.434	5th	50
1907	Patsy Donovan	65	83	.439	5th	40
1908	Patsy Donovan	53	101	.344	7th	46
1909	Harry Lumley	55	98	.359	6th	55½
1910	Bill Dahlen	64	90	.416	6th	40
1911	Bill Dahlen	64	86	.427	7th	33½
1912	Bill Dahlen	58	95	.379	7th	46
1913	Bill Dahlen	65	84	.436	6th	34½

It was enough to strip the joy from riding the Drop the Dips roller coaster at Coney Island. Ebbets needed a seasoned baseball man who could turn the team's fortunes around, one who knew how to win. So he turned to Wilbert Robinson. Uncle Robbie.

Before helming the Brooklyn team, Robinson succeeded as a player and again as a coach. A catcher, Robinson began his major league career with the Philadelphia Athletics from 1886 to 1890 and then played for the Baltimore Orioles from 1890 to 1899—his Baltimore tenure included the team's three consecutive National League championships from 1894 to 1896.

After playing for the St. Louis Cardinals in 1900, Robinson returned to Baltimore to play for the second incarnation of the Orioles in 1901 and 1902 before retiring from playing. When the Orioles' player-manager John McGraw flew Baltimore's baseball nest to become the Giants' player-manager for in the middle of the 1902 season, Wilbert Robinson took his place. When the season ended, so did Robinson's playing career in the major leagues, although he played for the Baltimore team in the Eastern League until the summer of 1904. McGraw continued as player-manager of the Giants, hanging up his spikes after the 1906 season but staying in the skipper position until his retirement from baseball in 1932.

Robinson helped the Giants informally as a pitching coach in 1909 and 1910, bringing incalculable knowledge about the art and science of pitching developed during more than 1,300 games behind the plate. He joined the Giants' coaching staff in 1911.

Between 1903 and 1913, the Giants won five National League pennants, but never captured a World Series championship. After losing a third consecutive World Series in 1913, McGraw and Robinson had an argument that neared Pier Six brawl status.

It happened at a bar where some Giants gathered to drown their sorrows.

It began with criticism from McGraw and Robinson about each other's coaching.

It ended when Robinson poured a glass of beer on McGraw and the now-soaked, pugnacious Giants manager chased Robinson out of the bar all the way to Ebbets Field, figuratively.[4]

Charles Ebbets hired Robinson to manage the Brooklyn team, beginning with the 1914 season. The relationship between owner and manager flourished. "There seemed never to be friction between them," wrote Jack Kavanagh and Norman Macht in the biography *Uncle Robbie*. "In later years, Robinson would be caught in a crossfire between the heirs of Ebbets and the McKeever family. But as long as president Ebbets lived, he and Robbie formed a strong and compatible combination."[5]

Nicknamed "Uncle Robbie" because of his genial disposition, Robinson contrasted with his predecessor, William "Bad Bill" Dahlen, who earned his "Bad Bill" nickname with an arguing style that had the finesse of a 300-pound ballerina. It propelled 65 ejections for Dahlen in his playing and managerial careers, a figure in the all-time Top Ten. Dahlen was a journeyman ballplayer with a career spanning 1891–1911 for the Chicago Colts, New York Giants, Boston Doves, and the Brooklyn team with interchangeable names. During his second tenure with Brooklyn—1910–1911—Dahlen also managed the team, a post he held for two more seasons after retiring as a player. His player statistics include[6]:

Games	2,444
Hits	2,461
Doubles	413
RBI	1,234
Batting average	.272

Dahlen's baseball career ended when Ebbets fired him in November 1913. Ebbets said, "His judgment in handling the players under contract of the Brooklyn club has been wonderful. During his first three years as manager he dispensed with the services of many players who were either incompetent, misbehaving or troublesome, rarely misjudging a player, as is evidenced by the fact that of all the men he passed up only one was of major league caliber."[7]

Brooklyn's managerial void led to press speculation about Jake Daubert taking the reins as a player-manager. Daubert, a solid first baseman, was the National League's MVP and leading hitter in 1913 with a .350 batting average.

In his career from 1910 to 1924, Daubert notched 2,326 hits, including 250 doubles and 165 triples. He ended his career with a .303 batting average.[8]

Ebbets' choice of Wilbert Robinson gave the team yet another name: Robins. Sports editors and writers interchanged "Robins" with "Dodgers" and "Superbas" as the team's moniker, sometimes within a story. "Flock" became another addition to the roster of names. The "Robins" label lasted for the duration of Robinson's managerial term, ending with the 1931 season.

While Robinson took over the team, the Federal League began, its operations lasting two seasons—1914–1915. Deriving its team name from owner Robert Ward's Tip Top Bakery, the Federal League's Brooklyn Tip-Tops played at the second Washington Park.

During Robinson's inaugural spring training as the Brooklyn skipper in 1914, he claimed that he could catch a baseball dropped from higher than 504 feet—the distance from the observatory in the Washington Monument. Pop Schriver of the Chicago Colts first accomplished the feat in 1894, followed by Washington Senators catcher Gabby Street in 1908 and White Sox catcher Billy Sullivan in 1910.[9]

Ruth Law, a Florida aviatrix, piloted Robinson's challenge. A tourist attraction for Daytona, Law's exhibition flights gave passengers a pilot's eye view of the area to create interest for the Nautilus Casino. When Law realized that she left the baseball in her room at the Clarendon Hotel, she needed a substitute item. "While I was considering the dilemma," Law said, "a young man working in my outfit brought me a small grapefruit that he had intended to have with his lunch and suggested that I drop that. It looked about the size of a baseball and I thought what difference would it make if I dropped the pretty yellow fruit? Dummy that I was, I hadn't thought of the difference in weight of its juicy interior."[10]

The grapefruit splattered Robinson with pulp and juice, causing him to exclaim, "Help me, lads, I'm covered with my own blood!"[11] Casey Stengel received mistaken credit for replacing the baseball with a grapefruit. One version depicts Dodgers trainer Frank Kelly flying with Law as an accomplice of Stengel. Another version has Kelly not realizing the object was a grapefruit.[12]

Robinson brought Brooklyn to the World Series in 1916, his third year as manager. But 1916 belonged to the Boston Red Sox. He led Brooklyn to the World Series again in 1920, a watershed year for baseball because of a scandal that rocked the sport harder than a Walter Johnson fastball.

The Black Sox.

A few days before the 1920 World Series between the Brooklyn Robins/Dodgers and Cleveland Indians began, Eddie Cicotte and Shoeless Joe Jackson graduated rumors to fact about gamblers reaching their tentacles into the White Sox clubhouse to choke the oxygen of purity from baseball. Cicotte and Jackson testified before a Chicago grand jury that eight White Sox players "fixed" the 1919 World Series in exchange for payment from gamblers betting heavily on Chicago's opponent, the Cincinnati Reds. The White Sox became the "Black Sox" because of the black mark they placed on the game.

Another dark event occurred in 1920 baseball, tragic because of its finality. On August 16, Cleveland Indians shortstop Ray Chapman got hit in the head by a Carl Mays pitch in a Yankees-Indians game. Thinking the ball hit the bat, Mays fielded the pitch and threw to first baseman Wally Pipp. Chapman took three or four steps and then collapsed. Although he walked off the field with assistance, the Indians shortstop died early the next morning in the hospital.

Yankees manager Miller Huggins surmised that Chapman could not avoid Mays' pitch because his left foot spikes got caught in the dirt.[13] Perhaps Chapman did not see the ball. After a few innings, the round, white baseball became a less than circular orb discolored by dirt and grass, plus a pitcher's marring the ball with substances like tobacco juice, sandpaper. Custom dictated that a ball be used for multiple innings, so the ball got increasingly discolored as a game progressed.

The Indians persevered through the Chapman tragedy, meeting Brooklyn in the 1920 World Series. In the first inning of Game 5, Elmer Smith knocked a grand slam off Burleigh Grimes. Ignominy furthered for Brooklyn when, in the fifth inning, Indians second baseman Bill Wambsganss made an unassisted triple play, the only one in World Series history.

Brooklyn lost the 1920 World Series to Cleveland five games to two. After the season, Ebbets shipped Rube Marquard to Cincinnati because of Marquard's arrest for scalping World Series tickets in a Cleveland lobby. "A judge gave him what amounted to a slap on the wrist, but Dodgers owner Charles Ebbets vowed that Marquard would never pitch another game for Brooklyn," states baseball historian Lyle Spatz.[14]

The Dodgers might have faced the White Sox instead of the Indians in the World Series had White Sox owner Charles Comiskey responded differently to the testimony of conspirators turned confessors Cicotte and Jackson. Or not responded at all. Instead, Comiskey suspended seven of the eight players allegedly involved in the 1919 World Series fix—the eighth, Chick Gandil, had already left the team. Comiskey's decision emptied the White Sox roster of its star players during the final days of the 1920 American League pennant race. Tied with the Indians in late September, the White Sox lost two of their last three games to the St. Louis Browns and, in turn, the American League pennant to the Indians.

Getting to the World Series was not the only high mark in Brooklyn's 1920 season. The Robins set a major league record when a game against the Braves went 26 innings and ended in a tie. The *Brooklyn Daily Eagle* reported that the game lasted three hours and 50 minutes before darkness ended it.[15] It remains the longest major league game gauged by innings.

To infuse integrity back into baseball's bloodstream, the owners appointed Judge Kenesaw Mountain Landis as the first baseball commissioner. Landis, with a face as craggy as the Georgia mountain that inspired his name, had busted billionaire John D. Rockefeller's Standard Oil monopoly. Certainly, the owners thought, Landis could revive baseball's image.

Despite the acquittal of the eight White Sox players at trial in the summer of 1921, Landis confirmed his autonomy by banning them from baseball.

> Regardless of the verdict of juries, no player who throws a ball game, no player who undertakes or promises to throw a ball game, no player who sits in confidence with a bunch of crooked ballplayers and gamblers, where the ways and means of throwing a game are discussed and does not promptly tell his club about it, will ever play professional baseball.[16]

The Roaring '20s were off to a less than propitious start for baseball.

Hitters gained a tremendous advantage when the baseball powers outlawed the spitball in 1920. Plus, they could see the ball better thanks to a new rule inspired by the Chapman incident—a baseball must be replaced if it gets dirty. Despite Major League Baseball's spitball ban, Brooklyn's Burleigh Grimes enjoyed permanent exemption from the ruling along with other selected pitchers[17]:

Doc Ayers, Detroit Tigers
Dutch Leonard, Detroit Tigers
Ray Caldwell, Cleveland Indians
Stan Coveleski, Cleveland Indians
Red Faber, Chicago White Sox

Jack Quinn, New York Yankees

Allan Russell, Boston Red Sox

Urban Shocker, St. Louis Browns

Allen Sothoron, St. Louis Browns

Bill Doak, St. Louis Cardinals

Phil Douglas, New York Giants

Dana Fillingim, Boston Braves

Ray Fisher, Cincinnati Reds

Marv Goodwin, St. Louis Cardinals

Burleigh Grimes, Brooklyn Dodgers

Clarence Mitchell, Brooklyn Dodgers

Dick Rudolph, Boston Braves

Grimes, a well-traveled pitcher elected to the Baseball Hall of Fame by the Veterans Committee in 1964, played for seven teams in his career from 1916 to 1934: Pirates, Dodgers, Giants, Braves, Cardinals, Cubs, and Yankees. He threw the last legal spitball in Major League Baseball when he appeared in relief for the Pittsburgh Pirates on September 20, 1934, against the New York Giants. Grimes won 270 games, compiled five seasons of 20 victories or more, and earned a World Series championship with the 1931 Cardinals. He won two games in the Series.[18]

Still, the grand slam ball to Smith in the 1920 World Series irked him, such is the wont of athletes suffering a moment replayed by memory, recounted by historians, or revived by fans. Grimes biographer Joe Niese uncovered a story in which Grimes relived the grand slam nearly 60 years after it happened, while patronizing a bait shop close to his home on Lake Holcombe, Wisconsin. A beer sign's daily trivia question challenged baseball fans to name the player who hit the first grand slam in World Series history.

Grimes spit out the answer before the man had finished reading the question. "Elmer Smith."

"I knew he'd know it," said the owner proudly as Grimes paid for his bait.

As Grimes was about to exit the shop, he stopped at the door and turned toward the group at the counter. "And do you know who surrendered that home run?" The men responded that they didn't. "One Burleigh A. Grimes," replied Grimes, leaving the shop before the men could react.[19]

Grimes' Brooklyn tenure exemplified the borough as a community with the baseball team being its center. Baseball historian Harold Seymour, a Brooklyn native who was a batboy for the Robins in the 1920s, recalled Grimes' familiarity:

> Burleigh Grimes sometimes passed by on his evening stroll with a great black cigar in his mouth while youngsters were playing punch ball in the street. It was a thrill to be able to recognize him and say "Hiya Burleigh!" and have him reply "Having a workout son?" This simple exchange imparted the feeling that we, too, belonged to the wonderful world of baseball, even though on a different level.[20]

Charles Ebbets' death in 1925 severed the remaining link joining Brooklyn to the team's first season. After spending the winter at the Ebbets southern home in Clearwater, Florida, where the Brooklyn Robins trained, Ebbets returned to New York City on April 5, 12 years to the day since

From left to right: Philadelphia Phillies player-manager Jimmie Wilson, Brooklyn Dodgers part-owner and president Steve McKeever, Brooklyn Borough President Raymond Ingersoll and Brooklyn Dodgers manager Casey Stengel, circa 1934 (Brooklyn Public Library—Brooklyn Collection).

Ebbets Field debuted. Rather than go to his Brooklyn home at 1466 Glenwood Road, Ebbets stayed in his suite at the Waldorf-Astoria. On April 17, Dr. Robert Adams—the Waldorf-Astoria's house physician—reported, "Mr. Ebbets is a very, very sick man. I consider him to be in immediate danger. He has been troubled with heart disease for many years but never before has his condition been so serious. He has been sinking rapidly today. His trip South this Spring apparently did him no good at all."[21]

Ebbets died peacefully in his sleep at 6:00 p.m. on April 18.[22]

He knew every aspect of the team, starting his career on Day One as a jack-of-all-trades office boy, escalating to the president's office with mentor George Chauncey's endorsement, and sacrificing his self-interest to finance the building of Ebbets Field. Baseball incarnate, Ebbets had the passion for baseball that Steve Jobs had for computer technology, Henry Ford had for cars, and Galileo had for astronomy. The *New York Herald Tribune* eulogized, "Virtually the whole of Mr. Ebbets' life was devoted to baseball. His sole interest was baseball and all his money was in it. He served the game wholeheartedly, with a fixed purpose which finally brought fulfillment."[23]

Ebbets' innovations revolutionized baseball. He's credited with inventing the rain check and the draft system, allowing the weakest teams to get the first choice of minor league players. He also advocated for creating a permanent World Series schedule and the extending the National League schedule to include the Columbus Day holiday.[24]

Baseball, like Brooklyn, adored Ebbets as it did Byrne. National League president John Heydler said, "Mr. Ebbets was probably the best beloved man in baseball, not only in his own league, but in other leagues as well. He was highly regarded everywhere and stood for the best interests of the game."[25]

Reach Baseball Guide praised, "He never played baseball 'politics,' was without guide, and so universally popular that he may be truly said to have been the best loved man, not only in his own league, but throughout the entire realm of baseball. Ebbets was one of the comparatively few old time magnates whose interest in the affairs of the game never faltered."[26]

On April 19, the Dodgers played the Giants in the second game of a two-game series, prefaced by a "silent tribute" to Ebbets before the game. Wearing black arm bands, the rival teams lost no love between them. "Otherwise, the party was as nice and friendly as a mass meeting of blood enemies," reported the *New York Times*.[27]

Heydler cancelled all National League games scheduled for April 21, the date of Ebbets' funeral.[28] Two thousand people shuffled into Trinity Church to pay their respects while another 2,000 remained outside.[29] Before arriving at Greenwood Cemetery, the funeral procession circled Ebbets Field and Washington Park.[30] There was no eulogy, but the choir sang *Now the Laborer's Task Is Over*, *Lead Kindly Light*, and *Nearer, My God, to Thee*.[31]

Co-owner Ed McKeever took over as team president; he got sick at Ebbets' funeral and died 11 days later.[32] Wilbert Robinson was elected to the presidency while Steven McKeever co-owned the team with the Ebbets estate—its executors were the Brooklyn Trust Company, Joseph A. Gileaudeu, and Grace Slade Ebbets, the owner's widow.

When Robinson ascended to the Dodgers presidency in 1925, a team statement recounted Robinson's boyhood days in Hudson, Massachusetts, where he organized a game against Bedford at the age of 12. "I went to our livery man and hired a horse and wagon," said Robinson. "We placed boards across the wagon bed and I hauled the whole nine over to Bedford, proudly driving the old hoss myself."[33]

Robinson also recalled how he learned the game of baseball with a contraption that Rube Goldberg would have copied, had he been a baseball fan.

Funny how I learned to catch behind the bat. I rigged up a clothes line in our back yard and fixed it just as high as my face when I leaned over and then I would have a boy throw a ball to me, trying every time to hit that clothes line. That was how I came to be the catcher for the first nine in our town when I was three years younger than any other boy on the team.

You see, after I had blinked at that clothes line and been banged up by those foul tips off the line I got so I could catch any kind of a ball and the waving of a bat meant nothing to me at all. Our team played the first nine on which two of my older brothers played. After the second inning their catcher got hurt by a foul tip and they insisted that I catch for both teams. I did. And I was so steamed up over catching that I worked the seventeen innings and never thought till afterwards that I had not "had by bats" at all.

After that I caught regularly for the first nine and that was the proudest, happiest summer of my life. Joining the Orioles never gave me the thrill I had when those boys said after that game that I could catch for the "first nine."

They may elect me president of the Brooklyn club but I can never have as high honor as I had back in Hudson when I was pointed out as the kid that caught for the first time.[34]

A long-standing joke represents the fans' humorous outlook during the bleak times for Brooklyn in the 1920s. A cab driver has his radio tuned to the game when a pedestrian inquires, "How's the game going?" The driver says, "The Dodgers have three men on base." The pedestrian inquires further, "Which base?"

Sometimes, the roles are reversed with a cab driver passing Ebbets Field and shouting the inquiry to a spectator. Still, the event referenced in the joke actually happened in a game against the Boston Braves in 1926.

One bright spot was Zack Wheat, the Brooklyn left fielder who racked up hits with the consistency of an assembly line. In a 19-year career from 1909 to 1927, Wheat churned out 2,884 hits. Eleven of those seasons saw Wheat amass hit totals exceeding 150, with three seasons exceeding 200 hits. But he reached the 100-RBI plateau in only two seasons—1922 and 1925—a testament to Brooklyn's absolute frailty in putting runners on base.[35]

Robinson left his front office duties as team president in 1929, but stayed in the manager job through the 1931 season. Before he stepped down, the September 1931 issue of *Baseball Magazine* surmised that 1931 would be Robbie's last season. It chastised the press for lambasting Robinson and spotlighted his managerial skills given the resources he had.

> Robbie, so it is said, is neither a good coach nor a good field general. Admitted. He has been called conservative. Correct. But with a minimum of financial backing he has for many years given Brooklyn fans a good run for their money. He has won pennants and come near to winning pennants. While exaggerating his faults and defects to the point of absolute nausea, why not give a fleeting glance to his good points?[36]

Future Hall of Famer Zack Wheat, a rare example of excellence in Brooklyn's lean years during the 1920s (National Baseball Hall of Fame Library, Cooperstown, New York).

Robinson's departure led the team's management to solidify a mercurial attitude toward the team's name. It turned to the Brooklyn chapter of baseball writers, which balanced the pros and cons of the various labels. On January 23, 1932, the *Brooklyn Daily Eagle* conveyed the team's permanent name with a banner headline across page 14: Brooklyn Baseball Club Will Officially Nickname Them "Dodgers."[37]

Thomas Holmes detailed the decision's logic:

> "Bridegrooms" and "Superbas" were unwieldy names. The weakness of 'Robins' as a nickname was the name's natural link to Wilbert Robinson. Through the years, 'Dodgers' has hung on pretty well. Since the passing of Mr. Robinson, there has been agitation in various quarters to settle upon a nickname that would be universal and unchanging. Alive to the discussion, Ebbets Field last week notified the Brooklyn baseball writers that it would officially adopt any nickname that the writers desired. Yesterday, the scribes voted for "Dodgers," preferring it to "Kings," which was the only other nickname that received serious consideration.[38]

When Wilbert Robinson died in 1934, players lauded his mentoring beyond the baseball diamond. "Robbie's death is a shock to baseball but to me it is a great personal loss. I worked with him seven years. He taught me how to play the sun field. He was like a father to me and the others under him," said Casey Stengel, a Brooklyn Dodgers outfielder who managed the Dodgers in the mid–1930s and later guided the New York Yankees to several World Series championships against his former team."[39]

National League president John Heydler said, "His fair fighting, his support of the umpires, his philosophy and good humor relieved the grind and stress of many a championship team."[40] Giants president Horace Stoneham said, "He was an outstanding figure in the sport, one of those who grew up with it. A pleasing personality, a disposition that seldom ever became ruffled, a capable player, manager, and club executive, he embodied the highest ideals of baseball."[41]

But the gentle and genial Uncle Robbie was not always gentle and genial. Sportswriter Damon Runyon saw the darker side of Robinson during their first meeting when Robinson was a Giants coach. It happened on a New York Giants train trip to Texas for the Giants' training camp. Runyon disclosed the story—which included a potential crux for Robinson's metamorphosis into an avuncular fellow—in his *The Mornin's Mornin* column in the September 19, 1915, edition of the *New York American*.

> "Robbie" was along in his capacity as coach of the young pitchers, and we thought of him then, and afterward, as we saw him bulked down in a Pullman seat, roaring rude jests at all and sundry, as a very rough and a very coarse old man.
>
> We remember that we marveled somewhat at the camaraderie that seemed to exist between the old fellow and the ball players, as manifested in mighty

scufflings in the aisles, and over the seats, and in ribald banterings; but we remember, too, that we felt that here was a character whose room would ever be much pleasanter than his company. He was too heavy-handed; too uncouth.[42]

Tragedy turned the harsh coach into a merciful angel offering comfort to an athlete dying young—Tom Hanley, a minor league pitcher with a mediocre record trying to break into the major leagues. Hanley had an 8–6 record with the Zanesville Potters of the Central League in 1911 and a 14–14 record with the Newark Skeeters of the Ohio State League in 1912.[43]

Hanley stood out because he did not fit into the paradigm of a training camp filled with activity, banter, and chatter. Runyon wrote, "The writer recalls him, vaguely enough, as a tall, thin blond young fellow, with very old eyes, who was generally found seated, always off by himself, out in the sunlight that sprays the verandas of the Arlington in the Spring—a lonely-looking figure in the rush and bustle of the camp."[44]

Runyon witnessed Robinson's consolation of Hanley, forced to bed by an illness preventing him from rejoining his teammates. "It was too late to save Hanley but for hours and hours old 'Robbie' kept watch and ward at the bedside of the boy, now talking to the lad in a voice as soft and soothing as a woman's, and now growling with indignation because of the neglect in the case."[45] Wilbert Robinson's expression of quiet kindness during Hanley's illness showed that toughness is not reserved for sliding into second base with spikes high, brushing back a batter from the plate with a high and tight pitch, or arguing with an umpire.

Toughness. That's the Brooklyn way.

The Dodgers played the role of National League spoiler in 1934, a delicious position considering the victim was a blood enemy—the Giants. In January, Giants player-manager Bill Terry told the press that the Giants' competition for the pennant would be the Pittsburgh Pirates, the St. Louis Cardinals, and the Chicago Cubs. When a reporter followed with a query about Terry fearing the Dodgers, Terry responded, "I was just wondering whether they were still in the league."[46]

Terry may have been trying to be funny rather than hurtful. It boomeranged on him and the Giants at the end of the season when the Dodgers proved that they belonged in Mr. Terry's league, National and otherwise. In a pennant race with the Cardinals, the Giants crumpled—they lost 11 of 19 games before facing the Dodgers in a two-game series to end the 1934 season. The Dodgers won both games and the Cardinals won their last four games to gain the NL pennant, beating the Tigers in the World Series.

The Giants would have to wait 17 years to turn the tide against the Dodgers. By that time, Casey Stengel had become a Yankees icon.

To say that Casey Stengel was a colorful character is to say that the Sistine Chapel is a nice work of art.

Stengel's tether to Brooklyn began in 1912, his rookie year in the major leagues; Stengel played in a Brooklyn uniform for six seasons. He notched tenures with the Pittsburgh Pirates, New York Giants, and Boston Braves before hanging up his spikes in 1925 with a .284 career batting average in nearly 4,300 at bats.[47]

Managing the Brooklyn team from 1934 to 1936, Stengel ignited a feature story in the *New York Times* about a bidding war during Stengel's playing days in Brooklyn. Charles Ebbets fought with fists full of dollars against the Chicago Feds and the Kansas City Feds of the Federal League to secure Stengel's services for 1915.[48]

Playing in Brooklyn remained a source of affection for Stengel, inspiring him to draw a distinction between full-throated Brooklynites and timidly vocal Manhattanites in a 1934 interview with the *New York World-Telegram.* "They didn't bother me much, of course. I was getting up and they was very well satisfied with me. But I knew as soon as I heard them yell, so clear, so healthy, not with weak city lungs, like in Manhattan, that I would love playing ball in Brooklyn."[49]

Stengel also figured that the Brooklyn team got a bum rap from an image rooted in silliness.

> So, naturally, our mistakes get more attention. Like in the all-star game between the two leagues, Al Lopez, our catcher, caught two of those American League managers off base on one run-down play. Cochrane and Cronin, both of them supposed to be master minds. I suppose they was so busy congratulating each other on being smart that they was not paying any attention. But if a couple of Dodgers got caught like that you would never hear the end of it.
>
> But give me a fellow that don't care for anybody and bears down all the time, and when he sees another fellow he will fly into that fellow and plow down, and if he has any petty grievance or contract trouble he will take it out on those Giants, and Brooklyn will love him and he will not wish to go anywhere else.[50]

Stengel's mental gymnastics recall a play that did not happen. Lopez picked off Cronin in the 1934 All-Star Game, but Cochrane was not even in the game when it happened. That's not the oddest play in Stengel's humorous though flawed—in this instance—recollection. During World War II, Private Joe Hasel interviewed Stengel for the Armed Forces Radio Services; a transcript of the show's rebroadcast features Stengel recounting a bizarre play from the bottom of the ninth inning in game circa 1915 against Philadelphia. A line drive over the first baseman's head approached the right field wall "and proceeded like it had legs, climbed the wall and laid up on top, all the spectators were quiet for about a half a minute, and then the ball rolled on the outside."[51] Under today's rules, the ball would be a ground rule double. Back then, it was a home run.

Stengel's verbal outbursts were not limited to quips, quotes, and sound bites. He was a ribber, the person on the team capable of making fun of the other team's players with verbal darts that, on occasion, hit an emotional vein that exploded with fury. On May 12, 1936, the ribbing escalated to fisticuffs with Leo Durocher, the Cardinals' shortstop, under the Ebbets Field stands. Because the teams shared common access to the locker rooms, physical proximity made fights easier on an impromptu basis.

Versions differed. Durocher alleged that seven Brooklyn ballplayers began attacking him with baseball bats. The Dodgers denied this, claiming the Cardinals assisted Durocher by pounding on Stengel. Faithful yet hyperbolic, a Brooklyn fan said, "I was standing there minding my business when 25 Cardinals, led by Frisch and Durocher, leaped on Mr. Stengel all at once. Mr. Stengel knocked out 15 of them before the cops stopped it."[52]

No matter the verbal or physical arrows slung from the competition, Brooklyn would not be swayed from its nexus to the Dodgers in mind, heart, and spirit. A full-page ad sponsored by the Brooklyn National League Baseball Club on the occasion of baseball's 70th anniversary of baseball in Brooklyn in 1936 celebrated team president Steve McKeever who, along with his brother, helped fund Ebbets Field. The ad's text began with a simple yet eloquent description: "Brooklyn is loyal to baseball because baseball has been loyal to Brooklyn."[53]

Loyalty shouldered the burdens of ignominy, sorrow, and defeat as a gloomy aura continued to envelop the Dodgers. During the Depression, fans became inured to rooting for a less than venerable team exhibiting a Keystone Kops quality. Ebbets' Pigtown warren became a site inspiring disgust, but not dismay. Frowns, but not tears. Relentless fealty saturated the Ebbets Field kingdom, whether the Dodgers were bumbling jesters or victorious princes.

Before the 1938 season began, Brooklyn lost another icon. Steve McKeever, a.k.a. "the Judge," died of bronchial pneumonia on March 7, 1938. Horace Stoneham acknowledged McKeever's ability to supersede the conflicts between the denizens of the Polo Grounds and Ebbets Field. "The Giants are and always will be natural rivals. Yet our relationship with Brooklyn has been friendly, thanks to poor Judge McKeever, a 100 percent sportsman, whose passing was a blow to our national game."[54] Joe Sartori, the owner of Joe's Roman Gardens restaurant and a self-described diehard Brooklyn fan, said, "Whenever anybody mentioned the Dodgers you just had to think of McKeever."[55]

McKeever signified the Brooklyn attitude of neighborliness with his standard "How's your heart?" query upon meeting someone.

Neighborliness. That's the Brooklyn way.

McKeever's death broke another link between the Dodgers' past and present. Nostalgia cordoned the former from ridicule; chaos exposed the latter. Though beloved for its history, the Dodgers' culture of ineptitude did not stop at the baseball diamond. It permeated the Dodgers' management.

Reeling from debt to the Brooklyn Trust Company, the Dodgers turned to Larry MacPhail, the general manager of the Cincinnati Reds possessing the next best thing to a godly endorsement—the commendation of National League president Ford Frick. "When MacPhail first walked into the Dodgers' office, at 215 Montague Street, Brooklyn, he felt that he had taken a position in which there was a great opportunity for the right man," wrote Robert Lewis Taylor in a two-part profile of MacPhail for the *New Yorker* in 1941. "The Dodgers were in a low state. The Administration was disorganized, the telephone service had been shut off, office employees were out looking for jobs that paid a salary every week, and the waiting room was filled with bill-collectors and process-servers."[56]

There was a deficit everywhere MacPhail looked—in the financial ledgers, on the ball field, and in Brooklyn's psyche. It was a mess begging for structure, order, and discipline. Taylor further described the consequences of mismanagement. "The club was heavily in debt, owing one creditor—the Brooklyn Trust Company—half a million dollars. The bank, as the most interested creditor, was practically running the team. The League executives were worried that the Dodgers might actually go out of existence."[57]

MacPhail initiated night baseball in Brooklyn during his rookie year in the front office after pioneering it in Cincinnati. Its Brooklyn debut provided the background for a baseball record that still stands—Johnny Vander Meer of the Cincinnati Reds pitched two consecutive no-hitters in June. He first blanked the Boston Braves, then the Brooklyn Dodgers in Ebbets Field's first night game.

About a month after Vander Meer's feat, the Giants-Dodgers rivalry turned violent when a post office worker avenged verbal taunts about the Dodgers by shooting his tormentors. On July 12, 1938, Robert Joyce basked in the Dodgers' 13–5 victory over the Giants earlier that afternoon. It was a bright moment in a dull season for the sub-par Dodgers. Joyce celebrated with 18 glasses of beer at Diamond's Bar and Grill, owned by Patrick J. Diamond, Democratic leader of Brooklyn's 8th Assembly District. "The prisoner, police said, is an enthusiastic Dodger baseball fan and resented some of the jibes at his favorite team made by the 30 other patrons in the place," reported the *Brooklyn Daily Eagle*.[58]

Police quoted Joyce as saying he was "going out [to] get two guns and shoot up the place."[59] And that's just what happened. Joyce had access to the post office, knew where the guns were located, and focused on vengeance with his anger fueled by alcohol. "According to Postmaster Francis J. Sinnott, Joyce had the keys to the post office because he was the early man assigned to open it at 5 a.m."[60]

Joyce did not execute his revenge immediately. The *Eagle* reported that Joyce started drinking around 9:00 p.m., left the bar, and waited until the late clerk closed the post office branch at 12:30 a.m. to retrieve the gun. Joyce returned to the bar a couple of hours later.[61]

William J. Diamond—the bar owner's son—was the first victim, followed by Frank Krug, a 39-year-old accountant in the Albany office of the Emergency Relief Bureau visiting his family in Brooklyn during his vacation. "He killed Krug instantly with a bullet through the heart. Young Diamond, 28, who lives at 420 8th Ave., was shot twice through the left side. A fourth shot went wild,"[62] the *Eagle* reported.

Joyce's journey of unbridled revenge did not happen smoothly, however. After shooting Diamond, Joyce attempted to intimidate Krug and a waiter, Charles Miller, after they "pounced on the clerk and wrested the revolver from him."[63] Joyce used the second gun to shoot Krug. When questioned by police the next morning, Joyce claimed he didn't remember the incident.[64]

Using fists instead of guns, Frankie Gennaro took action against those threatening the welfare of the Dodgers. Gennaro's target was George Magerkurth, an umpire. After the final Reds-Dodgers game of the 1940 season, Gennaro protested Magerkurth's reversal of a call by fellow umpire Bill Stewart. It cost the Dodgers the game in the tenth inning. Roscoe

McGowen of the *New York Times* explained, "Pete Coscarart had muffed a force-play throw from Johnny Hudson in the tenth. Stewart called Ival Goodman out on the play, and when [Reds Manager Bill] McKechnie and the Reds protested he appealed to Magerkurth, who promptly ruled Coscarart had muffed the ball, not dropped it as he was about to throw it."[65]

Dodgers manager Leo Durocher protested, once again earning his nickname "Leo the Lip" from the fans, press, and baseball brotherhood. When the game concluded, hundreds of fans funneled on to the field. The 21-year-old Gennano, described by McGowen as "a stocky 200-pounder," confronted Magerkurth, a 6'3" behemoth exceeding more than 200 pounds. "Only a word or two was exchanged, then Gennaro swung on the umpire, who struck back just as promptly," reported McGowen. "In the flurry of

Leo Durocher justifying his nickname "Leo the Lip" in one of many arguments with an umpire (National Baseball Hall of Fame Library, Cooperstown, New York).

blows the umpire went down on his back with his opponent on top of him, dealing lefts and rights briskly at Mage's face. Then the crowd closed in, with several uniformed ushers and special park policemen in the van."[66]

A scene in the 1942 movie *It Happened in Flatbush* mirrors the incident. While only mentioning "Brooklyn" but not the team's name, the movie clearly takes place at Ebbets Field.

The Dodgers' fortunes changed from jackpot to lemons as they approached a World Series championship in 1941. After edging the Cardinals to win the National League pennant by 2½ games with a 100–54 record, the Dodgers met the Yankees in the World Series. Down two games to one, the Dodgers owned a 4–3 lead going into the top of the ninth inning in Game 4 at Ebbets Field.

With two outs, Dodgers pitcher Hugh Casey worked Tommy Henrich to a full count. Then Henrich swung at a pitch and missed. The game was seemingly over. But catcher Mickey Owen could not hold on to the ball. As the ball treaded the ground on Owen's right, Henrich sprinted for first base and beat Owen's throw. The Yankees scored four runs to take a 7–4 lead, stopped the Dodgers in the bottom of the ninth to secure a 3–1 lead in games, and won Game 5 to take the World Series championship.

News about Owen's error traveled at the speed of light throughout Brooklyn's neighborhoods.

> The Dodgers permeated Brooklyn. The women who were housewives used to sit with their elbows on a pillow on the windowsill and you could follow the game while walking down the street. When Mickey Owen dropped the third strike in Game 4 of the '41 World Series that allowed the Yankees to rally and win the game, it broke up a punch ball game because someone had a radio hanging out the window."[67]

The 1941 World Series held special significance for Private Murray Waldenburg—a red, white, and blue Brooklynite. Stationed at Camp Wheeler in Macon, Georgia, Waldenburg confronted an officer who made a sarcastic remark about the Dodgers' National League pennant chances. Waldenburg said, "Look, mister. I don't know you and you don't know me. Call me names. You can put me on k.p. for a week and it'll be a pleasure. You can even take away my passes for a holiday. But please, mister, don't make humorous remarks about them Dodgers."[68]

Waldenburg's tale reached the offices of the *New York Journal-American*, inspiring a phone call to Camp Wheeler's commander, Brigadier General John Hutchison Hester. With a Georgia accent that could have placed him in the cast of *Gone with the Wind*, Hester gave permission

Pre-game ceremony at Ebbets Field during World War II (National Baseball Hall of Fame Library, Cooperstown, New York).

for Waldenburg to leave camp. "Suh, I'm from Jawjuh myself, but I'm rootin' for them Dodgers,"[69] explained Hester to the *Journal-American* envoy. Camp Wheeler was the latest stop for Brigadier General Hester in a storied military career that included commanding the 43rd Infantry Division in the South Pacific Theater in World War II.[70] But when he answered his telephone on a mid–September day in 1941, he became a hero to Brooklyn.

Larry MacPhail offered tickets to Waldenburg for two World Series games if the Dodgers won the National League pennant. On his journey northward, Waldenburg praised the Dodgers' generosity. "Oh, yeah, it's wonderful what dem bums will do for a guy,"[71] said Waldenburg, whose experience was not the only unexpected occurrence in the Dodgers' annals of September 1941. The aurora borealis and sun spots knocked out a radio broadcast of a Dodgers-Pirates game for 15 minutes. When the radio signals went down, the teams were in a scoreless tie. The Pirates led by four runs when the broadcast resumed.[72]

Despite the full-throated support of Waldenburg and the rest of Brooklyn, urban popinjays basked in the warm glow of pinstriped victory while a cold feeling of haplessness pervaded Brooklyn like the fog shrouding Dickensian London at the beginning of *Bleak House*. Brooklyn would always be second best. Or so it seemed.

Still, the 1941 World Series appearance was a salve for Brooklyn, which had not seen a Dodgers team in the World Series in more than two decades. Since MacPhail took over the club management in 1938, he fortified the roster, improved the finances, and restored Brooklyn's psyche. "He realizes that Brooklyn, without much in the way of tall buildings and plushy night clubs, feels inferior to Manhattan, and he has capitalized on the borough's sensitivity by giving it a powerful baseball team. Every time the Dodgers defeat the Giants, the people of Brooklyn forget their rural condition,"[73] wrote Taylor. Practicality was MacPhail's yardstick, not sentimentality.

By the time 1941 turned into 1942, the exclamation point in the phrase "Play Ball!" became a question mark with the nation at war in two theatres, European and Pacific. Commissioner Landis sought counsel from President Roosevelt regarding baseball as a continuing industry. The commissioner's missive of January 14, 1942, shows deference with a hint of wonder in the closing.

> Dear Mr. President:
> The time is approaching when, in ordinary conditions, our teams would be heading for Spring training camps. However, inasmuch as these are not ordinary times, I venture to ask what you have in mind as to whether professional baseball should continue to operate. Of course my inquiry does not relate at all to individual members of this organization whose status in this emergency, is fixed by law operating upon all citizens. Normally we have, in addition to the sixteen major teams, approximately three hundred and twenty minor teams—members of leagues playing in the United States and Canada.
> Health and strength to you—and whatever it takes to do this job.[74]

President Roosevelt responded the next day with "solely a personal and not an official point of view." He refused to issue a presidential fiat, but he encouraged Landis to continue baseball.

> I honestly feel that it would be best for the country to keep baseball going. There will be fewer people unemployed and everybody will work longer hours and harder than ever before.
> And that means that they ought to have a chance for recreation and for taking their minds off their work even more than before.
> Baseball provides a recreation which does not last over two hours or two

hours and a half, and which can be got for very little cost. And, incidentally, I hope that night games can be extended because it gives an opportunity to the day shift to see a game occasionally.

As to the players themselves, I know you agree with me that individually players who are of active military or naval age should go, without question, into the services. Even if the actual quality of the teams is lowered by the greater use of older players, this will not dampen the popularity of the sport. Of course, if any individual has some particular aptitude in a trade or profession, he ought to serve the Government. That, however, is a matter which I know you can handle with complete justice.

Here is another way of looking at it—if 300 teams use 5,000 or 6,000 players, these players are a definite recreational asset to at least 20,000,000 of their fellow citizens—and that in my judgment is thoroughly worthwhile."[75]

Roosevelt's "green light" letter legitimized baseball as a component of the World War II home front morale machine while names like Okinawa, El Alamein, and Normandy became as familiar as the names in the Dodgers lineup, more so if a family on your street had a son serving overseas. Fans who once prayed in the grandstands of Ebbets Field for the Dodgers to win the World Series now prayed in congregations at churches and synagogues for the safe return of the servicemen.

A veteran of World War I, MacPhail gave structure to Roosevelt's vague but encouraging missive. His opportunity came during the annual dinner of the New York chapter of the Baseball Writers' Association at the Commodore Hotel in Manhattan, less than a one-minute walk from Grand Central Terminal. More than 1,000 people attended, including New York City mayor Fiorello LaGuardia, former New York City mayor James J. Walker, United States Navy Commander John Reynolds (Head of Morale), and United States Army Major Theodore P. Bank (Head of Morale). The date was February 1, 1942, less than two months after the Pearl Harbor attack.[76]

MacPhail urged his brethren to refuse a "business as usual" approach to baseball. "We are expected to do more than provide recreation for twenty million workers. We are expected to work out a definite program of unselfish co-operation with agencies of government needing help. If we keep the faith, the workers will agree with the President that baseball has its place in an all-out effort to win the war."[77]

MacPhail outlined specific actions for Major League Baseball:

- Create a second All-Star Game to be played by one team consisting of players already enlisted in the armed forces against the winning team of the first All-Star game;

- Move the All-Star game scheduled for Ebbets Field to the Polo Grounds because its bigger seating capacity would lead to more money generated and donated to the armed forces
- Dedicate a percentage of the revenue generated by ticket sales to be allotted for the purchase of a bomber for the Army or Navy; and
- Encourage anybody employed in baseball to receive part of his income in war bonds or stamps.

The bomber idea never reached fruition, but the dual All-Star Games did. The country also enjoyed a boost in subscriptions to war bonds and stamps, and baseball's donations across the major and minor leagues amounted to $1,294,958.67 for the Army and Navy.[78]

As MacPhail stirred up patriotism, the Dodgers played outstanding baseball. Their 1942 record was 104–50, but it was not good enough to beat the Cardinals for the National League pennant. With a record of 106–48, the Cardinals went to the World Series and beat the Yankees in five games.

There were a couple of low moments for the boys from Brooklyn, too. Pete Reiser suffered a concussion after thundering into the outfield's concrete wall while pursuing an Enos Slaughter fly ball in a Dodgers-Cardinals game in St. Louis. Though he missed only four games, his batting average plummeted from .350 to .310. In addition, MacPhail resigned from the Dodgers on September 24, 1942, nearly a year after Owen's dropped ball. Duty to country trumped duty to baseball—Lieutenant Colonel would be MacPhail's new title as a member of the Service of Supply.[79] Taylor's *New Yorker* piece captured the bond between the MacPhail and Brooklyn.

> Bellicose, red-faced, and clownish, he is the idol of a community which demands such qualities of its heroes. The people there are comfortable in the knowledge that MacPhail will take care of all disparagers of their baseball team. He never disappoints them. His command of vituperation and eagerness to battle for the Brooklyn team have made him, by extension, a kind of borough defender.[80]

Along with the Dodgers board of directors, MacPhail brushed off rumors that financial mismanagement caused his departure.

> I have spent about a million for ballplayers, and this year alone, I spent $250,000 on repairs to the ball park. But I leave the Brooklyn club with $300,000 in the bank and in a position to pay off the mortgage. We have paid off $600,000 we owed the Brooklyn Trust Company and have reduced the mortgage another $600,000, to $320,000. I have sold the radio rights for 1943 for $150,000.[81]

MacPhail received a gift from the Dodgers players for his efforts—a watch with the inscription "Larry—From His Players—1942."[82] MacPhail's exit opened the door for his mentor, a lawyer turned baseball executive with an impressive résumé including World Series championships, unparalleled baseball know-how, and an idea that would revolutionize the game. And America.

Branch Rickey.

4th Inning: "Democracy has finally invaded baseball"

A veteran Dodger said of him, "Having Jackie on the team is still a little strange, just like anything else that's new. We just don't know how to act with him. But he'll be accepted in time. You can be sure of that. Other sports have had Negroes. Why not baseball? I'm for him, if he can win games. That's the only test I ask." And that seems to be the general opinion.[1]—Arthur Daley, *New York Times*, April 16, 1947

The address 215 Montague Street was more important to Dodgers fans than 1600 Pennsylvania Avenue to Washington, D.C., politicos. It was, of course, the address for the headquarters of the Dodgers. On the fourth floor of this ten-story building in the Brooklyn Heights neighborhood, Dodgers executives dictated trades, salaries, and manager hirings. Fans, too, paraded to the fourth floor, where they could purchase tickets to Dodgers' home games.

When Branch Rickey walked into 215 Montague Street for the first time as Dodgers general manager, he closed a 25-year chapter in St. Louis and opened a new one that he hoped to fill with changes to baseball, not merely victories, pennants, and World Series championships. In 1942, Rickey's last year in St. Louis, the Cardinals won the World Series championship—his fourth—a final jewel in an already sparkling crown of achievement, including sports marketing; Rickey pioneered promotions to create the next generation of Cardinals fans. A 1932 article in the *Cleveland Plain Dealer* reported,

> One of his early ideas was the "knothole gang"—a plan whereby he built up interest in the Cardinals by giving membership passes, good five days a week, to youthful St. Louis fans. Not only did their enthusiasm spread to their elders, increasing gate receipts, but knothole members became cash customers as they grew up.

Walter O'Malley (left) and Branch Rickey (Brooklyn Public Library—Brooklyn Collection). Rickey became the general manager of the Brooklyn Dodgers in 1942. At the time, O'Malley was the team's attorney. Both owned stock in the team. Rickey left the Dodgers in 1950 in a boardroom squabble with O'Malley. Eventually, O'Malley became the sole owner of the Dodgers.

Supplemented by frequent "ladies' days," the passes to the "gang" helped build up a following for the team long before pennants materialized.[2]

A letter contract dated October 28, 1942, detailed Rickey's duties and compensation with the Brooklyn Dodgers, with a qualifier related to World War II.

Term: 5 years

Services: Exclusive

Salary: $25,000 per year and 15% of profits, but when the war is over, then the salary increases to $50,000 and profit share reduced to 10% if National League baseball is in existence. If NL ball does not exist when the war is over, then the compensation is not increased until January 15th of the year after the war ends or 30 days before the next NL season, whatever date is earlier.[3]

Harold Parrott, later to become the Dodgers' public relations man, wrote a five-part series of articles for the *Brooklyn Daily Eagle* introducing Rickey to Brooklyn. It was an exercise in salesmanship—no wonder Rickey plucked him from the *Eagle* to spearhead the Dodgers' publicity efforts.

Characters? Say, buddy, we've had 'em!

But we haven't had 'em all. Not yet—not until we've had Mr. Rickey. Branch Rickey, Sr., Mr. Baseball himself.

He follows MacPhail, and ordinarily they'd call that bad theater. Coming after the Dodger Dynamo onto the Brooklyn stage is like following Toscanini with a tin horn. Or would be for almost anybody I can think of.

But Rickey—well, he's a card! He may not make Brooklyn fans forget MacPhail—but I guarantee he'll make 'em remember Rickey.[4]

Parrott also praised Rickey's negotiating skills by quoting a source familiar to Dodgers fans—Casey Stengel.

"There is only one way to get the best of that Rickey in a deal," said Stengel. "You let B.R. Talk for two hours on the strong and weak points of the player he wants to get from you and the player he wants to sell you and then when he leans back and says 'Is it a deal' you snap 'No!' and walk out of danger."

"But nothing happened," complained one of Casey's listeners. "You do not get the best of Rickey by walking away—"

"Oh no?" Casey snorted. "That shows how little you know that man. Any time you can confer with Rickey and come out with your shirt, your watch and the fillings in your teeth you have outsmarted him!"[5]

A lawyer who turned away from the practice of law early in his career, Rickey brought his analytical training to the game he loved. Branch Barrett Rickey, president of the Pacific Coast League, recalls his grandfather's career as an emblem of success resulting from dedication:

My grandfather was quintessentially a lifelong baseball loyalist. He spent over 50 years in the game. He didn't look for the easy way on anything and he loved to innovate. But he had so much energy, he never had to shy away from taking on hard challenges.

He needed money to support his wife and young child while he was studying at the University of Michigan Law School. The head coaching job opened up for the university's baseball team, but the law school dean didn't think it was an appropriate job for a law student. He didn't think the coaching would leave him enough time for his studies. So, the dean refused my grandfather's request to be allowed to apply. My grandfather began a very earnest campaign signing up anyone of influence to lobby on his behalf. Finally, the dean okayed my grandfather taking the job on one condition—stop the letters flooding his office!

The results speak for themselves. My grandfather is the only student, even now over 100 years later, to have graduated the University of Michigan Law School one year early. And during his coaching career, the Michigan baseball team had its greatest winning percentage.

This anecdote may give you a sense of how contagiously stimulating he was as a grandfather, as well. Subsequently, I learned many others who weren't his grandson also felt the same.[6]

Rickey also played baseball, though his talents were better suited for management. He was a catcher with the St. Louis Browns from 1905 to 1906 and the New York Highlanders in 1907, when he allowed 13 stolen bases in a game against the Washington Senators. Rickey got a front office job with the St. Louis Browns in 1913, managed the team for the last 12 games of the season, and compiled a sub–.500 record as manager for 1914–1915. After serving in France during World War I, Rickey went to St. Louis' other team, the Cardinals, where he became team president and manager.

Rickey's circle included George H. Williams, a powerful Missouri attorney who became a judge and a United States Senator. Williams met with Rickey in Washington, D.C., before the latter's departure from New York for Europe to serve his country. In a letter to Rickey's wife, Alice, Williams praised Rickey's decision to don a uniform: "Men of Branch's capacity and aspiration must assume leadership in problems of peace. The country will be run after the war by those who have participated in it. The leaders in peace will come from those who have served in war."[7]

Rickey's reign as team president lasted the 1919 season, but he stayed as manager under new owner Sam Breadon till 1926, when Rogers Hornsby took over managing duties as player-manager. Returning to the front office, Rickey devised an infrastructure for baseball—the farm system. "Rickey visualized a chain of minor-league teams of various classifications—a kindergarten, grade school, preparatory school and a university of baseball—which eventually would graduate shining Phi Beta Kappa students of the game—Hornsbys, Frisches, Sislers, Cobbs, Speakers and Mathewsons,"[8] explained St. Louis sports writer J. Roy Stockton.

The Cardinals vanquished the Yankees to win the 1926 World Series, the culmination of a season determining baseball loyalties for one branch of the author's family tree because of a contrarian rooter in the Ebbets

Field stands during a Cardinals vs. Dodgers game. I'm reminded of it every Passover when a three-bedroom home in East Brunswick, New Jersey, is transformed into Seder Central for the Krell family. Ellen, my second cousin and the youngest of my great-aunt Gloria's four daughters, hosts both nights of *seder* with a complete reading of the Haggadah, the booklet containing the Passover story with accompanying prayers

At some point during the "festive meal"—as described by the Haggadah—her husband, Eddie Seckler, will dash to his home office to monitor the Cardinals game on KMOX.com. Or MLB.com. Or Cardinals.com. Eddie, a dead ringer for Gary Sandy from *WKRP in Cincinnati*, has Cardinal Nation in his blood.

> My father, Sheldon Seckler, was six years old in 1926. My grandfather took him to a game at Ebbets Field where the Dodgers were playing the Cardinals. For no apparent reason, my father rooted for the Cardinals. He followed them through the Gashouse Gang days and kept rooting for them until he died. Following the Cardinals in the '30s was easy because other teams were colorless. The Cards had Dizzy Dean and Joe Medwick and Leo Durocher. They were characters.[9]

Characters, indeed. The 1930s Cardinals became known as the "Gashouse Gang," a nickname attributed to their rough appearances making them look like they could be part of the gang that roamed Manhattan's Gas House District—it wasn't an area populated by the tuxedo and martini crowd of Park Avenue. They dominated the National League, reflecting Rickey's acuity for analysis of a baseball player's value. The Cardinals won the World Series in 1931 and 1934.

Rickey utilized his analytical skills at home, too. Fifteen-year-old Sue Rickey, for example, got a $5 allowance with an explanatory letter discouraging the "absent-minded pick-pocketing out of mother's purse or my pants pockets."[10] In exchange, Rickey asked "to be invited to the picture show occasionally."[11]

Family. That's the Brooklyn way.

Rickey stepped up his involvement in the Dodgers operation by investing in it. So did Walter O'Malley, Attorney at Law. On November 1, 1944, O'Malley, Rickey, and Brooklyn insurance executive Andrew Schmitz collectively bought 25 percent of the Dodgers stock from the Ed McKeever estate.[12]

On August 13, 1945, O'Malley and Rickey enhanced their ownership when they joined with John L. Smith, president of Pfizer Chemical Company, to buy 50 percent of the Dodgers stock through the Brooklyn Trust

Company, one of three executors of Charles Ebbets' estate. In this transaction, Schmitz sold his stock to Rickey, O'Malley, and Smith. That left 25 percent of Dodgers stock owned by Steve McKeever's daughter—Dearie McKeever Mulvey.[13]

Portfolio fortified, Rickey began his quest to shut down the unofficial yet formidable ban of black players from the major leagues. It was a battle against entrenched separatism nationwide. The United States of America, a society built upon the foundation that all men are created equal, relied on a military to protect its citizens, guarantee its freedoms, and secure its liberties from all enemies, foreign and domestic. Paradoxically, the United States military remained segregated until 1948, when President Truman issued Executive Order 9981. The U.S. Army did not take formal steps toward segregation, however, until 1951.

Anecdotally, Commissioner Landis shoulders the blame of segregation in baseball, though he responded with immediacy to a racial slur invoked in the 1930s. Jake Powell, a Yankees outfielder, described his activities as a policeman during the off-season in Dayton, Ohio, when WGN announcer Bob Elson interviewed him before the July 29, 1938, game against the Chicago White Sox. The *New York Times* stated, "Powell is reported to have remarked in a jocular manner that he derived considerable fun out of his job 'cracking niggers over the head' [with his nightstick]."[14]

Powell denied making the statement. Yankees manager Joe McCarthy accompanied Powell to a meeting with Landis and defended his player. "I don't know what Powell said, but whatever it was, I'm pretty sure he meant no harm. Probably just meant to get off a wise crack. So the radio people ran out cold with apologies and I'm out a ball player for ten days in the think of a pennant race."[15]

Landis suspended Powell for ten games.

Powell came to the Yankees from the Washington Senators in 1936 in a trade for Ben Chapman, a ballplayer who would figure prominently in Dodgers lore because of his venomous remarks during Jackie Robinson's rookie season. Powell died in a police station in 1948 when he shot himself after getting arrested on charges of passing bad checks.[16]

Still, the major leagues remained segregated under Landis' governance with a clear line banning black players. When Landis died in 1944, the gates of segregation creaked with vulnerability. The import of law kicked them open.

On March 12, 1945, New York governor Thomas A. Dewey signed

the Ives-Quinn bill into law. Written by Irving M. Ives and Elmer F. Quinn, respectively the State Assembly majority leader and minority leader, the bill created an anti-discrimination commission. New York's Chamber of Commerce opposed the bill. Julian S. Myrick, the Chamber of Commerce's Public Health and Welfare Committee Chairman, claimed it would lead to "a loss of existing business to New York State and the loss of other businesses which might later locate here. Loss of industry means loss of jobs."[17]

Myrick was also concerned with the burden on employers. "The charge of unfair employment practice is easy to make and difficult to disprove because it involves a state of mind. The bill provides no definite criteria for the determination of such charge."[18]

The State Assembly passed Ives-Quinn after a debate lasting more than six hours. The vote was 109–32. The Senate passed it on March 5 by a vote of 49–6. On March 12, 1945, Chapter 118 of the Laws of 1945 became official when Governor Thomas Dewey signed it; the law took effect on July 1, 1945, created the New York State Commission Against Discrimination, and outlawed the refusal to hire someone based on race. Employers violating the law were subject to misdemeanor charges punishable by a $500 fine, one year in prison, or both.[19]

Baseball was one of the law's first beneficiaries. With Ives-Quinn as a fulcrum, Rickey could leverage its import to change baseball's racial exclusion. An oft-told tale involves Rickey's Ohio Wesleyan University teammate Charles Thomas being discriminated against at a hotel during their playing days. He rubbed his hands and said the color wouldn't come off. Ives-Quinn gave Rickey a chance to exorcise the ghost of discrimination.

After the Ives-Quinn announcement, Rickey approached Red Barber, the Dodgers' venerable radio announcer. Branch Barrett Rickey explains:

> My grandfather took Red into his confidence. Red was a deep southerner, but my grandfather said, "I am going to find a Negro player to play for the Brooklyn Dodgers. I know your background and I know your character. I don't want to put you in an awkward position. If you feel that this is something you cannot reconcile with a Negro player on the field, I want to give you time to make the necessary judgments."[20]

Born in Mississippi in 1908, Barber moved with his family to Sanford, Florida, in 1918. With Southern-bred attitudes about race influencing him, Barber leaned toward the exit door.

> And my first reaction was, when I came home, and told Lila that I'm going to quit. I don't think I can go through with this. And she said, well, a very wise woman, "You don't have to quit right now. Let's have a martini."

And I began to think about it as the days went by and I had to understand that it was by chance that I was born white. I could have been born black. I could have been born to any parents. Any place, any time.[21]

Jackie Robinson met his future at the Stevens Hotel in Chicago in the form of Clyde Sukeforth, a Brooklyn Dodgers scout. On orders from Rickey, Sukeforth scouted Robinson at a Kansas City Monarchs game against the Chicago American Giants. Rickey also had Robinson under evaluation by George Sisler, Tom Greenwade, and Wid Matthews. All praised him. "Tom Greenwade called him the best bunter he ever saw. Sisler said he could make it at second base, but not

Branch Rickey signed Jackie Robinson to the Dodgers' AAA Montreal Royals team in October 1945. Robinson won the 1946 International League Most Valuable Player Award and debuted with the Brooklyn Dodgers in 1947 (National Baseball Hall of Fame Library, Cooperstown, New York).

at short on account of his arm. Matthews said he protected the strike zone and was 'one of the best two-strike hitters he had seen in a long time,'" wrote Rickey biographer and confidante Arthur Mann.[22] Greenwade, not Sukeforth, was the primary scout who assessed Robinson. In a 1993 interview, Sukeforth confirmed, "I didn't see him play before we signed him. [Rickey] knew a lot about Robinson. He just sent me down there to check out his arm."[23] Greenwade was also instrumental in scouting Silvio García, a Cuban shortstop telescoped by Rickey as a contender to be the first "colored" player in the major leagues.[24]

Visiting Chicago for the 1945 Tigers-Cubs World Series, Rickey wrote Mann about his article positioned to reveal the desegregation strategy. The October 7, 1945, letter stated that the article "The Negro and Baseball:

The National Game Faces a Racial Challenge Long Ignored" could not be published, at least not until Rickey could confirm other players in his sights—Roy Campanella, Roy Partlow, John Wright, Don Newcombe, and Sam Jethroe.[25] With a November 1 deadline, Rickey informed Mann about attempts to push the deadline to January 1 "to give me plenty of time to sign other players and make one break on the complete story. Also, quite obviously, it might not be so good to sign Robinson with other and possibly better players unsigned."[26]

Mann lent his unpublished article to Jack Guenther, managing editor of *Look* magazine, for background information concerning an article by Tim Cohane. When *Look* published Cohane's article *A Branch Grows in Brooklyn* in its March 19, 1946, issue, Mann fumed. Betrayed by a fellow scribe, he alleged that Cohane lifted quotes from the unpublished piece. But plagiarism was not Mann's only worry, or even his biggest one. Rickey's trust in him became suddenly vulnerable.

In a letter to the Authors' Guild dated April 6, 1946, Mann stated his reluctance to pursue a legal recourse because money could not replace "the continued faith of a man who trusted me above all the sports writers in America. That faith and trust is far more important than a single magazine market—in fact, more important than all the markets put together."[27]

Rickey, in an example of compassionate leadership, you shall not be given any further concern about the Look article." He closed the letter with a turn to the future: "There are a lot of bigger things ahead of us. On to them, I say."[28]

Baseball's unofficial color line could have been broken in 1903, but Billy Williams rejected an offer from Ned Hanlon, manager of the Baltimore Orioles, to play first base because his parents "feared racial prejudice."[29] When Brooklyn rose from its slumber on October 24, 1945, it discovered that Robinson had fulfilled the promise that Williams denied— the day before, Branch Rickey signed Jackie Robinson to a contract with the Dodgers' AAA team, the Montreal Royals.

Robinson's Negro Leagues team did not welcome the news.

"We won't take it lying down," said T. Y. Baird, co-owner of the Kansas City Monarchs. "Robinson signed a contract with us last year and I feel that he is our property. He would have brought approximately $50,000 in the open market. If [Commissioner] Chandler lets Montreal and Brooklyn get by with this, he's really starting a mess."[30]

Rickey responded, "Negro leagues as administered at present are a racket."[31] He reacted to a query about why he didn't bring Negroes on to the Cardinals. "In St. Louis, Negroes are not allowed in the grandstand and I wanted that situation cleared up before bringing them on the field," said Rickey.[32]

Baird retracted his statement. "We would not do anything to hamper or impede the advance of any Negro ball player, nor would we do anything to keep any Negro ball player out of the white major leagues."[33]

Meanwhile, Robinson expressed assuredness, saying that he was "pretty confident that I'll be on the Dodgers."[34] When asked about his emotions, he acknowledged the responsibility upon his shoulders.

> I don't guess any one realizes how I actually felt. My emotions were deep and complex. I guess they were a little bit impersonal. I thought of colored kids playing sandlot ball and never hoping to get on a big team; I though [sic] of the way my people have wanted to see a Negro on a big league team. Most of all, I knew their aspirations were tied up with me. I got to make good.[35]

Harold Parrott, now with the Dodgers' front office, warned his former brethren in the press that signing Robinson was based on ability, not social justice. He said that "it was not a sudden move to be interpreted merely as a gesture toward solution of a racial problem. Robinson was signed on his merits as a shortstop after he had been scouted for a long time."[36]

An obvious issue involved players on the Dodgers roster with a Southern upbringing. Would they play with a Negro ballplayer? Branch Rickey, Jr., a Dodgers executive on his father's staff, told the press that these players would come to their senses. "Some of them, particularly if they come from certain sections of the South, will steer away from a club with colored players on its roster. Some players now with us may even quit, but they will be back in baseball after they work a year or two in a cotton mill."[37]

Besides racial attitudes, Jackie Robinson and Branch Rickey faced claims that they breached Robinson's contract with the Kansas City Monarchs. If this were proven in a lawsuit, Rickey's idea of integration would collapse. On July 13, 1946, Robinson wrote a handwritten letter to Rickey clarifying that he did not have a written contract with the Monarchs.[38]

Rickey's reification of the "Great Experiment" lowered the drawbridge across the moat of racism dividing baseball. Acquisition of players from the Negro Leagues did not occur holus-bolus, however. The New York Yankees, for example, did not integrate until 1955. The Boston Red Sox took until 1959—it was the last major league team to integrate. With its rosters depleted by integration, the Negro Leagues folded by the end of the 1950s.

Brooklyn fans, while appreciative of Robinson's civil rights trailblazing, looked forward to rooting for a championship team. "One did not go to Ebbets Field for sociology," wrote Roger Kahn in the 1972 landmark book *The Boys of Summer*. "Exciting baseball was the attraction, and a wonder of the sociological Dodgers was the excitement of their play."[39]

To sign Robinson, Rickey needed a distraction. So he announced plans to create the United States League as an alternative to the established Negro Leagues. It had the side benefit of allowing Rickey and his scouts to evaluate black players under the guise of Rickey's entry in the USL— Brooklyn Brown Dodgers. When Robinson met Rickey in late August 1945, the UCLA track and football standout presently playing for the Kansas City Monarchs of the Negro Leagues naturally presumed that Rickey wanted his services for the Brooklyn franchise in the USL. Half of his presumption was true. Rickey wanted Robinson, but he wanted Robinson for the Dodgers.

"He said that he sensed that this was a man who was going to stand behind him. It was not just a gimmick, just a trial, or an experiment," said Rachel Robinson of her husband's assessment. "This is a man who believed in things like family, like commitment, like, you know, he wanted him on the team. And he was going to help him stay there."[40]

Black media outlets welcomed Rickey's out-of-the-box thinking.

The *Atlanta Daily World*: "Acceptance of Jack Roosevelt Robinson by the great Brooklyn Dodgers for service with the Montreal club of the International League is a major advance in the cause of American liberalism and democracy presaging a new era of opportunity and growth for Negroes of the sports arena."[41]

Fay Young of the *Chicago Defender*: "Democracy has finally invaded baseball, our great national pastime."[42]

NY Amsterdam News: "The cracking of baseball jim-crow, one of the most flagrant anti–Negro institutions, is just the drop of water in the drought that keeps faith alive in American institutions."[43]

Meanwhile, Rickey rebuffed press allegations that the Ives-Quinn law motivated him:

> I've been checking on Negro ball players for more than three years, long before the bill ever came up. On the other hand, some of these owners who declare that they're not going to hire Negro players are going to run into difficulty. I hope they won't be forced into it by legislation because that is always undesirable. However, it's coming. This is a movement that cannot be stopped by anyone. They may be able to detain it for a while, but not for long. The world is moving on and they will move with it, whether they like it or not.[44]

Arthur Mann and Lawrence Taylor fictionalized the Robinson canon in their script for the 1950 movie *The Jackie Robinson Story*. For example, it shows Jackie getting a letter from the Black Panthers, a Negro Leagues team that never, in reality, existed. His performance on the Black Panthers leads to an invitation from Brooklyn Dodgers scout Clyde Sukeforth to come to Brooklyn for a meeting. Robinson blows it off, thinking the invitation is a prank. Sukeforth, angry at the dismissal, pounds on Robinson's door to wake him up. Robinson's ignorance is also fictional.

Sukeforth recalled his experience for Rickey in a meeting on January 16, 1950, to discuss *The Jackie Robinson Story*. Rickey, according to Sukeforth, mandated an evaluation of Robinson's throwing ability. If it met Sukeforth's standard, then a quiet transport to Brooklyn should follow without other teams catching on to the scheme.[45] Sukeforth also mentioned that in the August 1945 meeting at Dodgers headquarters, Rickey peppered Robinson with queries about reactions to racial taunts. Robinson assured Rickey that he could withstand the abuse without incident.[46]

On April 18, 1946, Jackie Robinson made his first appearance in the minor leagues when the Montreal Royals opened the season with a game against the Jersey City Giants at Roosevelt Field in Jersey City. Robinson went 4-for-5, hit a home run, stole two bases, and scored four times. The Royals won, 14–1. Robinson was a cornerstone of the Royals' championship squad that won the 1946 Little World Series against the Louisville Colonels.

The United States League never got off the ground.

Jackie Robinson's breaking of the color line, historic by any measure, was neither automatic nor certain. It didn't happen in a vacuum, either. Six months before Jackie Robinson voyaged to 215 Montague Street, a 22-year-old college student at the College of William & Mary opened the door of integration. And the university power brokers slammed it shut.

Marilyn Kaemmerle was the Editor-in-Chief of *The Flat Hat*, William & Mary's student-run newspaper. Looking for an editorial subject, she found a source of inspiration in the anniversary of Lincoln's birthday in 1945. Kaemmerle went beyond preaching against prejudice, racism, and segregation. She suggested blacks and whites socialize together for everything from education to marriage. It was a call to social progress, anathema to some quarters of the South. A scandal erupted.

Kaemmerle's editorial was titled "Lincoln's Job Half-Done."

> When Lincoln freed the slaves, he undoubtedly hoped the Negroes would someday be accepted as equals by the other colors of people in this country. Today we find the Negroes released from formal bondage but not equalized.

Racial Intermarriage...

We believe and know that Negroes differ from other peoples only in surface characteristics; inherently all are the same. The Negroes should be recognized as equals in our minds and hearts. For us, this means that Negroes should attend William and Mary; they should go to our classes, participate in College functions, join the same clubs, be our roommates, pin the same classmates, and marry among us. However, this cannot and should not be done today, or tomorrow,—but perhaps the next day. Neither they nor we are ready for it yet. Only chaos such as the Southern states experienced during the Reconstruction would result if such a plan were initiated before both Negroes and others were educated for it.

The One Human Family...

Through education we learn of the spread of early man to all corners of the globe. Those who settled nearer the equator, whether in Europe, Asia, or in the Americas, developed a darker skin color than those who settled north of them. People's hair often remained the same over great areas. Europeans remained quite hairy, but body hair almost disappeared in some parts of the world. Blue eyes appeared in the north, and in Asia a fold of skin developed over the inner corner of the eye, forming a slant eye.

Northern Negroes And Southern Whites...

There is little difference in heighths [sic] or head shapes; whites, Negroes, Mongols, and all races have the same four blood types. Tests show that Negroes in this country made a lower score than whites on intelligent tests; they also show that Northerners, *black and white*, had higher scores than Southerners, *black and white*, and that Northern Negroes had higher scores than Southern whites. *The differences did not occur because people were from the North or the South, or because they were white or black, but because of differences in income, education, cultural advantages, and other opportunities.* Equal opportunities must therefore be offered to all peoples in all sections of the country.

Prejudice, A Nazi Strategy...

The most important work, however, must be done in educating ourselves away from the idea of White Supremacy, for this belief is as groundless as Hitler's Nordic Supremacy nonsense. We are injuring our personalities with arrogance; we are blocking our own emotional growth. Not until we eliminate Nazi race tactics in our own everyday life can we hope for a victory which will bring peace for the universal Human Race of the One World.

Do you *really* want peace? Is *your conscience* clear?[47]

The Board of Visitors pressured university president John Pomfret to expel Kaemmerle. He refused, then upped the ante by threatening to resign. As a compromise, Pomfret removed Kaemmerle from her editorial position. But he wanted more. Kaemmerle recalled, "And then he asked that I sign a statement saying I thought a censored paper was in the best interest of all concerned. And I said, 'Well I can't do that. I'm not the editor.'"[48]

Kaemmerle's dismissal brought attention from the national press. William & Mary's student body remained uninterested, even though Kaemmerle sought to stir debate rather than dissension. Kaemmerle "hadn't even heard a ripple from any of them."[49]

A test of Robinson occurred without him knowing. When Emil Joseph "Buzzie" Bavasi spied on Jackie Robinson's background, he chose the person who knew Robinson best—Rachel Robinson. Bavasi, a Dodgers executive, discarded Rickey's initial idea of traveling to Robinson's hometown of Los Angeles in favor of going to Montreal. He sat behind the players' wives during a night game at Delorimier Stadium, where he witnessed Rachel Robinson's comportment informed by maturity, manners, and grace. Bavasi reported, "Mr. Rickey, if Jackie Roosevelt Robinson is good enough for Rachel Robinson, he is good enough for the Dodgers."[50]

As Jackie Robinson and his wife, Rachel, got accustomed to Montreal, Gerald Stern had a different task thrust upon his 11-year-old shoulders in the spring of 1946 when his widowed mother ushered him from the kitchen to the living room in their home at 3807 Oceanic Avenue in the Sea Gate section of Coney Island. She explained that Gerald was about to meet the man who might become his second father. Although Gerald pieced together what was happening before his mother's gentle warning, he had only one thing on his mind as he approached the gentleman. "Are you a Dodgers fan?" he asked, Indeed, Sam Zaslow was.

> Sam had a soft spot for Leo Durocher, even when Durocher crossed rivalry lines and went to the Giants. But he still remained a Dodgers fan. We shared a ritual. When the Dodgers won an afternoon game, he gave me money to get the afternoon editions of the *Daily Mirror* and *Daily News*, plus fifty cents for a pint of Breyer's ice cream. I'd race down to Sonny & Lou's on West 36th Street, right outside Seagate, to get the papers. It was a seven or eight minute walk, but faster on the bike. We'd eat, read about the day's game, and switch papers with each other. When the Dodgers lost, we didn't get the newspapers at all.[51]

Stern has a link with Jackie Robinson that goes beyond fandom. They share the same birthday. Sort of. Stern was born on April 15. Jackie Robinson's debut with the Dodgers was on April 15, 1947. And Stern was witness to a Robinson act that was one part retaliatory, one part didactic, and one part practical joke.

> Sam took me to a ballgame at the Polo Grounds on 1952 on a hot August night. It was a 15-inning game. We had the best seats that I've ever had at a baseball game—second row behind the Dodger dugout. Every time Robinson returned to the dugout, a fan raced down into the section and ran up to the barrier that

separated fans from players by just a couple of feet. He screams, "Showboat! Showboat!" Dodger fans in that area were yelling at the Giant fan that he was a racist. The guy's defense was that he was commenting on Robinson's style of play, not his race.

He does this two or three times. Late in the game, Robinson returns after his at-bat very slowly. He goes to the water fountain on the home plate side of the dugout, apparently to quench his thirst. On cue, the fan comes running down the aisle just as Robinson times the finish of his drink. The fan is now a few feet from Robinson, who sprays the guy with a mouthful of water and gets him all wet. We all cheered. The guy turns and I remember to this day the look on his face was a beaten look.[52]

Stern's brother David Zaslow shares the passion for the Brooklyn Dodgers through Campaign 42, a grass-roots effort to have all baseball players wear the number 42 on Jackie Robinson Day—April 15—no matter the player's age or level of play. Zaslow, a rabbi, attributes the program's success to higher powers. "I do think it was an inspired idea. It didn't come from me. It came from Ebbets Field up above. The spiritual Brooklyn Dodgers in the other world descended down and said, 'Do this.'"[53]

The Jackie Robinson Story shows Robinson having difficulty in getting anyone to warm up with him. Sukeforth denied this occurrence, stating for Rickey, "No embarrassing moment at all. Several boys were ready to keep them busy, to take them right into a bunting game. They want that in the picture about difficulty in warming up. Nobody gave that story to them. It was not true at all. No incident like that at all."[54]

Rickey, in fact, suppressed a revolt from within the Dodgers' ranks by an enclave of Southern-bred Dodgers voicing their opposition to Robinson. Or any black player for that matter. The players were: Hugh Casey—pitcher (Georgia), Kirby Higbe —pitcher (South Carolina), Bobby Bragan—catcher (Alabama), and Dixie Walker—outfielder (Alabama). Carl Furillo, an outfielder from Reading, Pennsylvania, also opposed Robinson's playing for the Dodgers. In his 1967 memoir *The High Hard One*, Higbe claimed that he, along with Walker, Bragan, Furillo, and shortstop Pee Wee Reese, complained to Rickey. Higbe alleged that Reese "[c]hanged his mind about playing with Robinson."[55]

The South being a nidus of bigotry, notwithstanding Mr. Lincoln's proclamation more than 80 years prior, the protestors formalized their opposition with a petition during spring training in Panama. It was a snowball threatening to become an avalanche capable of burying Rickey's integration design. Rickey benefited from Harold Parrott, the *Eagle* scribe turned publicity hawk for the Dodgers. Ever alert for a scoop, Parrott discovered the petition effort from Higbe, who exclaimed, "Old Hig just can't do it; Old Hig just can't be a part of it."[56] Beer loosened Higbe's tongue in a bar and the former newspaperman turned Dodgers public relations guru listened with ears at full attention before springing into action.

> I phoned Rickey in Brooklyn, and the Old Man jumped into a plane within the hour, heading to Panama to quell the rebellion.
> Rickey wasn't needed this time. Durocher handled the whole thing. When I told Leo about the plot, he had exploded. He called the midnight meeting in the barracks, and I can still hear him as he challenged the mutineers. He was wrapped in a yellow bathrobe, and he looked like a fighter about to enter the ring. He stared down Walker and Bragan and started punching out the words.
> "I don't care if the guy is yellow or black, or if he has stripes like a fuckin' zebra. I'm the manager of this team and I say he plays. What's more, I say he can make us all rich. An' if any of you can't use the money, I'll see that you're traded!"[57]

Durocher's verbal tirade would have made General George S. Patton take out a pencil and pad to take notes on speaking with authority to underlings. According to Durocher, though, Sukeforth informed him of the mutiny, not Parrott.

> From everything I hear, he's only the first. *Only the first, boys!* There's many more coming right behind him and they have the talent and they're gonna come to play. These fellows are hungry. They're good athletes and there's nowhere else they can make this kind of money. They're going to come, boys, and they're going to come scratching and diving. Unless you fellows look out and wake up, they're going to run you right out of the ballpark.
> So, I don't want to see your petition and I don't want to hear anything more about it. The meeting is over; go back to bed.[58]

Durocher's nickname wasn't "Leo the Lip" for nothing. Meanwhile, the storm of protest quieted. Rickey traded Higbe to the Pirates, but he kept Bragan because of Bragan's Solomonesqe solution. "Bragan had at least promised Rickey that while he would not welcome a Negro with open arms, he would not put any more stumbling blocks in his way," wrote Robinson biographer and collaborator Carl Rowan.[59]

Dixie Walker, a Brooklyn favorite, presented an obstacle for Rickey bigger than the other protestors because of his stature summarized by the fans' moniker for him—"The People's Choice," pronounced "Cherce" in Brooklyn. A year prior to Robinson's debut, Harold C. Burr underscored Walker's popularity in the *Eagle's Brooklyn Man of the Week* column.

> There's something wrong with this title. Not only is Dixie Walker the man of the week, but the man of the months and the years in the hearts of Dodger

fans. Ever since he came to the Brooklyn club in 1939 he has been at odds with the front office, but if any attempt were made to take him out of right field now his millions of friends in the stands would burn down Ebbets Field.[60]

When Rickey signed Robinson in October 1945, Walker dismissed it. "As long as he isn't with the Dodgers, I'm not worried," said Walker.[61] But that was 18 months prior. Robinson proved himself as a ballplayer with the 1946 Montreal Royals, winning the International League's Most Valuable Player Award with a .349 batting average, 66 runs batted in, and 113 runs scored. Plus, the Royals won the 1946 Little World Series against the Louisville Colonels.

Walker refused to have his picture taken with Robinson. In the 1950 meeting with Rickey, Sukeforth explained that Walker had concern about a potential negative effect on his hardware and sporting goods business in the South.[62] In a 1981 interview with sportswriter Ira Berkow, Walker claimed that he did not initiate the petition against Robinson[63]; prejudice was passive rather than proactive, rooted in the color of money rather than the color of Robinson's skin. Or so Walker posited in the interview."[64]

In *The Era*, Roger Kahn recalled a conversation while Walker was a batting coach with the Los Angeles Dodgers in the mid–1970s. According to Kahn, Walker took responsibility for the boycott.

> I organized that petition in 1947, not because I had anything against Robinson personally or against Negroes generally. I had a wholesale business in Birmingham and people told me I'd lose my business if I played ball with a black man. That's why I started the petition. It was the dumbest thing I did in all my life. If you ever get a chance, sometime, please write that I am deeply sorry.[65]

After the 1947 season, Rickey traded Dixie Walker to the Pirates, a heretical act for Dodgers fans, who remained unaware of Walker's attitudes contrasting their acceptance of Robinson. Dixie Walker without the word "Dodgers" in blue script across his jersey would be like Joe DiMaggio without pinstripes. Arthur Daley of the *New York Times* wrote, "From a strictly sentimental standpoint the Flatbush Faithful will grieve deeply at his departure because no Dodger ball player could create such electric sparks or generate more enthusiasm than the soft-spoken, friendly, gracious and obliging Southerner."[66]

Walker hit .316 for the Pirates in 1948, the highest batting average on the team. He retired after the 1949 season. In the Berkow interview, Walker said, "The other night I watched a television program and heard mention of a number of people who were important in the blacks gaining advantages in America. And the name of Jackie Robinson never came up. It surprised me. I mean, how soon people can forget."[67]

On the morning of April 10, 1947, Jackie Robinson fielded a phone call in Room 1169 of the McAlpin Hotel. Resting in the shadow of Manhattan's Herald Square—the finish line of the Macy's Thanksgiving Day parade in Manhattan—the McAlpin served as a temporary home for Robinson, who received orders to come to Brooklyn immediately to sign a contract with the Brooklyn Dodgers.

During an exhibition game that afternoon with the Yankees, Rickey authorized a statement to be released to the press box. He chose Arthur Mann as his Mercury to deliver the missive: "The Brooklyn Dodgers today purchased the contract of Jackie Roosevelt Robinson from the Montreal Royals."[68]

Jackie Robinson's breakthrough should have dominated Brooklyn's attention.

It didn't.

5th Inning:
Silencing the Lip

"Antagonism toward us goes back to Leo Durocher's day as manager. Leo wasn't satisfied to beat the other clubs. He wanted to enrage them, so they'd play hardest against us. He figured it was a good way to keep us sharp."[1]—Pee Wee Reese

Leo Durocher argued with umpires like balls and strikes were matters of life and death. In Brooklyn, they were.

So, when baseball commissioner Albert Benjamin "Happy" Chandler suspended Durocher for the season on April 9, 1947, he silenced the borough's loudest advocate. "Durocher has not measured up to the standards expected or required of managers of our baseball teams," said Chandler, whose ruling stemmed from a blood feud between the Yankees and the Dodgers.[2]

Chandler's decision rocked Brooklyn. This was not an unassisted triple play or a dropped third strike. It was downright tragic. Leo Durocher personified everything Brooklyn held dear—pride, boisterousness, and toughness. An assault on one Brooklyn Dodger, after all, was an assault on the borough.

The chain of events leading to Durocher's suspension began the previous fall with coach Charlie Dressen fleeing Brooklyn for the Bronx. Rickey alleged that Dressen, by taking a coaching job with the Yankees, violated a verbal agreement requiring him to stay with the Dodgers for an additional two years, unless a major league team offered him a managing job. Further, when the Yankees announced Bucky Harris as the team's manager on November 6, 1946, Larry MacPhail—now general manager of the Yankees—claimed that Durocher had expressed interest in managing the Yankees. "I replied that if Leo were free to act he could come and see me. He never came," said MacPhail.[3]

Durocher claimed otherwise. At a sports luncheon featuring Jack Benny later that month, Durocher said, "About a month before the season ended Larry MacPhail called me at my apartment in New York and asked to see me. I went over and he offered me the Yankee job. I told him I had a verbal agreement with Mr. Rickey and couldn't take it. That was the last I heard of it."[4]

On November 25, Branch Rickey announced that Durocher had signed a one-year contract to manage the Dodgers for a $70,000 salary. Responding to questions about MacPhail's offer, Durocher said, "He offered me a longer contract and more money than I signed for here a while ago."[5] He also said, "It's just as I told you fellows in the clubhouse when the season ended: Mr. Rickey has been like a father to me and I want to manage the Dodgers the rest of my life."[6] MacPhail fired back, again claiming that Durocher asked for the Yankees job.[7]

About a month before 1947's Opening Day, Rickey faced another Durocher crisis—the Catholic Youth Organization withdrew from the Dodger Knothole Club because of Durocher's romance with Laraine Day while she was married. Day, an actress living in California, filed for divorce from Ray Hendricks on the grounds of extreme cruelty. Judge George Dockweiler granted the request with a condition—Day could not marry another man and she must live in California for one year.[8]

The CYO cared not about legal technicalities, only its version of morality. It said, "The present manager of the Brooklyn baseball team is not the kind of leader we want for our youth to idealize and imitate."[9] Consequently, the boycott had potential to destroy the present box office and the future fan base. Rickey's frustrations increased in Havana, Cuba, during spring training. Although the Dodgers won 1–0 against the Yankees in front of 10,000 people at Stadia Grande, Rickey focused not on the field, but on MacPhail's box, where two known gamblers sat—Memphis Engleberg and Connie Immerman, in defiance of Chandler's crackdown on baseball's association with gambling. Rickey hinted to Herbert Goren of the *New York Sun* and Arch Murray of the *New York Post* that MacPhail entertained gamblers.[10]

Gambling was a sore spot for the clean-living Rickey; it tarnished the game, destroyed players, and risked integrity. He saw gambling infecting the Dodgers clubhouse during his early days in Brooklyn, a sign that the team's problems did not stop at the foul lines. Arthur Mann wrote:

> There were salary advances of a month, two months, and even on futures. One young player had borrowed half of his next year's income. There were weeping wives and bewildered children, innocent victims of clubhouse gambling fever, which, Rickey believed, had cost the Dodgers an easy 1942 pennant.[11]

Rickey's accusations regarding MacPhail became public through the New York City press, causing Chandler to hold a secret hearing in Sarasota, Florida. Evidence included Durocher's *Brooklyn Eagle* column, ghostwritten by Harold Parrott, particularly the March 3 edition slamming MacPhail and Dressen. "He [MacPhail] tried to drive a wedge between myself and all these things I hold dear. When MacPhail found I couldn't be induced to manage his Yankees, he resolved to knock me and make life as hard as possible for me."[12]

Although MacPhail accused Durocher, Rickey, and Parrott of "conduct detrimental to baseball,"[13] his actions were not innocent. "Significant is the fact that neither MacPhail nor Chandler ever challenged the truth of the castigation," observed Mann.[14]

In addition to suspending Durocher, Chandler ruled that Dressen had agreed to continue working for Rickey before taking a job with the Yankees. He suspended Dressen for 30 days, fined the Yankees $2,000, fined the Dodgers $2,000, and fined Parrott $500 for his role in publicizing Durocher's beliefs about MacPhail. Rickey respected Chandler's authority; an appeal seemed unlikely.[15]

Since 1939, Durocher had helmed the Dodgers. Cleaving him from the team was a crime against Brooklyn. Arthur Daley wrote, "The Lip is in a comparable position to the chap hauled into traffic court for driving through a red light and then being sentenced to the electric chair."[16] With the ink still drying on the Chandler ruling, Durocher walked into a familiar setting on the evening of April 10—the Dodgers' annual Knothole Dinner at the Hotel St. George. "It was a dramatic entrance that electrified the crowd," wrote Tommy Holmes in the *Brooklyn Daily Eagle*.[17] Brooklyn, about to make history with Jackie Robinson, suffered with fury at Chandler's swiping a member of the family from the Dodgers.

Never shy, Brooklynites voiced their attitudes on the pages of the *Eagle*[18]:

Might as well throw him out of baseball altogether. It's a scheme to get him out.—Edward Baker

A great injustice to the team. He's a Brooklyn hero. They'd better have a squad of extra police on hand when Chandler visits Ebbets Field.—George Pfeifer

This is unfair to the Brooklyn team, rank injustice to our borough.—Frank Pagano

Great injustice. Chandler had no business kicking him out for a year or for a day. It was only a private feud.—Erwin Althol

Chandler may have been a good United States Senator, but as a judge of baseball I don't think much of him. Sure, Durocher may have been a little hot-headed.

Everybody knows that. He had an argument with Larry MacPhail. They're both old champions and both know one another's ways. It was a case of one man taking revenge on another.—Peter McGuinness

Durocher, no stranger to scrapes on and off the baseball diamond, knew that a battle with the commissioner's office was a sure-fire loser. Virulent and verbal, passionate and pugnacious, Durocher emerged victorious from other skirmishes. In 1945, a fan named John Christian accused Durocher and Joseph Moore—a special patrolman at Ebbets Field for 29 years—of assaulting him with a "blunt instrument" in the players' runway during a Dodgers-Phillies game at Ebbets Field. At six feet and 200 pounds, Christian had "a broken jaw, a black eye and two head bruises."[19] Moore, too, was a burly man.

With only one member that had never been to Ebbets Field, a Kings County jury took 38 minutes to acquit Durocher and Moore. Following

Left to right: Leo Durocher, Branch Rickey, and attorney John J. Breslin after a jury acquits Durocher of assault charges involving a rival fan (Brooklyn Public Library—Brooklyn Collection).

his lawyer's advice, Durocher had settled a civil suit with Christian for $6,750, though the judge advised the jury to disregard it.[20]

Christian's version depicted Moore removing him from the stands after he cheered loudly against the Dodgers. Then, Moore and Durocher broke his jaw "in a room near the Brooklyn dugout."[21] Durocher's testimony about the incident swayed the jury, assuming Dodger loyalty hadn't already swayed them. While Durocher testified that he spoke with Christian about "vile language," he refuted any link to Christian's injuries. "The manager insisted that Christian was injured when he fell after running out of the room a moment after calling Durocher a vile name,"[22] reported the *New York Herald Tribune*. Judge Louis Goldstein advised, "I'm glad for the sake of the Brooklyn baseball team that their manager has been vindicated. No discredit has been placed on the great American game of baseball."[23]

In 1949, Durocher received another suspension from Happy Chandler because of an assault accusation. Now the manager of the Giants, Durocher resumed deflecting claims, only this alleged incident did not take place in a room. It happened in the stadium proper. After a Dodgers-Giants game, Fred Boysen went onto the field to attempt shaking hands with Jackie Robinson. Boysen alleged that Durocher "had struck him on the neck, knocking him down, and had then kicked him."[24]

Durocher, of course, argued otherwise. And he had witnesses. Julius November, for example, had an unparalleled view from his perch in Section 16, with a seat directly behind Boysen. "This belligerent customer was loud and insulting. He made insulting remarks about Durocher and about his wife," said November. "He exceeded the bounds of decency. I wondered why he was not ejected from the park.

"After the game this man jumped over the railing onto the playing field and ran after Durocher. As he approached he raised his hand over Durocher's head, maybe to grab his cap, maybe for some other reason. Durocher turned and pushed him and went on his way. He positively did not strike him or kick him."[25]

Chandler reinstated Durocher. Boysen dropped the assault charge.

Durocher's suspension in April 1947 consumed Brooklyn as the black press prepared its readers for Jackie Robinson's debut. While Robinson's breakthrough could be the first step toward shattering prejudice in baseball, black journalists warned their readers that rude behavior at Ebbets Field could be detrimental, if not disastrous, to desegregation.

In *The Chicago Defender*, Walter White wrote:

Jackie Robinson has demonstrated his ability as a ball player and his level-headedness and courage as a man. The best help we can give him to smash for all time the color line in highly lucrative professional baseball for himself and for others is to act like civilized human beings.[26]

The Pittsburgh Courier urged:

We are sure that he would prefer to be regarded as just another major league baseball player trying to do his best rather than an idol on a pedestal.

Again, over-enthusiastic Negro fans who can see only Jackie Robinson do not help him to get on any better with his teammates who will become better adjusted to the unprecedented situation in the degree that they regard him as an individual rather than a symbol of the Negro group.[27]

On the same day the *Courier* ran the editorial, it published a story by Wendell Smith about Rickey's concerns regarding Robinson's popularity. "If these people who are always coming to him and asking him to make an appearance at different places are his friends, they will leave the alone and give him time to adjust himself," Rickey said. Then he exercised authority, stating, "He will not appear at any affair or go to any public place from now on unless he gets approval from this office."[28]

Rickey, a Methodist with devotion that could rival a preacher's, also received praise from religious media, for example, *Christian Century*:

Now that Brooklyn has broken the taboo, and the press reports that the fans have greeted the first appearance of Robinson in a Brooklyn uniform with cheers, other clubs may be expected to give Negro athletes their fair chance. But don't forget that it was Branch Rickey, the much derided churchman, who took the first, decisive step. Perhaps Mr. Rickey's religion is not such a humbug after all.[29]

Jackie Robinson was not the first black player in the major leagues, though he is often credited with that honor. On May 1, 1884, Moses Fleetwood Walker donned a uniform for the Toledo Blue Stockings in the American Association, then a major league. When he stepped onto the field for the Blue Stockings' game against the Louisville Eclipse, Walker stepped into history, only to be overshadowed by an unwritten, unspoken racial ban in succeeding decades. Weldy Walker joined the Blue Stockings during the 1884 season. He, too, became a footnote in history until baseball scholarship revived the brothers' acclaim.

Moses Walker played 42 games for Toledo, compiled a .263 batting average, and notched 40 hits.[30] Major League Baseball's web site describes him as a "good-field, no-hit catcher."[31] After the 1884 season, he bounced around the minor leagues until he retired in 1889.

Still, the Walkers' claim on racial history does not, in any way, subtract from Robinson's courage, discipline, and emotional stamina. Having successfully fought a court martial while stationed at Fort Hood, Texas, for not moving to the back of a bus in 1944, Robinson knew the naked harshness of bigotry whether expressed by bans, segregations, or words burnished with hatred. His was a mission of destroying ignorance endorsed by societal norms reflected beyond ballparks in a "separate but equal" mentality.

In 1934, Nat Trammell posited the question of desegregation in his periodical *Colored Baseball & Sports Monthly*. Trammell certified the skills of Negro Leagues players while arguing that desegregation yielded economic benefits: "We are living in a very strenuous age, and our economic adjustment must compel us to do away with many of our obsolete social customs. Ill feeling toward any group is not wise through this period of economic unstableness."[32]

Trammell's vision, while practical, could not penetrate the wall of racial separation. In 1942, Jackie Robinson and Nate Moreland tried out for the Chicago White Sox, but baseball's racial structure remained firm.[33] Wendell Smith worked to move desegregation forward by aligning with Boston councilman Isadore Muchnick, a politician looking to get the increasingly dominant black vote in his geographic corner of Beantown.[34] Muchnick and Smith lobbied the Red Sox to arrange a tryout for Jackie Robinson, Marvin Williams, and Samuel Jethroe; their efforts culminated on April 16, 1945.

Acting as an unofficial liaison between the Red Sox and the trio, Smith wrote to Eddie Collins, the Red Sox general manager, expressing the players' appreciation for the tryout."[35] Could a broken leg have been the cause of the Red Sox not signing a black player or at least avoiding the issue? Collins responded to Smith on May 11, 1945, explaining that Red Sox manager Joe Cronin broke his leg "shortly after the time you were here." Cronin's condition "threw everything out of gear as far as our plans were concerned," added Collins."[36]

It took the city that birthed the American revolution with bedrock principles of liberty, equality, and freedom till 1959 to introduce its first black player—Elijah "Pumpsie" Green.

Jackie Robinson, the black knight who rescued baseball from the claws of segregation, overcame a gargantuan burden of entrenched bigotry, racial taunts, and blind ignorance; he accomplished his mission neither immediately nor solitarily. Smith took on the responsibility of documenting Robinson's travails, in essence becoming both a confidante and a conduit. The relationship strengthened from mutual admiration as both men realized the monumental task of breaking baseball's color barrier. Robinson had to do it, Smith had to write about it, and they both had to complete their tasks without glorification, grandstanding, or theatrics.

Robinson knew the deep value of a reporter representing the black press, one with a keenness to sift exaggerations, misstatements, and misinterpretations. In a letter to Smith on October 31, 1945, Robinson expressed his gratitude to Smith and the *Courier*.[37] Along with being a conduit for Robinson with readers of the black press, Smith was also a gateway of information for Branch Rickey. Smith's information pipeline became extraordinarily helpful to Rickey during the delicate period after the 1946 season when Rickey needed to decide whether Robinson's temperament would reach the level of moderation mandated by the responsibility of being the first 20th-century black player in the major leagues.

On November 27, 1946, Smith wrote to Rickey inquiring about Robinson's spring training status for the 1947 season. It was a question of practicality as Smith wanted to know about the Dodgers' logistics of hotel reservations for writers.[38] Smith offered succor in the November 27 letter, detailing an endorsement of Robinson by Winfield Welch, then the manager of the Cincinnati Crescents and formerly the manager of the Birmingham Black Barons.[39]

Jackie Robinson took the field for the Dodgers' 1947 Opening Day game against pitcher Johnny Sain and the Boston Braves at Ebbets Field. Robinson went 0-for-3 in his Dodgers debut. Thus, history was made on April 15, 1947.

Rickey believed in him. The Dodgers played with him. The fans cheered for him. Yet, he was alone on the field, in the dugout, and in the clubhouse as the only black baseball player in Major League Baseball.

Alone to receive the taunts and not fight back.

Alone to live up to Rickey's expectations.

Alone to set the standard for every Negro Leagues player who thought of following him.

And it was about to reach a breaking point.

At an Ebbets Field home stand against the Phillies, the Dodgers consolidated behind Robinson when Phillies manager Ben Chapman led a diatribe of racial slurs. In HBO's 2007 documentary *The Ghosts of Flatbush*, Dodgers pitcher Ralph Branca recalled Chapman's abuse: "Hey boy, come over here and shine my shoes. Hey boy, why ain't you out picking cotton?"[40]

Those were the most benign comments.

A native of Alabama, Chapman crossed over the undrawn line of bench jockeying. He defended his treatment of Robinson because, in his view, it was the price of doing business as a ball player:

> You fellows want Robinson to become a real big leaguer, I suppose. Well, so do we, and we're treating him just the same as we do any other player on a rival club. When we're playing exhibitions with the Yanks, DiMaggio is always "The Wop"; and when we meet the Cards, Whitey Kurowsky is "The Polack." The phils ball club rides the devil out of every team it meets. That's our style of baseball. We hand it out and we expect to take it too. If you want us to lay off Jackie and treat him like a guy who can't take his medicine the way the rest of have to in this slam-bang game of baseball, then we'll do it—but that isn't the way a big leaguer is made. And remember, all that stuff is forgotten the minute the ball game is over.[41]

Eddie Stanky, the Dodgers' second baseman, reached his own breaking point by the third and final game of the series. "Listen, you yellow-bellied cowards," he cried out, "why don't you yell at somebody who can answer back?"[42] The Dodgers' front office stood up for Robinson, too. Under the stands, Chapman confronted Harold Parrott, the Dodgers' publicity chief. He teased, "Poor Parrott. Know how you're going to end up? You'll be the nursemaid to a team of twenty-four niggers and one dago." Parrott responded with Chapman's "Winslow" nickname, based on a bridge bidding system that Chapman called the Winslow System: "If I was short a hotel room, and had the choice of bunking with you or with Number 42, know what I'd do? I'd room with Robinson, Winslow."[43]

Dan Parker publicized Chapman's tirade in the *New York Daily Mirror*:

> Ben Chapman, who during his career with the Yankees was frequently involved in unpleasant incidents with fans who charged him with shouting anti–Semitic remarks at them from the ball field, seems to be up to his old trick of stirring up racial trouble. During the recent series between the Phils and Dodgers, Chapman and three of his players poured a stream of vile abuse at Jackie Robinson. Jackie, with admirable restraint, ignored the guttersnipe language coming from the Phils' dugout, thus stamping himself as the only gentleman among those involved in the incident. Chapman isn't adding to this stature either as a man or as a manager by not only tolerating this sort of stuff, but setting the bad example for his players. Is he the type of "sportsman" Baseball wants to hold up as a model for American youth?[44]

Robinson, however, put aside any ire. Most men would have failed to do this. But Branch Rickey did not select most men—he selected Jackie

Robinson. In a prime example of taking a punch and remaining standing, Robinson granted a request by Rickey to pose for a photograph shaking hands with Chapman. "I have to admit, though, that having my picture taken with this man was one of the most difficult things I had to make myself do,"[45] admitted Robinson.

No wonder. Chapman was not a sole offender; he had a backup chorus in the team symbolizing the City of Brotherly Love. Robinson, though shaken, refused to let being distraught lead to disaster:

> The first time I stepped up to the plate, they opened up full blast. "Hey, you black Nigger," I heard one of them yell. "Why don't you go back where you came from?" Then I heard another one shout: "Yeah, pretty soon you'll want to eat and sleep with white ball players!" As the jockeying continued on this level, I almost lost my head. I started to drop my bat and go over and take a sock at one of them. But then I remembered Branch Rickey's warning me of what I'd have to take without losing my temper. So I pretended I didn't hear them. I gritted my teeth and vented some of my anger on a solid single.[46]

In his *Pittsburgh Courier* column *Jackie Robinson Says*, Robinson took a softer approach. "Some of the Phillies bench-jockey's [sic] tried to get me upset last week, but it really didn't bother me," wrote Robinson. "I got used to that kind of stuff when I was playing last year with Montreal. The things the Phillies shouted at me from their bench have been shouted at me from other benches and I am not worried about it."[47]

Robinson further downplayed the Chapman incident two weeks later in his column: "I was glad to cooperate and when we got over to the Phillies' dugout, Chapman came out and shook my hand. We said hello to each other and he smiled when the picture was snapped. Chapman impressed me as a nice fellow and I don't think he really meant the things he was shouting at me the first time we played Philadelphia."[48]

After the *Pittsburgh Courier*'s Jack Saunders revealed that Chapman encouraged the Phillies to mock Robinson with racial jeers, Chandler legislated the banning of racial taunting.[49] "Mr. Chandler said that no favors should be granted Robinson from the bench, but there is a limit to everything and he thought that hurling racial epithets was beyond that limit. The Commissioner also said that if the Phillies continued their 'tirade,' he'd be forced to take more drastic action,"[50] explained Walter Mulbry, the secretary-treasurer of the commissioner's office.

Rickey's old team presented another obstacle—the St. Louis Cardinals planned to strike. Under a cover story of traveling to New York City to meet with Cardinals manger Eddie Dyer about the team's poor record, Cardinals owner Sam Breadon voyaged to the New Yorker Hotel to find out more about the rumored National League strike, supposedly beginning with his team on May 6, the date of the Cardinals' first 1947 game against the Dodgers. Breadon confirmed the rumor. National League president Ford Frick responded with the force of Zeus:

> If you strike, you will be suspended from the league. You will find the friends you think you have in the press box will not support you. You will be outcasts. I do not care if half the league strikes. Those who do will encounter quick retribution. All will be suspended. I don't care if it wrecks the National League for five years. This is the United States of America and one citizen has as much right to play as another.... You will find if you go through with your intention that you will have been guilty of complete madness.[51]

Stanley Woodward broke the story in the May 9, 1947, edition of the *New York Herald Tribune*. Commending Robinson's comportment, Woodward wrote, "It is not generally known that other less serious difficulties have attended the elevation of Robinson to the major leagues. Through it all, the Brooklyn first baseman, whose intelligence and degree of education are far beyond that of the average ball player, has behaved himself in an exemplary manner."[52]

One problem, though. A St. Louis version of events depicts the strike story as a fantasy. Bob Broeg, a St. Louis native and sportswriter, claimed that Breadon's fears ignited the strike rumors rather than hard evidence. Breadon had drinks with Dr. Robert F. Hyland and said, "Jeez, I'm worried about this black guy. They're going to strike. Things like that are distracting."[53] Rud Rennie of the *New York Herald Tribune* knew Breadon and Hyland; when Rennie arrived in St. Louis to cover a Yankees road trip, he asked Hyland about the Cardinals owner. Hyland responded that Breadon was worried about a strike. Rennie, in turn, informed his editor, Stanley Woodward. Rennie could not write the story because he had a friendship with Breadon that he wanted to protect. Woodward then wrote the story in the *Herald Tribune*.[54]

A game against the Cardinals on July 18, 1947, gave more fodder for solidarity on the Dodgers. When Enos Slaughter spiked Robinson's foot at first base on a ground ball, Ralph Branca wanted to retaliate from the pitcher's mound with a beanball. Robinson dismissed the idea, attributing the act to hyper-competitiveness rather than racism. Slaughter denied the spiking was intentional, but Robinson didn't go that far, saying, "I think Slaughter would cut his mother if he thought it would help him win a ball game."[55]

Robinson proved Rickey's baseball instinct correct, to the dismay of the other National League teams. In 1947, Robinson played in 151 of 154 games, had a .297 batting average, got 175 hits (including 12 home runs), stole a league-leading 29 bases, drew 74 walks, scored 125 runs, and struck out 36 times. For his efforts, effectiveness, and efficiency, Robinson received the 1947 National League Rookie of the Year Award.

Essentially, Robinson and Rickey were partners. Robinson, gracious to the point of shyness, praised Rickey's contribution to his career, long after he retired from baseball. On November 20, 1969, a 50-year-old Jackie Robinson was the mystery challenger on the television show *What's My Line?* Host Wally Bruner said, "You know, we all, Jackie, owe you a deep debt of gratitude for what you started when you joined the major leagues because you've made baseball a much better and interesting and exciting game. And it began with you."[56]

Appearing pensive, almost uncomfortable with Bruner's sincere compliments, Robinson responded by turning attention to Rickey: "He had a much more difficult role than I had and I like to give him credit for the role that he played in helping us and guiding us through our careers."[57]

Unsurprisingly, Rickey showed similar immodesty in a 1960s interview with Cubs broadcaster Jack Brickhouse on Chicago television station WGN.

> No credit should come to me or anybody else about that thing. Montreal deserves credit. And above all, Jackie Robinson deserves credit. But you see, the man that carried the load during those first two, three years, more than that, was Jackie himself. He's not a natural in that field. Naturally, he's very resentful of any kind of mistreatment or insult or discrimination. He carries chips on his shoulders chipping at it. And when he talks in anger, he talks regretfully. He is a great character in that he was able to impose upon himself the restrictions that were necessary to carry that load for his race. He sensed that, he realized that, and he did it. And nobody knows what he had to take. He's a wonderful person, that fella.[58]

Not everyone who opposed Robinson did so on the basis of race, particularly the ballplayer he replaced—"Big Ed" Stevens. In his autobiography *The Other Side of the Jackie Robinson Story*, Stevens alleged that Robinson was handed the position of Dodgers first baseman from Rickey instead of earning it.

> We were not competing. I began to realize that Jackie's playing time was being programmed from the front office, and every move he made was directed by

Branch Rickey and his staff. People began asking me what I thought about the situation. I didn't hold anything against Jackie Robinson because he was doing exactly what he was told. But this would never have happened without Branch's tinkering. You go to spring training and fight for a job. That's how it worked. But Jackie never competed for first base.[59]

Even if Stevens' version is correct, Rickey needed a warrior to fight the battle against prejudice on America's baseball diamonds to ensure a flow of the top Negro Leagues players to the major leagues. If not in 1947, when? If not Robinson, who?

Marty Adler kept the legacy of Robinson and Rickey alive through his creation of the Brooklyn Dodgers Hall of Fame, an informal association. Adler, an assistant principal at Jackie Robinson Middle School (I.S. 320) for 23 years, retired in the mid–1990s. The school is across the street from the old Ebbets Field site. Adler passed away in 2013.

The Brooklyn Dodger Hall of Fame began as a gimmick to get the kids interested in math," he said. "We had a 10th birthday party for the school in 1977. It coincided with the 30th anniversary of Jackie Robinson's breaking the color line. We began to use baseball statistics like batting averages and slugging percentages to ignite an interest in math.

Brooklyn was the place for Robinson to break through. It couldn't have happened in Pittsburgh because the city was too blue collar. Detroit had the influence of Father Coughlin and Ty Cobb. The Phillies had Ben Chapman. St. Louis and Cincinnati had the southern view of race. The Yankees were conservative.

There's a definite political element, too. From Reiser to Snider to Koufax, from Charles Schumer to Barbara Boxer to Ruth Bader Ginsburg, Brooklyn loved its lefties![60]

When Robinson debuted, racism appeared entrenched in the stands. Robinson found an antidote of acceptance from his fellow infielder, a Kentuckian shortstop with a nickname attributed to being a marbles champion who mastered the use of a pee wee marble.

The time in Boston when the Braves were heckling him in infield practice and he put his arm on my shoulder. And the time in Cincinnati when all our white players got letters saying if they don't do something, the whole team will be black and they'll lose their jobs. Pee Wee got on the bus and brought it up and we started discussing it and pretty soon we were all laughing about it. Pee Wee was the captain, he knew how to handle everything.[61]

In the 1950 biography *Jackie Robinson*, Bill Roeder documented the Reese-Robinson display as happening around the National League during Dodgers warm-ups. "The result was that the kidding ceased, and a great

Pee Wee Reese threw an arm around Robinson during warm-ups before several National League games during Robinson's rookie year of 1947. Reese's gesture represented acceptance, quieted hecklers, and symbolized brotherhood on the Brooklyn Dodgers. Reese is shown here signing autographs for young fans (National Baseball Hall of Fame Library, Cooperstown, New York).

many players around the league formed a new respect for Robinson as an individual. If Pee Wee likes him, the players concluded, the guy must be all right," wrote Roeder.[62]

It happened in Fort Worth, too, during an exhibition game. In one of the deepest parts of the South, Reese deflated—or at least deflected—racism volleyed with venomous opinions. New York City sportswriter Roscoe McGowen recounted, "Reese called time, walked over, dropped an arm around Robinson's shoulders and started talking to him. What he said doesn't matter. The gesture said everything."[63]

A statue at MCU Park, home of the New York–Penn League's Class A Brooklyn Cyclones, immortalizes the Reese-Robinson incident as does the 2013 film *42*.

A golf course in a Danville, Illinois, country club became another sports venue where racial fences buckled. Pee Wee invited Jackie Robinson and Wendell Smith to join him, pitcher Rex Barney, Harold Parrott, and McGowen. Pee Wee's group played ahead of Robinson and Smith at the club. After about four holes, Reese said, "Why don't you two join us? We can make this a six-some, although that's against the rules. There aren't many people out here today and it won't make much difference."[64]

Acceptance. That's the Brooklyn way.

The Dodgers revived under Rickey, whose vision transformed the way baseball conducted its business. In 1948, Rickey began Dodgertown, a spring training complex on the site of a former Naval training base that stayed in the Dodgers organization for 60 years. Dodgertown was an icon, its Vero Beach, Florida, location famous because of its continuous link to the Dodgers while everything in baseball changed—integration of black and Latino players, domed stadiums, artificial turf, the designated hitter. In the music video for John Fogerty's 1985 hit song *Centerfield*, the first shot after a montage of baseball cards is a pan of the billboard for Vero Beach, winter home of the Brooklyn Dodgers and affiliated teams.

Dodgertown was also a place of learning, an innovative concept of uniting players before the season to practice the basics of baseball. Rickey drilled his players on the fundamentals, lest they develop, observe, or further bad habits. Roy Campanella said,

> I'd never seen anything like this. I never knew what a sliding pit was. To learn how to slide. Batting cages to hit a ball off a batting tee? Never did see one before. This was the first time I'd ever hit against a pitching machine. I was getting grounded in the basics that the Dodgers always practiced—of throwing the ball to the right base, of learning how to take a lead off first. And there were exercises before you started every day. This was a new challenge to me. This helped me to develop into the player I became.[65]

Dodgertown. Jackie Robinson. The Dodgers in the World Series. These were not days of the hapless bums who brought misery to the borough during the 1920s and 1930s. Anything seemed possible, even though the Dodgers lost the World Series to the Yankees in 1947 and again in 1949. Hope sprang eternal, a symbol of the Brooklynite's faith, perseverance, and toughness. "Wait Till Next Year" became the battle cry for those whose dreams brought joy but never achieved complete bliss, that achievement being a World Series championship.

Yankee hurler Bill Bevens approached a no-hitter in Game Four of the 1947 World Series only to see his masterful work of 8⅔ innings destroyed with a Dodger comeback in the bottom of the ninth inning. In Game Six, Al Gionfriddo robbed Joe DiMaggio of an extra base hit 415 feet from Yankee Stadium's home plate. Down 8 to 5 with two outs in the bottom of the sixth inning, the Yankees had two men on base when DiMaggio walloped the ball.

Baseball lore dictates that Gionfriddo prevented a home run, but that is a questionable theory because he took a few steps toward the wall after he caught the ball. "I put my head down and I ran, my back was toward home plate and you know I had it right," said Gionfriddo. "I had the ball sighted just right."[66] DiMaggio revealed his emotions about as often as a Republican advocates raising taxes. But, on this occasion, he grimaced as he kicked the dirt near second base.

Gionfriddo emblemized the scrappiness of the Dodgers. At 5'6" and 165 pounds, he had the heart, if not the physique, of a major leaguer.[67] The Dodgers were working class; the Yankees, highbrow. Oscar-winning actor and Brooklyn native Lou Gossett, Jr., said, "The Yankees symbolized that kind of life, that kind of ambience, that kind of thing we aspire to but never attain."[68]

Even though they lost to the Yankees, the Dodgers had something deeper that could not be quantified by batting averages, home runs, or championships. No team could match the affection bestowed on the Dodgers. It was tribal. "For ever so many years, the Yankees have been a great club, prosperous and respected and feared and, in some quarters, hated," wrote Red Smith. "But they have not been greatly loved.

"They have never, that is, won such an impassioned national following as the Dodgers have known."[69]

The 1949 Yankees, according to Smith, were a different breed because of challenges they needed to overcome. But Smith attached the word "adversity" to the Yankees, including the need to overcome "sixty-odd disabling injuries" to win. "People used to call the Yankees a team of business men ball players. They did a big business, and it involved approximately as much sentiment as the business of United States Steel."[70]

On May 4, 1950, Pee Wee Reese played in his 1,000th game. He got ejected from it after arguing a called third strike with Umpire Babe Pinelli. "Reese bristled up the arbitrator and finally flung his bat angrily in the air, starting out for his position, but Pinelli ran halfway to the pitcher's mound where Paul Minner, a former teammate of Reese stood, grinning, and told Reese he was through for the afternoon. Eddie Miksis replaced him," stated the *Brooklyn Eagle*.[71]

The Dodgers lost the 1950 National League pennant to the Philadelphia Phillies on the last day of the season, but it wasn't the only suffering felt by the Dodgers. John L. Smith died in July, leaving an ownership void impelling Walter O'Malley to unite power in the Dodgers front office, with Rickey and Smith's widow in the crosshairs.

Rickey, despite a sacred reputation in baseball circles, faced diminishing clout at 215 Montague Street. Knowing that an O'Malley monocracy would muffle his voice, Rickey plotted his escape. He found the key in the original 1945 partners agreement. If a partner wanted to sell his or her share of the Dodgers, the agreement mandated that he or she must offer the other partners an opportunity to match bids from outsiders. To further his plan, Rickey allied with John Wilmer Galbreath, a part-owner of the Pittsburgh Pirates.

Galbreath built his fortune on skyscrapers, those steel-and-glass symbols of 20th century progress. True to A-type business mogul form, Galbreath loved competition beyond the balance sheet. Winning a construction bid was nice, but Galbreath sought baseball and horse racing as additional outlets. "You haven't lived until you've crossed over the track to the infield to get a plate or a trophy,"[72] explained Galbreath.

Rickey was a baseball innovator who revolutionized the game; Galbreath, a real estate developer who created urban skylines. They were builders. And they both wanted to win. Galbreath's stake in the Pirates knocked out the possibility of purchasing Rickey's share of the Dodgers. Galbreath didn't want Rickey's shares, though—he wanted Rickey for the Pirates management team.

Galbreath conceived a scheme that would have gained grins from George Steinbrenner for the outcome benefitting the Pirates front office, Donald Trump for the artistry of the deal, and Jack Benny for the money involved. Galbreath collogued with a fellow member of the real estate brotherhood, New York City's William Zeckendorf, to bid on Rickey's share of the Dodgers. Zeckendorf was a decoy designed to boost the purchase price for Rickey's shares, then succumb to O'Malley's matching offer. Rickey would then be free to pursue other opportunities in baseball, specifically, a job with the Pirates.

The carnival shell game, corporate style.

Zeckendorf's initial bid for Rickey's share of the Dodgers was $1 million. Legally, O'Malley needed to bid the same amount or more, even if he thought the figure outrageous. The deal increased $50,000 because Zeckendorf's capital was "tied up" during the process. This was a smokescreen providing cover for Rickey getting an extra $50,000 while beginning a new baseball life in Pittsburgh.[73]

O'Malley controlled 50 percent of the Dodgers. Remaining percentages were owned by Smith's estate and Dearie McKeever Mulvey, heir to former Dodgers president Steve McKeever. "Later, O'Malley purchased stock from Smith's estate to increase his holdings to 66⅔ percent, and he became the sole owner with the acquisition of stock from the Mulvey family in the early 1970s,"[74] states the Los Angeles Dodgers web site.

Branch Rickey's departure created a fissure in the psyche of the Brooklyn Dodgers. It was Rickey, after all, who built the National League's dynasty at Ebbets Field. It was Rickey who created the Nashua Dodgers, a New Hampshire minor league team serving as an incubator for potential major league talent, including Don Newcombe and Roy Campanella. It was Rickey who visualized Dodgertown, the sprawling spring training complex in Vero Beach. And it was Rickey who propelled baseball on a new path of racial oneness by destroying the proscription of racial exclusion.

On stationery from the Hotel Jaragua in Ciudad Trujillo in the Dominican Republic, Robinson expressed sorrow, appreciation, and friendship to his partner leaving 215 Montague Street, while acknowledging that "finding the right words come hard."[75]

Rickey reciprocated, "I do not suppose that our paths will probably parallel again in any close fashion, but I do want you and Rachel to know that always I, and, indeed the family, will have a constant and lasting interest in your welfare and happiness."[76]

Appreciation. That's the Brooklyn way.

6th Inning:
"I guess we weren't
meant to win it"

*"When you're playing the Giants,
your manhood's on the line."*[1]—Carl Erskine

Macy's had Gimbel's. Hatfields had McCoys. Montagues had Capulets. And the Brooklyn Dodgers had the New York Giants.

After losing the 1950 National League pennant to the Phillies on the last day of the season, the Dodgers began 1951 looking for vengeance. Or vindication. Or both. Their cross-town rivalry with the New York Giants culminated at the end of the 1951 season, forming a tale belonging on a storyboard in the office of a Hollywood producer debating whether he should take his wife to Ciro's or his latest casting couch conquest to the Trocadero. Or vice versa.

The Giants-Dodgers rivalry traces back to October 1845, six months before baseball's ur-game in Hoboken between the Knickerbockers and the New York Club, credited as the first game with organized rules, thanks to Alexander Cartwright. The October 1845 game paired the New York Ball Club against a team of Brooklynites, each team having eight players.[2]

Ancestors to the Giants and Dodgers also met in an 1889 precursor to the World Series when the Brooklyn Bridegrooms of the American Association faced off against the New York Giants of the National League in a best-of-11 championship series. On October 18, 1889, the *New York Times* reported, "The rivalry between New York and Brooklyn as regards to baseball is unparalleled in the history of the national game. It is not confined to the players or attaches of the clubs, but the patrons take part in it."[3]

The Giants won.

What added to the 1951 drama was a traitor on par with Benedict Arnold in the eyes of Dodgers fans—Leo Durocher, manager of the New

York Giants. Dodgers fans didn't know the whole story, though. Durocher got his job with the Giants because of Branch Rickey, when both men were working for the Dodgers. After his 1947 suspension, Durocher returned to manage the Dodgers in 1948. In Peck Memorial Hospital with a bladder infection, Rickey sent Harold Parrott on a mission—tell Leo Durocher to resign as manager of the Dodgers. Rickey then left for his farm in Maryland.

On Independence Day, 1948, fireworks started early. Parrott went to the Dodgers clubhouse after Durocher got kicked out of the last game of a three-game series against the Giants at Ebbets Field. Roy Campanella clocked two of his career 242 home runs as the Dodgers battled the Giants to a 13–12 victory, but Durocher had another battle to fight. In *The Lords of Baseball*, Parrott described Durocher's outburst: "The Old Man will have to fire me himself, face to face, an' he hasn't got the guts!"[4]

Durocher's version is a bit more bland. In his autobiography *Nice Guys Finish Last*, Durocher wrote that he said, "See that phone right there on the desk, Harold? That goes right up into Mr. Rickey's office. If he wants to fire me, let him pick up that phone and send for me so that he can fire me in person. You and I are old friends, so take this the way I mean it, but you tell him I am not going to resign and nobody is going to fire me by messenger."[5]

Later, Parrott brought another message for Durocher to visit the Maryland farm. Durocher responded, "You tell Mr. Rickey that I'm not going to go all the way to Maryland to get fired. If he wants to fire me he can come up to Philadelphia."[6] The Dodgers started a three-game series against the Phillies on July 5.

Embraced by Brooklyn as one of its own, Durocher was more than a manager. He was a Dodgers institution with an us-against-the-world philosophy. From Canarsie to Coney Island, Brooklynites reveled when their mouthpiece argued with umpires about blown calls. Hell had no fury like Leo the Lip. The phrase linked to Durocher's personality—"Nice guys finish last"—is misunderstood, however. He never said, "Nice guys finish last." Not exactly. During Durocher's tenure with the Dodgers, Frank Graham of the *New York Journal-American* was interviewing him about Eddie Stanky when Mel Ott approached the batting cage for batting practice before a Giants-Dodgers game. "Take a look at that Number Four there," said Durocher. "A nicer guy never drew breath than that man there. Walker Cooper, Mize, Marshall, Kerr, Gordon, Thomson. Take a look at them. All nice guys. They'll finish last. Nice guys. Finish last."[7]

Durocher did not form a nexus between describing the Giants and predicting their place in the standings. His insight reflected a philosophy that nice guys needed to put aside niceties during competition. "Oh, Stanky's the nicest gentleman who ever drew breath, but when the bell rings you're his mortal enemy. That's the kind of a guy I want playing for me,"[8] said Durocher. Graham wrote it in Durocher's framework, if not the precise meaning. "But the other writers who picked it up ran two fragments together to make it sound as if I were saying that you couldn't be a decent person and succeed," said Durocher.[9]

Rickey saw an escape hatch for his battles with the opponent of nice guys when Giants owner Horace Stoneham called the Dodgers front office, looking to sign Burt Shotton for the Giants manager position. Rickey upped the ante by offering Durocher as an alternative choice. Stoneham jumped at the opportunity. Durocher, though not fired from the Dodgers, saw that continuing to manage the team would increase the tension between Rickey and himself.

After conversing with Stoneham, Rickey explained that the managing job at the Polo Grounds had Durocher's name on it. When Rickey did not give a definitive answer regarding Durocher's Dodgers tenure for the rest of the 1948 season, Durocher arranged a meeting with Stoneham at the former's Upper East Side apartment, where Stoneham arrived with Giants legend Carl Hubbell, the Hall of Fame pitcher who had dominated National League hitters with a screwball and had become a baseball icon by striking out Babe Ruth, Lou Gehrig, Jimmie Foxx, Al Simmons, and Joe Cronin consecutively in the 1934 All-Star Game.

> It wasn't that easy for me to click Brooklyn off. *Not* that easy for me, buddy," said Durocher. "For nine years, I had been charging off the bench whenever that battle cry "Leooooo!" filled the Brooklyn air. For nine years, I hadn't been able to drive up Bedford Avenue after a game without a knot of guys yelling at me from every corner to find out how we had made out. If we had won, they'd raise a cry of victory, and if we had lost they'd always say, "*Wha' happened?*[10]

But those who wear black and orange instead of blue and white were never welcome in the hearts of Dodgers fans, not even a baseball icon once embraced as the borough's favorite son.

Baseball's vernal ritual of Opening Day in 1951 held promise for Brooklynites savoring the Dodgers' efforts as part of their everyday lives. Children, especially, anticipated the beginning of the baseball season, for afternoons would soon be filled with freedom from homework, term papers, and assembly halls.

The Dodgers vanquished the ghosts of 1950 by tearing through National League competitors in 1951 like fire through kindling. They reached a 13½-game lead over the closest team, the Giants, in mid–August. The lead evaporated. After the last day of the season, the Dodgers and Giants were tied, forcing a three-game playoff to decide the National League title. They split the first two games—the Giants won the first game, 3–1, and the Dodgers retaliated, blanking the Giants, 10–0, in the second game.

Riding the momentum of rookie pitcher Clem Labine's six-hit shutout at the Polo Grounds, Dodgers fans voided the season's collapse from their memories. Shutting out the Giants was one thing. But a ten-run shutout? That was an exhibition of excellence, not a competition. Gray skies greeted the teams on October 3, 1951, but the threat of rain mattered not to the borough. With the pennant to be decided at the Polo Grounds that afternoon in the third playoff game, they found an emotional boost from the hometown press. Joseph Wilkinson of the *Brooklyn Eagle* wrote, "If you hear any one whistling 'I'll Never Smile Again,' he's probably a Giant fan."[11]

Would that it were so for Brooklyn.

In the bottom of the ninth inning of Game 3, the Dodgers led, 4–2. Giants' hopes rested on Bobby Thomson. With two runners on base, Dodgers manager Charlie Dressen called the bullpen, an activity he had not engaged in previously that day. "He started calling in the eighth and kept it up right into the ninth," said coach Clyde Sukeforth. "He must have called half a dozen times. He sounded frantic: 'Who's ready?' he would ask. I'd tell him [Ralph] Branca was ready and then he'd call again. 'Who's ready?' It kept up that way right until he made the change."[12]

Dressen's order to relieve Newcombe with Branca rested on a Carl Erskine pitch in the bullpen.

Clyde Sukeforth answered the phone. "They're both ready," he said. "However, Erskine is bouncing his overhand curve." Dressen said, "Let me have Branca." On Ralph's second pitch, Thomson hit a three-run homer to win the game and the pennant. Whenever I'm asked what my best pitch was, I say, "The curveball I bounced in the Polo Grounds bullpen,"[13] explained Erskine.

Newcombe, the 1949 National League Rookie of the Year, started the ninth with a 4–1 lead. But the Giants scored a run and had two runners on base when Bobby Thomson approached the plate. Born in Glasgow, Scotland, as the youngest of six children, Thomson grew up on Staten Island and stayed there after returning from Air Force service during World War II at various posts in the United States.

Branca pitched a called strike to Thomson. Then, it happened. "The Shot Heard Round the World." It was a punch to the solar plexus of Brooklyn's soul, like the time you discovered that your security blanket got ruined in the wash, your crush liked somebody else, and Santa Claus did not exist, all rolled into one swing of the bat that finished a battle of catastrophic proportions not seen since the Olympians overthrew the Titans.

When Bobby Thomson's home run flew over Andy Pafko's head into the left field stands at the Polo Grounds, Brooklyn came to a standstill. Even the fish in Sheepshead Bay stopped swimming.

If Shakespeare could return from the grave to document an event, the Dodgers-Giants game on October 3, 1951, might likely be the topic of his 38th play—it reflected the autumn of Brooklyn's discontent, the glorious feeling of summer warmth not to be extended as the metaphorical clouds that lowered upon the borough refused to be buried in the deep bosom of Sheepshead Bay. Who needed *Richard III* when real tragedy invaded every corner of Brooklyn?

Under the vise-like pressure of a deadline reinforced by Thomson's last-minute heroics, sportswriters did not have the luxury of waiting for muses to arrive. Baseball scribes who thought they had seen everything reflexively pounded typewriter keys, their creative instincts honed by years of reading great writers and writing great copy. They chronicled "The Shot Heard Round the World" for a readership stunned by an outcome once unthinkable to even the biggest long-shot bettor. The Giants won the pennant.

Hollywood's most imaginative writers on an opium jag could not have scripted a more improbable windup of the season that started in April and had its finish today in the triumph of Bobby Thomson and the Giants.[14]—Shirley Povich, *Washington Post*

Now it is done. Now the story ends. And there is no way to tell it. The art of fiction is dead. Reality has strangled invention. Only the utterly impossible, the inexpressibly fantastic, can ever be plausible again.[15]—Red Smith, *New York Herald Tribune*

Bobby Thomson completed the baseball miracle of miracles yesterday. With a three-run homer off Ralph Branca in the ninth inning, Thomson broke the hearts of the Brooklyn Dodgers and all the Brooklyn faithful.[16]—Rud Rennie, *New York Herald Tribune*

You're Leo Durocher, a fresh guy out of Springfield, Mass., and you didn't hit the home run. You stood there in the coach's box, helpless and yearning the way a crap shooter does when he's betting case money on the hard ten. You can't claim you anticipated it. No one could. But you didn't doubt it either.

A picture is worth a thousand tears—Dodgers pitcher Ralph Branca after Bobby Thomson smashed his pitch for a home run that became labeled "The Shot Heard Round the World" (National Baseball Hall of Fame Library, Cooperstown, New York).

You're a guy who doesn't believe in sure things. You wouldn't be playing the Yankees in the Stadium if you did.[17]—Jimmy Cannon, *Newsday*

After a campaign of vicissitudes and adventure, joy and despair, the Dodgers couldn't pick up the marbles. The miracle Giants snatched 'em out of their palsied fingers at the Polo Grounds yesterday to become champions of the National League for the first time since 1937.[18]—Harold C. Burr, *Brooklyn Daily Eagle*

I will miss the leather-lunged ladies who are a fixture at Ebbets Field, likewise the home talent bands emitting horrible sounds. But I don't believe these people represent the real Brooklyn. They represent the Brooklyn of the fictioneers and the magazine writers—a phony vision built up by adroit press-agenting to the virtual extinction of the neighboring Giants.[19]—Hal Burton, *Newsday*

Never had there been a finish like this. Nor will there probably be another in our times. There just couldn't be.[20]—Carl Lundquist, *Newsday*

The Giant addicts displayed their legendary bad taste, passing out black-edged cards of condolence, crying towels, and other vulgarities. Observant Brooklynites were able to avoid most of the Giant fans, who are readily spotted because of their weak, receding chins, beady, criminal eyes, and cretinous smiles.[21]—Joseph F. Wilkinson, *Brooklyn Daily Eagle*

Don't make mine vanilla on this round, I'll settle for cyanide and there must be thousands of people in our fair and unhappy town who feel about the same, as the Giants moved into action against the Yankees in the first game of the World Series today.[22]—Tommy Holmes, *Brooklyn Daily Eagle*

Ball clubs win big games in the last of the ninth all right, but the way it was won this unforgettable afternoon happens more often in fiction than in fact. Three runs behind starting the ninth. Then single, single, double and home run. The game that was lost almost beyond hope was suddenly won as dramatically as any ball game in the history of baseball has ever been won.[23]—Bill Lee, *Hartford Courant*

In *Newsday*, Jack Altshul profiled a Yugoslavian immigrant named Tony, a bartender at Felice's Restaurant in Westbury, New York.

Tony has lost seven pounds and at least seventy dollars following the fortunes of his team in the last few days. A homicidal gleam clouds his eyes when you mention the dirty word, "Dressen." Mention further such a treasonable utterance as "Durocher," in the same breath you are ordering a Martini, and accept the consequences. If you are lucky, you will get a Manhattan. If not, the drink may smell suspiciously of bitter almonds.[24]

The headline banner across the top of the *Brooklyn Daily Eagle's* sports section on October 4, 1951, summarized the feeling throughout Brooklyn: "Let's Not Talk About It Anymore."

Carl Erskine recalled,

The first thing Dressen did was take his shirt off. But he didn't unbutton it. He just ripped it off, popping all the buttons in one motion. Jackie looked totally disgusted and he fired his glove down. The rest of the team was quiet. Ralph plopped down on the steps leading up from the locker room to the trainer's room. He sat there leaning over with that number 13 shining on his back.[25]

Clem Labine said, "Oh, it was terrible. Like being in a morgue."[26]

Stuart Greenwald, an attorney in Middletown, New York, and a New York Giants fan with an unparalleled respect for the game that Abner Doubleday did not invent, celebrates "The Shot Heard Round the World" with an annual telephone ritual. He revels in his hypermnesia that allows him to relive one of baseball's greatest moments:

> For years, my friend John Krause and I call each other on October 3rd and we talk about it like it happened yesterday. One year, John calls me. The next year, I call him. The night before my daughter Nancy got married, my wife and I hosted a dinner for our family and friends attending the wedding. I spoke about my daughter and the wedding and how special it would be. Then, I risked marital capital when I said, "But up until this moment and tomorrow, the most special moment in my life was on October 3, 1951." My wife yelled, "We weren't married, then!" I responded, "I wasn't talking about you! I'm talking about Thomson's home run."
>
> A guy got up with tears in his eyes and said it was the saddest day of his life.[27]

Thomson's home run struck Ronnie Klein close to his heart. And his home. Klein grew up on West End Avenue in North Plainfield, New Jersey, rooting for the Dodgers. Thomson married Sue Colton, who lived on Klein's block. "We all followed the Dodgers, but we couldn't understand why Stanky and Durocher moved to Manhattan to be with the Giants,"[28] Klein says.

When Mr. and Mrs. Warren Poole emigrated from Oaudreut, Canada, for a baseball honeymoon, they wanted to see the Dodgers because they knew some of the players from their tenure with the Montreal Royals. "Now we've come to watch them in the series."[29]

Gamblers betting on the Dodgers lost money. Alice Hall of 94 St. Mark's Avenue made a bet of a different kind. She bet neighbor Jack Bader, "If we lose this one, I'll walk up and down Flatbush Ave. in a bathing suit … on a leash!" She made good on her bet. Their picture appeared in the *Brooklyn Eagle*.[30]

Four weeks after "The Shot Heard Round the World," Halloween caused a reminder, as if the loss wasn't already seared in the hearts and minds of Brooklynites. "I didn't like the Giant organization," said Duke Snider. "I didn't like the colors orange and black. In fact, I never have cared for Halloween because their colors are orange and black."[31]

Thomson's heroics, plus the drama of the moment, eclipse the display of baseball excellence by both teams, starting with Sal Maglie, the Giants' starting pitcher. Dodgers fans despised Maglie, nicknamed "the Barber" for pitching balls so close they could shave the batter's face. "They believed that, when I pitched against Brooklyn, I threw at the heads of the Dodgers. This was their belief and I can't really blame them for it. *They were 100 per cent correct*,"[32] admitted Maglie in a 1959 article for *Cavalier* magazine.

After Jackie Robinson drove in Pee Wee Reese with a single in the first inning, Maglie did not allow another Dodger run till the eighth inning, when Reese and Duke Snider singled and a wild pitch allowed Reese to score with Snider moving to third base. Maglie walked Robinson intentionally, strategizing for a double play. An Andy Pafko ground ball to Giants third baseman Thomson scored Snider. "Thomson knocked the ball down but could not get hold of it in time to catch any one,"[33] reported Rud Rennie in the *New York Herald Tribune*. Cox singled Robinson home, boosting the Dodgers lead to 4–1.

The Giants went three up, three down in the bottom of the eighth. Larry Jansen relieved Maglie in the ninth and retired the Dodgers in order. With a comfortable 4–1 lead, the Dodgers looked poised to meet the Yankees in the World Series. Alvin Dark scored on a Whitey Lockman double, closing the distance to 4–2. Then the unthinkable happened. "Many of the spectators just sat in their seats after it was all over," wrote Rud Rennie in the *Herald Tribune*. "Talk was incoherent. Words were inadequate because this was more than the winning of a ball game, this was the end of fourteen long suffering years for the Giant rooters. Every club in the league, except Pittsburgh, had won a pennant since the Giants won their last one."[34]

In consecutive years, the Dodgers lost on the last day of the season. Was the home run a numinous harbinger of baseball divinity? Baseball is a game rooted in superstition, ritual, and imagined power. A hitting streak will cause a player to wear the same socks until the streak ends, lest he lose the benefit of the socks' supposed influence. Ralph Branca wore #13 on his uniform, a traditionally unlucky number. If you add the number of the month of October to the number of the date, you get 13.

Doris Kearns Goodwin masked a superstition with a gesture of good will. As a child, she was a die-hard Dodgers rooter. Her household chores included taking her mother's order to the Bryn Mawr Meat Market. When Goodwin found out that butcher Max Knopf wore his faded Giants cap to bed after it adorned his head all day in the shop, inspiration struck the future political commentator and historian—she bought him a new Giants hat, hoping that it would break the Giants' good luck. Knopf refused to wear the hat in the shop, relegating it to his night table. Goodwin's plan crumbled, though foolproof in her imagination. "Thus Max continued to wear his battered old cap, and the Giants kept winning until their streak had reached an astonishing sixteen games,"[35] Goodwin wrote in her memoir *Wait Till Next Year*.

Goodwin, like many Brooklynites, attempted to avoid Giants fans.

"After almost a week had passed, a large bouquet of red roses arrived at my door addressed to me," Goodwin explained. "It was the first time anyone had sent me flowers. 'Ragmop, please come back,' the card read. 'We miss you. Your friends at the Bryn Mawr Meat Market.'"[36]

Was Thomson's home run a result of providence? Branca thought so. He said, "I guess we weren't meant to win it."[37]

Branca later found out that the source was neither magical nor supernatural.

It was immoral.

While the Scot from Staten Island leapt around the Polo Grounds base paths like King David when the Ark of the Lord came into Jerusalem, he ended the 1951 National League season that began with the Dodgers breathing fire, but falling victim to the Giants' extinguishment toward the finish line.

The "boys of summer" hit their career highs in various categories in 1951:

Roy Campanella in batting average (.325), doubles (33), and hits (164);

Carl Furillo in hits (197);

Pee Wee Reese in hits (176) and RBI (84).

Everywhere one looked, a Dodger compiled statistics, showcased strength, and felled opponents. A foregone conclusion pervaded the Dodgers' locker room in mid-season—they were going to the World Series. Ralph Branca denied that he goaded the Giants through the wall separating the teams' locker rooms, but Don Newcombe corrected him in a 1974 episode of *The Way It Was*. Newcombe said he heard Branca exclaim "Eat your heart out, Leo!" Branca shrugged and said that maybe it was Jackie Robinson who said it.[38]

After the Thomson home run, Carl Furillo said, "When you've got something right in your hand, and then you drop it yourself, with nobody pushing you—well, that ain't good, is it?"[39] Furillo's analysis placed the burden on a perceived Dodgers' failure. It was, however, an analysis omitting a factor unknown to the Dodgers—the Giants employed a spy to decipher the upcoming pitch by looking through a telescope in the center field clubhouse at the Polo Grounds.

Joshua Prager's breaking of the telescope story in *The Wall Street Journal* in 2001, followed by his comprehensive 2006 book *The Echoing Green*, defines investigative journalism.

Penetrating to the core of an omertà, Prager filled a lacuna in the Thomson home run story by tracking down details of alleged chicanery like a modern-day Sherlock Holmes.

Thomson, who homered off Branca in Game 1, denied until his death in 2010 that he had the sign of Branca's pitch. "When I looked at the films I was proud of my swing," said Thomson. "I jumped on the pitch, lashed out at it, hit it hard. Some say it would have been an out at Ebbets Field. Who cares? I hit it at the Polo Grounds over a 25-foot wall at the 315-foot mark and we beat the Dodgers. No need to say any more than that."[40]

Actually, there was. "The Shot Heard 'Round the World" possesses import bordering on myth. Although chronicled, it deserved to be investigated. It is, possibly, the most dramatic moment in baseball. Sports, perhaps. Thomson's home run was the apex of Brooklyn reaching for glory, but never quite capturing it. In essence, it symbolized the perceived destiny of the Dodgers to be also-rans.[41]

Of course, Prager's story fomented the eternal ire of Dodgers fans and Giants fans alike—because the Thomson home run was arguably fraudulent. Branca could not forgive the Giants, particularly Thomson, after Prager's revelation of Durocher's telescope scheme. Prager said,

> Some felt, however, that I had *already* demeaned a home run in newsprint. To them I say that what I reported was fact. I say that in these pages I took pains to place a telescope in the larger context of baseball thievery and to recognize those writers who long before me nibbled at a rumor. I say that I have intended to *honor* a home run, to make clear why for millions it remains a memory so unshakeable that one doctor used it to describe the limits of Wernicke-Korsakoff syndrome.[42]

Stealing signs is part of the game and has been since baseball's origins. The late Bill Veeck, a team owner known for flamboyant promotions, claimed that Charley Dressen was the self-proclaimed "world's greatest sign-stealer." Veeck also said that a spy in the Polo Grounds clubhouse during the John McGraw era used binoculars, then signaled the pitch to the batter by lowering or raising the shutters. Apparently, sign-stealing was in the Giants' DNA.[43]

With or without the signs, Thomson's home run was an incredible moment. But it was just that. A moment. Certainly, more significant, impactful, and lasting societal touchstones occurred in October 1951. Winston Churchill won re-election as Prime Minister of the United Kingdom after six years away from the position, CBS' trademark eye logo debuted, and a redhead named Lucy captured our hearts in her prime time debut less than two weeks after Thomson's home run. Plus, a true tragedy occurred daily as American soldiers got killed serving their country in the Korean War.

Also in October 1951, a college football game showed the Dodgers' beacon of social progress threatened by shadows of immutable ignorance in the Johnny Bright incident. Bright, a halfback/quarterback at Drake University, got his jaw broken by Oklahoma A&M defensive tackle Wilbanks Smith. In a 1980 interview with the *Des Moines Register*, Bright said, "There's no way it couldn't have been racially motivated." Bright added, "What I like about the whole deal now, and what I'm smug enough to say, is that getting a broken jaw has somehow made college athletics better. It made the NCAA take a hard look and clean up some things that were bad."[44]

Smith knocked Bright unconscious three times in the first seven minutes of the game. The jaw-breaking occurred after a handoff from Bright to fullback Gene Macomber. A photo sequence in the *Des Moines Register* illustrated the timing of the jaw-break—*Register* photographers John Robinson and Don Ultang won the Pulitzer Prize. Like Jackie Robinson, Bright plowed through the hate-filled nemeses by using athleticism as a weapon. He made first team as a college football All-American and finished fifth in the 1951 Heisman Trophy voting. Drake named its stadium after Bright—he is the only Drake football player to have his number retired.

"The Shot Heard Round the World," nevertheless, resonated as a moment of primary importance for baseball fans, particularly those in Brooklyn who cared not about politics, entertainment, or football on October 3, 1951. They cared for something they cherished, then lost. Hope.

A Giants pitcher benefited from Thomson's home run with a "W" on the scorecard—quietly, as is the wont of pitchers yielding glory to dramatic home runs, acrobatic fielding, and explosive base running. Even a baseball aficionado soaked in sobriety—the serious-minded kind, not the liquor abstinence kind—may not remember Larry Jansen, the pitcher who relieved Maglie in the top of the ninth inning.

Jansen was a native of Verboort, Oregon, a community founded by Father William Verboort for Dutch Catholic families in 1875, the year before the National League began. Jansen's affection for his Verboort brothers and sisters inspired him to return home after his playing days. He settled into a quiet, almost rural life compared to playing and living in the country's biggest cities. "Dad was always a family man. He never aspired to live anyplace else but Verboort,"[45] says Darlene Greene, one of Jansen's children.

Launching a baseball career from his small Dutch community, Jansen found success on Manhattan, the island settled by his Dutch ancestors after Peter Minuit bought it from the Indians in a real estate deal that would make Donald Trump blush with envy. Before joining the Giants in 1947, Jansen pitched for the minor league San Francisco Seals. During his rookie season, Jansen placed second in the Rookie of the Year voting to Jackie Robinson; he notched a 21–5 record and a 3.16 ERA. Greene recalls:

> During Spring Training, he got hit in the jaw by a line drive. For the first month of the season, he was laid up and drinking milkshakes. Joe DiMaggio got his last hit off dad. It happened in the 1951 World Series. When dad would come home from the night games, we always had baloney sandwiches. It was a ritual. I was the oldest of seven children, so I got to stay up later. He was usually back from the Polo Grounds by 10:30 p.m. We rented houses from schoolteachers who went away during the summer.
>
> We lived in New Rochelle and Pelham. In those days, we didn't have television at our home in Oregon. So, we were exposed to a lot more in New York City. By the time I was in 8th grade in the mid–1950s, the style in New York City wasn't in Oregon. Hairdos, skirt length, whatever. Mom and dad sacrificed so we were always in our Oregon home and our own school by the fall. In May, we went to New York and returned in the Fall to Oregon.[46]

Although Jansen may be a footnote to Thomson's eternal flame of baseball history, his Verboort lineage yields an omen, eerie perhaps, of the events leading up to Branca's fateful pitch. In the introduction to the biography *Verboort: A Priest & His People,* Father Scott Vandehey cites a verse from Hebrews 12:1–2 mirroring the mission, struggle, and victory in the 1951 Giants-Dodgers competition for the National League pennant. "My brothers and sisters: … since we are surrounded by so great a cloud of witnesses, let us … persevere in running the race that lies before us while keeping our eyes fixed on Jesus."[47]

More than six decades after Jansen's victory, Brooklynites still feel the pain. Their hearts adust, Dodgers fans relive the valediction of the 1951 season in documentaries, news footage, and sports journalism. It is considered *sui generis*—a moment of pain so deep, it cannot be rivaled by any moment in sports. On October 4, 1951, the *Eagle* ran a cartoon titled *Not According to Script* portraying a generic Brooklyn Dodgers player, bruised and sweating, poring over the book *Jack the Giant-Killer* as the proverbial Giant walks into the background clapping, leaving the Dodger to wonder, *Wha Hoppen?*[48] Bob Cooke parodied Thomas Macaulay's poem *Horatius at the Bridge* in the *New York Herald-Tribune*—Cooke called his offering *Bobby Thomson at the Plate*.

Whoever said time heals all wounds never enjoyed the rituals of eating at Toomey's Diner on Empire Boulevard and Rogers Avenue, watching Happy Felton's television show, and hearing the sounds of Hilda Chester's cowbell or the Dodgers Sym-Phony Band.

Red Barber announced the game on October 3, 1951. Ernie Harwell, too. Harwell entered the Dodgers broadcasting fraternity when Barber

Red Barber was a cornerstone of life in Brooklyn during the 1940s and the 1950s. You could walk down any block in Brooklyn and not miss a pitch because every storefront, every apartment window, and every car had a radio tuned to the game. In the photo, Barber is accepting the Jewish War Veterans Award, circa 1953. Left to right: Kings County Jewish War Veteran Commander Jerry Cohen, Red Barber, Sidney Laxmeter (Jewish War Veteran Chairman of the event), General Withers Buress and Mrs. Rose Schwager (Jewish War Veterans Ladies Auxiliary) (Brooklyn Public Library—Brooklyn Collection).

took ill in 1948, forcing Branch Rickey to find a replacement. He traded Cliff Dapper of the Dodgers' Montreal Royals AAA club to the Atlanta Crackers for Harwell, the Crackers' announcer. Dapper played for the Dodgers in 1942, but his major league career ended there. After serving in World War II, Dapper returned to baseball in 1946. He managed and played in the minor leagues, retiring in 1957.

Harwell broadcast for the Dodgers from 1948 to 1949 and the Giants from 1950 to 1953. He later became the voice of the Tigers from 1960 till 1991. Finding refuge in Anaheim after being ousted by Tigers radio station WJR, Harwell broadcast California Angels games on a part-time basis in 1992, then returned to Detroit when new ownership purchased the Tigers in 1993. He stayed till his retirement after the 2002 season.

Knowing the importance of broadcasting to the Dodgers community, Rickey assigned Arthur Mann to assess Harwell's broadcasting acumen in 1948. Mann wrote:

> His voice is clear and vibrant, but not shrill. He pitches it low, but it doesn't lose timber or clarity. It is really an unusual voice, and actually a bit soothing. It does not drip hominy grits and honeysuckle, though it does contain a trace of the ol' South. Understandably, his technique on play-by-play is almost flawless, relaxed and clear. He doesn't drink or smoke.[49]

Harwell and Barber were fixtures of Dodgers broadcasting, particularly Barber. Russ Hodges eclipsed them on October 3, 1951, however. "Nobody has come up to me over the years and said that they heard my broadcast. People talk about Russ Hodges and his broadcast," said Barber.[50] Indeed, what seals "The Shot Heard Round the World" as a hallmark of baseball history is the radio broadcast of Hodges screaming "The Giants win the Pennant!!! The Giants win the pennant!!!"

Hodges' call gained immortality because of 26-year-old Lawrence Goldberg, an unsung hero of baseball history. Goldberg lived on East 12th Street off Avenue J in Brooklyn with his parents. A Giants fan, Goldberg was a rare breed of Brooklynite. Unfortunately, work obligations in Manhattan prevented him from listening to the game. So, Goldberg did the next best thing. He taped it.

Rudimentary by today's digital standards, Goldberg placed a tape recorder next to the radio and instructed his mother to hit "Record" at the start of the ninth inning. He did not visualize posterity, nor did he vie for fame. Not a fanatic, Goldberg simply enjoyed baseball. And he wanted to listen to the game when he came home.

In World War II, Goldberg had served in the Air Force and fixed airplane radios in London. Before the war, he tried to be a radio announcer, then found himself in the travel agency business, where he remained for the rest of his life. After Goldberg moved to Atlanta in the mid–1950s, he became president of the men's club in his synagogue and stayed active in community theater, where he met his wife.

"He majored in drama at Ithaca College. He was focused on what makes great theater,"[51] says Debra Sifen, Goldberg's daughter. Radio. Theater. Goldberg's twin passions found themselves realized in an audio document of the biggest moment in baseball history. While aware of his contribution, Goldberg remained humble about it. Steve Goldberg says of his father:

> It just kind of happened and he wasn't the kind of person to brag. When he realized what he had, he called the radio station where Hodges worked and told them about his recording. He sent it to them, without trying to profit from it. I think he got box seats to Giants games and $100. The station licensed the recording and Chesterfield sponsored it. We would sit when I was a little boy with the reel-to-reel tape deck. We talked into the recorder. In fact, a recording of me may be on the same reel as the Thomson home run! My dad passed away in 2009. Coincidentally, the first game I took my son to after my dad's passing was a Braves-Giants game in 2010. I just felt like my dad was there with me, filling my heart.[52]

Sifen echoes her brother's sentiments. "He didn't make a big deal about it. He was just a mensch now remembered for being a nice guy. His favorite story was about the radio repair final exam in the Air Force. No one could figure out why the radio didn't work. Answer: It wasn't plugged in."[53]

John Drebinger of the *New York Times* claimed that memory would house the moment. "The clincher was a struggle that should live long in the memory of the fans who saw it, as well as those who had it portrayed for them by radio and television in a coast-to-coast hook-up."[54] Thanks to Goldberg, memory gets a boost. At the moment of Thomson's home run, fans rushed to the telephone to commiserate or tease the person on the other end of the line. It caused a surge in telephone usage from 4:00 p.m. to 4:25 p.m. that pre-empted telephone access for many businesses.[55]

What about the ball itself? *Eagle* writer Tommy Holmes said that it "landed in the lap of a lady in the left-field stands. The lady's name is unofficially reported to be Helen Gawn."[56] Brian Biegel tracked the ball's existence in *Miracle Ball: My Search for the Shot Heard 'Round the World*, concluding that a nun caught the ball but never told anyone because attending the game violated her convent's rules. Another possibility exists.

At the National Baseball Hall of Fame and Museum—baseball's treasure chest of memorabilia, information, and lore—the A. Bartlett Giamatti Research Center staff preserves files on every major league baseball player, from David Aardsma to Dutch Zwilling. In the Bobby Thomson file sits a 1991 telephone inquiry record and a letter from John Lee Smith of Ithaca, New York, indicating that a boy caught the ball.

Smith went to the Polo Grounds with a classmate from Yale the night before the October 3 game to be first in line the next morning when general admission tickets became available.

> We planned to camp out over-night at the Polo Grounds. When we arrived at the stadium three good ol' boys were already there with their blankets, lunch pails, and flashlights. We struck a deal: "save us a place at the head of the line and we'll bring you a fifth of whiskey tomorrow morning." We then left and booked a room in a third-rate hotel on the Grand Concourse.[57]

Booze in hand, Smith and his ally got tickets for the front row in the left field stands. He recalled that a boy about ten or eleven years old caught the ball as it traversed the playing field to the stands.[58]

Thomson's home run, though indelible in the minds of Dodgers fans, became a part of the past as soon as Pafko looked at the orb of horsehide destined for the left field stands. The next day, the Giants met the Yankees for Game 1 of the 1951 World Series. It was Joe DiMaggio's last World Series and Mickey Mantle's first. The Yankees won.

Dodgers fans wondered, "Is anyone going to beat those guys?"

7th Inning:
"Ladies and Gentlemen, the Brooklyn Dodgers are the champions of the world!"

"I know one of these days the good Lord is going to come calling and when that happens I certainly hope he sees fit to send me up to heaven. But heaven will really have to be something to be better than what we all had long ago in Brooklyn."[1]—Preacher Roe

Brooklyn is, in part, a state of mind. Walking down any block in the borough revealed fulfillment of the primal human need of belonging. The Dodgers propelled that fulfillment by giving the citizenry a center around which to cheer. When the voice of Red Barber, Connie Desmond, or Vin Scully floated from radios, Brooklynites could leave their homes secure in the knowledge that the entire neighborhood would be listening. Storefronts. Cars. Apartment building windows. The statement occurs so often, it is a cliché. But that does not invalidate its truth. Any Brooklyn Dodger fan will tell you that you could walk ten blocks, and not miss a pitch.

The Brooklyn Dodgers Sym-Phony Band in Section 8, Row 1, Seats 1–7 housed the musical representatives of the Dodgers fan base, playing "Three Blind Mice" when the umpires blew a call and other silly musical themes timed to the opposing players returning to the visiting team's bench—they blasted a huge note as soon as the player sat down. When a musicians union threatened the symphony with a picket line, the Dodgers respond with a Musical Appreciation Night. "Admittance is free as long as you bring a musical instrument. And so they come, more than thirty thousand strong, with harmonicas, drums, kazoos, and every conceivable type of portable instrument, including—yes!—even two pianos, which are brought into the rotunda at the main entrance. What a night for music!"[2]

A 1949 profile in the *New Yorker* cited the band members' working

The Brooklyn Dodger Sym-Phony Band provided musical accompaniment with humor at Ebbets Field. If an umpire blew a call, the band played *Three Blind Mice* **(Brooklyn Public Library—Brooklyn Collection).**

class backgrounds that would have made Ralph Kramden, Ed Norton, and Chester A. Riley feel at home.

> That Brooklyn Dodgers Sym-Phony Band is, to get right down to cases, composed of six amateur musicians: Lou Soriano (leader), snare drum; Phil Mason, trumpet; Bob Sharkey, clarinet; Patsy Palma, bass drum; Pete Norman, trombone; and Jo Jo Delio, cymbals—Brooklyn natives all. Soriano drives a small truck that juggles crates and bundles at the Brooklyn Army Base, Mason drives a full-sized truck on the streets of his borough, Sharkey is a maintenance man for the B.-M.T., Palma distributes beer, Norman is a paper cutter, and Delio is a grocer.[3]

Soriano created the Dodgers Sym-Phony after picnic plans went awry, thanks to rain that ended a picnic but didn't postpone a Dodgers home game.

> "My friend had his trombone with him," explained Soriano. "The Dodgers got a man on base, and I told him to go ahead and blow some notes. So he did,

and we had a good time. A couple of days later, I came with this fellow and a kid I knew that had a pretty good mouth. And we kept adding instruments till we got what we got now. Everybody except Pete and Bob are the original members."[4]

The band may have invented a musical staple at baseball stadiums—music geared to the moment. Norman said, "We play incidental music to the game. 'Army Duff' to walk a visiting player off the field, 'Hearts and Flowers' when the visiting team is hollering about something to the ump, 'Somebody Else Is Taking My Place' when a visiting pitcher gets knocked out."[5]

Hilda Chester needed no supporting instruments to make her musical statement. With her trademark cowbell, she became a fixture at Ebbets Field, as identifiable as Abe Stark's "Hit Sign Win Suit" billboard on the right field wall. Anne Berlin wrote a one-woman musical about the Dodgers' most famous fan; she titled it *Howling Hilda*. "The more I learned about Hilda, the more I could hear her," Berlin explains. "When I imagined Ebbets Field, I heard her shouts and cheers everywhere. This lady was a tireless one man band—in the early years banging on her frying pan and iron ladle, then later on clanging her trademark twin cowbells. Her 'noise and sound' were thrillingly musical to me."[6]

In 1952 and 1953, the Dodgers went to the World Series, competed against the Yankees, and suffered déjà vu. They lost each time, reinforcing the "Wait Till Next Year" credo embraced by the Brooklyn fans. Every season began anew in April with a clean slate of 154 games to be played, 154 opportunities to win, rejoice, and move one step closer to a World Series championship.

The 1954 season belonged to the Cleveland Indians, the New York Giants, and Willie Mays' over-the-shoulder World Series catch of a Vic Wertz fly ball to deep center field in the Polo Grounds. Mays' grab, 180-degree turn, and throw to the infield happened in a fluid motion, making the moment an archetype of Mays' athleticism.

Then 1955 came. And the Dodgers exploded with batting averages that National League pitchers feared. "It was a year of power for Brooklyn," said Walter Alston, the Dodgers' manager. "We led the league in batting, and our closest opponent in run-making was Cincinnati which scored ninety-six fewer times than we did. Campy made a big comeback and was the top hitter with .318; Carl Furillo batted .314, Duke Snider .309, but Jackie Robinson had his worst year ever with .256."[7]

When the Dodgers had a World Series championship in sight,

Thomas Oliphant watched Game 7 on television with his father. It was a different experience than if he were with his friends. "Had I been with contemporaries, I would have been shrieking and jumping; with my father and his still-inexplicable silence, I was experiencing the game, living it. There was an intensity and intimacy about our afternoon that blocked everything else out."[8]

In the sixth inning, Yogi Berra sliced a ball headed for the left field foul line that looked impossible to catch. Gil McDougald thought so, anyway. On first base, McDougald took off because Dodgers left fielder Sandy Amoros played Berra in a spot closer to center field than left. Running like he was Nike's son, Amoros sprinted, caught the ball, and wheeled around to fire it to Pee Wee Reese, who threw to Hodges to double off McDougald. It was a marvel of defense.

Brooklyn slaked its thirst for a World Series championship when Reese fielded a ground ball and made a low throw that forced Gil Hodges to stretch to catch it. Vin Scully announced, "Ladies and gentlemen, the Brooklyn Dodgers are the champions of the world!" Brooklyn erupted with glee—its zeitgeist's tectonic plates shifting with its victory over the Yankees—signifying that "next year" had arrived. It was a sockdolager expiating all previous sins, errors, or peccadillos.

In the gloaming that evening, Dodgers fans sat at their dinner tables to fill their stomachs. Their hearts were already filled. Gil Hodges drove in both runs in the 2–0 shutout of Game 7. It made people forget about his 0-for-21 performance in the 1952 World Series that inspired the Rev. Herbert Redmond to stand in front of his congregation at mass at St. Francis Roman Catholic Church with a mandate: "It's far too hot for a sermon. Keep the Commandments and say a prayer for Gil Hodges."[9]

Despite the 1952 slump, Hodges was a force in the Dodgers lineup, knocking in 100-plus runs for seven consecutive years. He blew a kiss to his wife in the stands after he crossed home plate in his home run trot. The tradition began after she gave him batting tips that honed his swing.[10] Johnny Podres, the winning pitcher of Game 7, earned *Sports Illustrated*'s "Sportsman of the Year" award. Podres emblemized the power of hope for Dodgers fans accustomed to their National League dynasty falling to the Yankees. "Campanella was calling the greatest game of his career. Every time he'd give me a sign, 'I want you to throw it here,' I was throwing it there. 'I want it up and in.' I'd throw it up and in. 'I want it low and away.' I'd throw it low and away. 'Curveball in the dirt.' I'd throw it in the dirt," said Podres.[11]

Relieving the Dodgers of the "always a bridesmaid" burden by pricking the balloon filled with sorrow hovering through the Dodgers' lineage, Podres was, in this moment of glory, the most popular player in Dodgers history—more popular than Hall of Famer Zack Wheat, Brooklyn's lone bright spot in the 1920s; more popular than Rex Barney, who pitched a no-hitter for the Dodgers in 1948; more popular than Campy, Oisk, Jackie, or Duke.

Podres did not win the game alone, of course. Amoros made a catch that redefined the word "spectacular," Hodges redeemed his 1952 slump by batting in both runs in Game 7, and the rest of the Dodgers outpaced the National League during the regular season to get to the World Series. But Podres, on his 23rd birthday, became the hero for leading the charge against the Yankees to bring the only World Series championship to Brooklyn. In the *New York World-Telegram & Sun*, Joe Williams wrote, "At precisely 3:43 in Yankee Stadium yesterday afternoon a king died and an empire crashed and from Greenpoint to Red Hook, from Sea Gate to Bushwick, from Coney Island to Flatbush, in fact, all over the teeming turbulent borough across the bridge, joy was at once unconfined and unrefined."[12]

Johnny Podres, unstoppable on the field earlier that day, showed no signs of slowing down at the team's celebration in Brooklyn's Hotel Bossert. Bill Roeder said, "One who came to stay was Johnny Podres, who turned out to be the life of the party in spite of the grueling game he had pitched a few hours before. He must have danced for two hours with Ann Thompson [Dodgers executive Fresco Thompson's pretty blond daughter]."[13]

Charlie Dressen, then the manager of the Washington Senators and an ex–Dodgers manager, analyzed the 1955 World Series for the *New York World-Telegram & Sun*. The Yankees, Dressen claimed, stole a sign that led to a victory in Game 2: "When Tommy Byrne came to bat in the fourth inning of the second game, Martin was on second base. He lifted his right leg as he stood there. I said to Cal Griffith, sitting with me: 'It's the fast ball—Byrne will murder it.' Byrne hit the single for two runs and the ball game."[14]

The Dodgers kept encountering opponents fond of stealing signs. Williams detailed a similar incident in the 1920 Dodgers-Indians World Series:

> Specifically, it was Jack McAllister, the Indians' third base coach, who, noting that Pete Kilduff, the Brooklyns' second baseman, bent over and scraped the base line dirt before each pitch, concluded this was something more than mere mannerism.

The convincer was that Kilduff went through the motion about as often with bare hand as glove hand. After he began checking with the hitters, McAllister was able to establish that a fast ball always followed a bare hand scrape, a curve when Kilduff went down with the glove.[15]

With Talmudic dedication, Dodgers fans followed the team's travails via radio and, later, television broadcasts. They complemented their recall with box scores and newspaper stories the day after a game. Strikeout totals of Carl Erskine, Don Newcombe, Joe Black, and Clem Labine became numbers as familiar as birthdays. Checking Pee Wee Reese's batting average, Billy Cox's hit total, or Duke Snider's home run total became part of the daily routine for a Brooklynite. Further, the Dodgers team was a national brand, underscored by their drawing power across the National League. *Eagle* columnist Tommy Holmes said, "There are fervent fans in Brooklyn and many of them; still the fact that the Dodgers hold the National League record for home attendance is a less glowing tribute to the appeal of a colorful ball team than the fact that they have drawn an even greater attendance on the road."[16]

When fans remember the Brooklyn Dodgers, their memories reveal an emotional bond that neither time nor distance can sever. Their emotions, with the tenderness of a glass egg but the endurance of a Greek monument, create a portrait of a simon-pure place governed by viridity.

Nick Kostis, owner of the Pickwick & Frolic Restaurant and Club in Cleveland, Ohio:

They weren't just a team. Brooklyn was a neighborhood and nothing contributed more than the Dodgers' presence.

Gil Hodges' brother-in-law owned the barbershop around the corner on of St. John's Place and Washington Avenue. Jack's Candy Place was also on the corner. Pee Wee Reese and Hodges sometimes held court with the kids there. The first time I saw a Cadillac, it was Hodges' Coupe de Ville. The longer Hodges stayed in the store, the longer the kids stayed there.

Once a year, my school had a track and field event with competing schools. They called it Field Day. Jackie Robinson would come and pass out sports pins. We also had an event called Brotherhood Week. This gentle giant would grace us with his presence. He dressed in a beautiful suit and tie. He epitomized what was happening in Brooklyn at the time when he talked about treating others as equals respectfully. Brotherly love was the message. You could hear a pin drop during the assembly.

But he wasn't a black man. He was an every man who took down the barriers that we could see and observe and discern about making us different. He made us feel like there was goodness and hope and that the world can be as one in harmony and peace. That's moving people a long way back then.

When he talked, he made you feel like he was putting his arms around you. He exuded humanity, but we didn't really understand what he went through until years after his playing career ended. He planted an image that has lasted for decades, an image of an intelligent, sensitive, giving, caring human being. At that moment, he stopped being any color. He was just a man and a man you wanted to be near and touch and be close to. A gift of humanity.[17]

Charles Lynde "Chip" Babcock IV, partner, Jackson Walker law firm, Houston, Texas:

My father and grandfather were rabid Brooklyn Dodgers fans. My grandfather had season tickets near the field on the third base side. He'd come home at noon to the house at 18 Montgomery Place, have lunch, then walk across Prospect Park. He took me to some games at Ebbets Field and some Spring Training games in Florida. He was very gruff and unapproachable. As soon as Hilda Chester saw my grandfather, she'd say, "Here comes the old grouch!" He responded, "Shut up, Hilda!" Hilda called my dad "Big Guy" because he was 6'5". She would say, "Hi beautiful!" to my mom. When I was five years old, I was allowed to walk up to the hot dog stand by myself, order a hot dog, and walk back to the seats.

I've always theorized that there's something in our DNA that's broader than the Dodgers. It's baseball. My grandfather was heartbroken when the team moved. My father said that it broke my grandfather's spirit. For people living in Brooklyn in the 1950s, the Dodgers formed a special attachment with them. For a long time, the Dodgers weren't very good. In the last years of the Brooklyn Dodgers, the team was solid.

The first Charles Babcock was a real estate mogul in Brooklyn. He owned property that he inherited from his father, Edward Howard Babcock who was married to Cynthia Lynde. Her father, Charles Lynde, was a New York Supreme Court judge and a New York state senator. My family comes back to Brooklyn every November to visit a mausoleum that I own. Sometimes, we'll take a tour of properties that used to be owned by a Babcock.[18]

Bob Greene, best-selling author, Chicago newspaper columnist, and CNN.com journalist:

I grew up in Bexley, Ohio, a suburb of Columbus. We never understood why people called them "bums" because they didn't seem like bums to us. They had Duke Snider. How could you do anything but love a team with Duke Snider?!

When I was a kid, the Dodgers seemed accessible. The Yankees seemed like Harvard or Princeton. The Dodgers seemed like Ohio State. You could imagine talking to Duke Snider or Pee Wee Reese. You couldn't imagine talking to Phil Rizzuto or Mickey Mantle. The Yankees weren't on the same human level.

Our minor league team in Columbus was the Redbirds, a subsidiary of the St. Louis Cardinals. The name changed to the Jets and the team affiliation changed to the Pittsburgh Pirates. I rooted for the Cincinnati Reds. But we didn't have much of a connection with baseball except for baseball cards, television, and radio. We bought our baseball cards at Roger's Drugstore on Main Street.

I remember one weekday afternoon when were on a playground after school We're standing on a basketball court outside Cassingham Elementary School. My best friend Jack Roth lived one block to the west at Elm and Ardmore. The court had a black top surface. One of the kids had a radio. I can remember so vividly the sun dying in the late afternoon. We would listen to the broadcast with Dodger names, like Duke Snider, and we didn't feel like the Dodgers were hundreds of miles away because radio and television brought them into our lives.

Baseball is there waiting for you. I have a feeling that anyone who hasn't gone to a game in years has a feeling that emerges when someone says, "Let's take in a baseball game." It doesn't have to be a specific team or game. It's feeling of taking you back to a place where you used to be.[19]

Branch Rickey III, commissioner, Pacific Coast League:

We were together on the day that the announcement was made that the Dodgers were leaving for Los Angeles. He said, "What a terrible betrayal of the finest fans in America." Any time I come across a Brooklyn Dodgers fan in Texas, Montana, Nevada, New York, or wherever, it is absolutely remarkable how accurate my grandfather's assessment was back then. Those fans seem to have had their hearts stolen when the Brooklyn club went to the west coast. We fall in love with our teams, much more so years ago when so many people shared the common denominator of their teams. Your team became part of the family.

What is perhaps the most undersold element of Branch Rickey is his tenacity in problem solving. He took the components and different sides into account when making a decision. Another undersold element is the combined force of two people working together. Jackie Robinson is a personal hero on many levels. So often, people ignore Robinson's ferocity as a competitor. Jim Brown stunned me when he said that Robinson was the most intense athlete to play sports. Robinson's partnership with my grandfather caused him to come to the equation prepared to turn the other cheek and excel. It was not done alone, but as part of a team.[20]

Dawna Amino, daughter of Duke Snider:

He always looked forward to putting on a Dodger uniform and belonging to the team. I went to a lot of memorabilia shows with him. People would stand in line all day long to get an autograph and thank him. He actually thanked them. I live in the Bay Area, so I meet people all over California who are from Brooklyn and they can't stop talking about it. My mom loved living there. None of the players wanted to leave for L.A. It was a really hard change to make. My dad missed Ebbets Field and Brooklyn. O'Malley later sold him to the Mets for the 1963 season. Then, the Mets sold him to the San Francisco Giants for 1964, which was his last season. O'Malley sold him to the Mets because he wanted my dad to finish his career in New York.[21]

Gerald Stern, instructor at Westchester Community College for a course targeted to seniors about Jackie Robinson and the integration of baseball:

I grew up at the tip of Coney Island in a place called Sea Gate. You have to go through Coney Island to get to the tip of the peninsula. My first game ever was in 1944 or 1945. My older brother was on leave from the Coast Guard, he's about eight years older. He took me to the doubleheader against the Reds.

The Red Sox, Giants, Tigers, even the Yankees don't compare for the enormous social community. Besides that, Jackie Robinson brought a Negro League style that baseball had not seen before. I remember a game in June 1947 when the Dodgers played the Cubs. Robinson was on first. He reached first on an error, took a lead, then Gene Hermanski, a lefty, bunts down the 3b line. The third baseman picks up the ball and throws to first, Robinson goes to third. The ball goes into left field and Robinson scampers home. I once saw him score on a pop up into short right field. His stats alone do not measure his impact.

That year, I watched the '47 World Series on television because my stepfather was a lease holder on a piece of property on Seagate beach that was a bar and had sandwiches and ice cream. He needed a TV for the bar. When the season was over, we got the TV in time for the World Series. It was his first business venture.

A professor did a statistical study that concluded Robinson's stealing of home 20 times was unnecessary and unhelpful because of stats with one or two outs, the chances of him scoring from 3b were that he would have scored more often. Total lack of understanding of Robinson's impact of stealing home. He danced off third and distracted the pitcher. He got the pitcher's attention. Then, the pitcher would groove the ball, putting the batter in a better position to keep the rally going. That was his greatness.

I used to insist to my friends that we get there no later than 9:30 in the morning for a 1:00 p.m. game because I knew where Dick Whitman and Eddie Miksis parked their car. We'd wait for them to get autographs. Jackie came to the park from the Prospect Park subway station. Usually, my friends and I would be the first ones around him. After the game, hundreds of kids waited for the Dodgers. I tried to sit next to Robinson on the subway. This was my routine 15–20 times a season.

My daughter lives in L.A. I couldn't care about the L.A. Dodgers when the team moved from Brooklyn, but I root for the Dodgers when I visit L.A. I have forgiven them, because my daughter is a fan.[22]

Ken Mailender, CEO of Mailender, Inc., a paper supplies company based in Cincinnati, Ohio:

The Brooklyn Dodgers are tantamount to the Green Bay Packers in terms of a team's connection to its community. Very close-knit. My dad was a small minority partner of the Reds in the early 1960s. His friends convinced the team to sell part of the Reds. Mailender, Inc. was a dairy supply company back then.

He used to skip school to watch the Reds at Crosley Field. The Brooklyn Dodgers remind me of the Big Red Machine of the 1970s. A good ball club. We use to listen to games on WLW or WKRC. Back then, there were only eight teams in the 1950s. You got used to seeing the same players against your team. It's not like that today. You can't bond with the opposition in three games today.[23]

Mark Cane, professor of Earth and Environmental Sciences at Columbia University's Lamont Doherty Earth Observatory:

I was a civil rights activist born in 1944. I grew up at 22nd Street and Farragut Road in Flatbush, very close to Brooklyn College. The Dodgers were our heroes. Where else in American life could you find black heroes in that era? Kids are color blind. They have no racial context. We keep reading about the Dodgers because have emotional resonance, like the *Titanic* or the Lindbergh baby kidnapping.[24]

Marty Appel, author, *Pinstripe Empire*, and former public relations director for the New York Yankees (1973–1977):

The real test of the Brooklyn Dodgers' staying power is still to come when all of us will have faded from the scene. Jackie Robinson will be remembered 50 years from now because he is a civil rights figure. But those who keep the Brooklyn Dodgers name alive will no longer be here, so it's hard to predict.

The look of Ebbets Field plus its location in the middle of neighborhood combined with the opportunity to encounter the players in the grocery store made the Dodgers a community team in a borough of communities, not merely a hometown team. My first real appreciation of the Brooklyn Dodgers was the 1955 World Series. I had turned seven in the summer. People danced in the street when the Dodgers won the world championship. Everyone was talking about the Brooklyn miracle, so I decided that the Yankees were the underdogs and that's why I decided to root for them!

When I worked in the Yankees public relations department, I brought a love of baseball history and a love of the Yankees franchise. On Old Timers' Day, I cared about getting the uniform right for the guys on the '21 Yankees. And in those days, we regularly invited a lot of Brooklyn players. We knew they were special in the city. Not that many people in my generation were interested in baseball history. When I wrote a letter to Bob Fishel, I assumed he got 1,000 a day. Mine was the only one.

We need to look back at baseball history. Baseball stories tell better, last longer, and are worth talking about 12 months a year. The 1950s are glorified in our minds, though. Ebbets Field was not comfortable. It had narrow seats. It was not clean or well kept. But you felt that you were there with family. Unless the opposing team was the Giants, there weren't arguments. It was a lovely place to be.

In 1955, my dad took me to my first game. He was born in Brooklyn in 1916, but his friends were not baseball fans. So, it was his first game, too! I grew up on St. John's Place. I can't say I appreciated it yet, because I was just becoming familiar with the game. Our seats were a little bit to the right behind home plate. Most of the day, I was amused by Roy Campanella's chubby body. My dad didn't really get back into baseball until I started working for the Yankees in 1968.[25]

Jerry Wiskin is a customs and international trade lawyer:

I grew up in Flatbush within walking distance of Ebbets Field. Two memories stand out. In 1956, I saw Carl Erskine throw a no-hitter against the Giants at Ebbets Field. It's the only no-hitter that I ever saw. With one out in the ninth inning, Whitey Lockman belted a foul ball that hit Bedford Avenue. Our hearts were in our mouths because it only went foul by a foot! About a month after the Erskine no-hitter, I was at a Reds-Dodgers game when Don Zimmer got beaned by a Hal Jeffcoat pitch. It broke his cheek bone. I can still hear the thud of the ball hitting Zimmer's head.[26]

Ralph Hunter is the director of the African American Heritage Museum of Southern New Jersey:

I was in the Philadelphia school system where 75 percent of classmates were not African Americans. When my safety patrol won the opportunity to go to Connie Mack Stadium to see the Phillies play the Dodgers, it was the touching moment of my life because I got to see Jackie Robinson play. In my group of friends was a guy named the Dipper. He was Wilt Chamberlain. From that point on, Jackie Robinson changed the way Americans think and he changed me. As a young, black kid, I knew that I could reach any goal out there. Knowing that a black man put on a jersey and didn't fight back just resonated with me. Robinson chose to take the humiliation and the people not liking him. He knew he was hated and he got through it. I never had any problems dealing with people of any color because I knew achievement was right around the corner.

Jackie Robinson paved the way for latino players, too. He had to do his job in front of 50,000 people. And I believe that's what inspired me to start collecting black history memorabilia.[27]

Ron Bittel has a Ph.D. in modern European history from the University of Massachusetts:

I had a Dodgers uniform when I was about 12. I had a fierce loyalty to the Dodgers. I went to Ebbets Field with my father for a game around 1954 or 1955. We sat in the right field seats opposite the bullpen. At that time, Don Drysdale was a relief pitcher. When I was a freshman at Bishop Loughlin High School near Flatbush Avenue and the Williamsburg Building, the Dodgers won the 1955 World Series. For the seventh game, I raced home on the BMT from Lafayette Avenue to East New York and then East New York to Chauncey Street. Nobody else was in the house. I got home in the eighth inning.

I sat on the couch for the end of the game. I remember falling back into the couch when the Dodgers won. I bawled with joy. It was one of the most emotional and dramatic times I remember from my childhood. That night, there were celebrations and noise all over. About three blocks away from our house, there was a bar called Grim's owned by the father of Bob Grim, an ace Yankee relief pitcher. A crowd formed and they hung an effigy of a Yankee of the nearest lamppost. The feeling was topped off the next morning when the *New York Daily News* had a caricature of the bum smiling wide with the headline *Who's A Bum.* You could see the uvula. That summed the sense of release and long-denied triumph and vengeance.[28]

Ron Schweiger is the Brooklyn borough historian.

When the minor league Class A Brooklyn Cyclones debuted in 2001, I wore my Dodgers cap and Dodgers shirt on Opening Night. Within two minutes of walking into the ballpark, I had to stop counting how many people were in Dodgers attire because there were too many to count!

In the 1970s, there was an empty area in the East New York section of Brooklyn. The Department of Transportation built a small street just a couple of blocks long from Linden Boulevard, a six-lane main thoroughfare, into empty fields. The DOT workers who mapped out the street named it after their favorite Dodgers pitcher—Carl Erskine. When the Gateway Shopping Center was built right near the Queens border, they extended the original Erskine Street a couple of blocks so people had an entry into the center.

I don't think there is any franchise in sports that left its city and still enjoys the following that the Dodgers have. I'm amazed at how many people still follow that team. By the way, the Brooklyn Dodgers never moved, they're on an extended road trip![29]

Ronnie Klein is a high school history teacher:

My grandfather was from Brooklyn. He was a big Dodgers fan. I was a baby during the war years, so the men were off fighting while my family lived in a small Cape Cod house in Dunellen, New Jersey. There must have been three aunts, my mother, an uncle who didn't go to fight, and my grandparents in the same house. I used to listen to all the Dodger games on the radio sitting on my grandpa's lap.

My dad played in the minors as a catcher for Cincinnati, and coming from Southern Indiana was obviously a big Reds fan. But because of my grandfather and our Brooklyn roots, I became a HUGE Dodger fan. We got our first television set, a 12" blond Dumont, when I was seven or eight years old and I'll never forget watching one game with my grandfather, when the Dodgers scored 15 runs in the first inning. We went nuts and were jumping up and down. It was like it happened yesterday. Jackie Robinson was my idol and every Dodger from Preacher Roe to Duke Snider were my boyhood heroes. I had a Dodgers uniform, the yearbooks, baseball cards, and other memorabilia. I loved the bum logo. I was such a big fan that I had a duplicate set of the 1952 Dodgers baseball cards. I traded it away.

If you were a Yankee fan, you probably came from money. The Dodgers were down to earth. They were the common man's team. I liked that fans could see the Dodgers walking around Brooklyn. People could relate to them. But we couldn't understand why Stanky and Durocher moved to Manhattan for the Giants.

In those days, the world was different. All the guys in the neighborhood would go to games by ourselves. We needed $10 for the day. We'd take a bus to Port Authority and then the subway. Dreyer's Sporting Goods in Plainfield, New Jersey, sponsored a semi-pro team. Joe Black played for the team, so my love for the Dodgers got accentuated when he got called up.

Happy Felton read a question of mine on the *Talk to the Stars* segment of his show. It was a technical question about baseball. Hodges couldn't answer it, so I won a watch, two cartons of Tareyton cigarettes and four tickets to a Giants-Dodgers doubleheader at Ebbets Field. It couldn't get any better than that. I was the envy of all the kids in the neighborhood. I couldn't do anything with the cigarettes because I was just a kid! This was in 1953. We got there early and I met the Dodgers in the clubhouse. We had box seats for the game, first or second row behind the dugout. I felt an aura of importance around me.

Before the game, my dad, my uncle, my cousin, and I went to the hot dog stand. While we were in line, I turned around to say to my cousin, "Guess who's standing behind us?" It was Willie Mays wearing a yellow banlon collared shirt. I asked him for his autograph and he graciously gave it to me! Try that with the top stars of today.

I followed the Dodgers when they moved to Los Angeles, but it wasn't the same. Even today, over 60 years later, I still get depressed when I think of the Thomson home run. I couldn't even watch the Giants/Yankees World Series in '51. My happiest baseball day ever was, of course, when we finally beat those damn Yankees in 1955.[30]

Samuel Roberts is a former CBS News producer:

There's a particular gestalt about Brooklyn and the Dodgers were at the center of it. Baseball in the 1940s and 1950s was unbeatable. I grew up in a largely Italian neighborhood. My friends rooted for the Yankees because of Berra, DiMaggio, Rizzuto. Jews were for the Dodgers. But the Giants had no discernible ethnic group. I became a Giants fan when I discovered a Giants game suddenly on the radio. The arguments happened in every neighborhood. Who was a better outfielder, Mays, Mantle, Snider or DiMaggio? Who was a better catcher, Berra or Campanella?

Fifty years from now, they'll be studying the Dodgers because of the racial aspect. It was clearly a turning point in American history and a forerunner of what happened 10–15 years later in civil rights.[31]

Scott Andes operates the Lasorda's Lair web site:

I've known since I was a kid that I loved the Dodgers. I like to say that I was born into blue. I'm a third-generation Dodger lifer. My grandfather was a

Boston Braves fan because he lived in Boston. He stopped following the Braves and started following the Dodgers. He moved to LA about the same time that the team moved. My uncle was at Sandy Koufax's perfect game. He was thirteen years old. He's seen four no-hitters. In fact, his very first game was Koufax's no-hitter against the Mets. The next game he saw was the perfect game.

Baseball is steeped in tradition. The Dodgers are one of the oldest teams. They've been around since 1883. The Dodgers' tradition is very important to Dodgers fans. But more than the history and tradition, there's a Dodgers culture. If you go to Dodger Stadium, not much has changed since 1962. A few luxury boxes, some seats closer to the field, Diamond Vision. But mostly unchanged. Vin Scully for 65 years. It's rooted into the Dodgers culture to know the history and tradition. Roger Owens is the peanut guy who started throwing peanuts behind the back and under the leg. He's been with the team since 1958.

Nancy Hefley is the organist since 1988. Gladys Gooding trained her. When I go to sleep at night, I hear her organ in my head. I think that a lot of the Dodgers' tradition, spirit, and passion followed them from Brooklyn to Los Angeles. Sad for Brooklynites, but geographical expansion was a sign of the times.[32]

Stan Goldberg is a native Brooklynite and the owner and operator of Trail's End Camp in Pennsylvania:

I knew the address of the Dodgers office at 215 Montague Street better than my home address. That's where we got tickets to the game. If you had a certain amount of ice cream wrappers, you could trade them for a ticket. This was reflected in one of my brother's episodes in *Brooklyn Bridge*. We would go early to games for batting practice because the ushers would let you go to the stands behind home plate and talk to the players.

We lived in Bensonhurst and played stickball in the schoolyard. We matched the Dodgers lineup against the Yankees.[33]

Robert Garfinkel is a retired teacher who worked in the New York City public school system for 35 years:

Toomey's Diner on Empire Boulevard and Rogers Avenue had the best hamburgers in Brooklyn. Sometimes, you would see Dodger players there. I loved them all, but my favorite was Duke Snider. There was always the debate about the best center fielder in New York City baseball. Mantle, Mays, or Snider. By statistics, Mantle and Mays won that argument every time. But Snider didn't get enough credit for his contribution to the Dodgers.

Across Bedford Avenue beyond Ebbets Field's right field fence, a car dealership had glass windows. But the home runs that Snider smashed never reached the windows because guys were waiting on Bedford for a home run. Nobody ever fulfilled Abe Stark's "Hit Sign Win Suit" offer on a right field wall billboard because Carl Furillo dominated that area. I bought an Ebbets Field brick for a quarter when they left. The bricks went first. They wanted five dollars for a chair. One thing that people forget is Sal Maglie pitching a great game for the Dodgers when Larsen had his perfect game in the 1956 World Series. The Yankees only got five hits in that game. The final score was 2–0. But the Dodgers play I always remember is a ground ball to Reese and the throw to Hodges for the last out of the 1955 World Series. Brooklyn was different in those days. I want to go back, but I can't.[34]

Howard McCormack is an admiralty lawyer and a former Navy officer who grew up in Bay Ridge, where several Dodgers lived:

I learned about the Dodgers moving to Los Angeles when I was serving on a destroyer, the U.S.S. *Robert A. Owens*, DDE 827. The Dodgers left Brooklyn in 1957, the same year that I came out of the Navy after a three-year tour. I was a Lieutenant Junior Grade and the ship's gunnery officer. When you're on a ship, you don't have access to news unless you're in the Mediterranean Sea. Then, the bigger ships might send a news summary via radio. I was so annoyed because the Dodgers were part of my life. As a varsity baseball player in high school, baseball held a tremendous interest for me. At Ebbets Field, you paid sixty cents for a bleacher seat. Yankee Stadium and the Polo Grounds didn't have seats in those days, only planks. World War II depleted the rosters. By and large, though, the stands were still filled. It was a community.[35]

Paul Parker is the Colorado Rockies club historian:

My family moved to Bedford Avenue in 1949. I was born a couple of years later, in 1951. Gil Hodges lived on the same block. He must have moved to Bedford Avenue sometime prior to 1963 because he lived there when he managed the Washington Senators and the New York Mets in the 1960s and early 1970s. I started college in the fall of 1969, the same year Hodges managed the Mets to a World Series championship,

Hodges was the strong, silent type, not overly expressive like Earl Weaver or Casey Stengel. He has compelling numbers compared to other first basemen who are in the Hall of Fame. For example, he hit 372 home runs. Plus, he missed three seasons because he served in World War II. Without the three-year absence, his numbers would be even higher. Campanella, Snider, Robinson, and Reese are all in the Hall of Fame. Apparently, the Hall of Fame voters tired of having so many Dodgers from the 1950s inducted. Hodges absolutely belongs there, but he died young. So, there was no chance to actively campaign for himself. It's fitting, though, that Hodges drove in both runs in Game 7 of the 1955 World Series against the Yankees to give the Dodgers their only championship in Brooklyn.[36]

Stuart Greenwald is an attorney in Middletown, New York:

Why should we care about the Brooklyn Dodgers? The Brooklyn Dodgers represented America. It was the only game in town that people would talk about at the barber shop, the shoeshine stand, or the tavern. It was in the fabric of America. The Giants attracted theatrical people. The Dodgers attracted blue collar people. It's difficult to put the emotions into words. I went to hundreds of games at Ebbets Field and the Polo Grounds. The Giants and Dodgers had an intensity, acrimony, and rivalry between them that makes the Red Sox-Yankees relationship pale in comparison. Baseball back then had a richness about it. Players weren't isolated from fans by attorneys and agents.

What the Dodgers contributed to baseball and America should be remembered like any other historical point. Jackie Robinson breaking the color line showed a beginning for blacks to get into other areas of business. But to me, the Dodgers were poison because I was a Giants fan! However, Robinson was the most electrifying player. You couldn't look at anyone else when he was on base. It wasn't until I matured that I realized what a phenomenal team this was with the personalities.

I was a Dodgers fan in the early 1940s, but then Reese and Reiser went into the service, so my father suggested I become a Giants fan. I saw Carl Hubbell pitch his last game. I love baseball, so I didn't walk away from it when the Giants and Dodgers left for California. There's a ten-year-old boy in an old man's body, but the little boy doesn't want to get out! I still enjoy the game and I follow the Mets.[37]

Ted Hollembeak is a municipal judge in Emporia, Kansas:

I grew up in Arkansas City, Kansas. The closest team was the St. Louis Cardinals, so I read everything about them in the newspaper. But the first baseball book that I ever read was about the Brooklyn Dodgers. I'm the youngest in my family of eight. One of my sisters was 17 years older and she married a guy who was a second father. They had two little kids and they would take me two or three times during the summers to Sportsman's Park when the Dodgers played the Cardinals. It was a nine-hour drive. A friend's mom brought me back a 1955 autographed Dodger baseball from a trip to New York City. One day, when we didn't have a baseball to play with, we used it.

When I went to my first game, probably about 1952, I had never seen a major league game on television. We didn't get a TV until '53. I didn't want the game to end. I was devastated when the Dodgers lost the playoff against the Giants in '51. I felt like I knew the Dodgers personally. The personalities of the players were unique and so were the fans. With the Dodgers Sym-Phony band and the personalities, it was like listening to a family. When they hurt, I hurt. I listened to games on the radio and every time a Dodger was at bat, I squeezed a rubber ball. When they were in the field, I put on a glove. I listened on KMOX, it connected to KSOK in Arkansas City.

My daughter was a bat girl for Emporia State University. I helped coach my son's baseball teams. So, they saw all the books I had about the Dodgers. I talked to them about the history. In my baseball-themed man cave in the house, the first thing you see is a blown up photo of Jackie Robinson after a game, completely exhausted. He's holding a bottle of Coke. If you look at his face, you saw that nothing was undone. He hated to lose more than any other competitor. I don't know if they won or lost that game, but he left nothing on the field.

My son died during the Persian Gulf War. He served in the Army. He played third base in high school and American Legion ball. I played semi-pro when

134

I was 16, then went into the Army and played the Midnight Sun game in Alaska that starts at Midnight. I played second base. This was in my final assignment in Alaska from April 1, 1960, to mid July 1961. When I went to the Royals fantasy camp, I played 2nd base and the outfield. To honor my son, I wore his #23.[38]

Arnie Korfine is a semi-retired sales executive:

I've had a really good life, but that era from around 1947 to 1956 was a different world. It was a world that was safe to grow up in.

Baseball was our life well before pro football took off in television. The Brooklyn Dodgers were the lifeblood. Just an amazing period. You felt like everyone was a friend. My mom loved Campy's smile. It came from his soul. You knew this was a happy man. When the camera was behind the plate, my mother and aunt Bella would goose him.

When I was about ten years old in the late 40s, I would go to the day games between July 1 and Labor Day. Sometimes, I went with a friend, sometimes I went by myself. I always went with one dollar. My mother would write my name, address, and phone number on a piece of paper and attach it to my shorts with a safety pin. My dad made me two salami sandwiches and one tuna sandwich. I walked 14 blocks to Ocean Avenue and took the trolley to the a intersection of Empire Boulevard and Flatbush Avenue, four blocks from Ebbets Field. It cost 60 cents to get into the bleacher seats, so that left me with 30 cents. I would sometimes give an usher my sandwich and he let me into a $1.25 seat. Sometimes, I'd sell a sandwich to a cop so I could buy something like a hot dog. A peanut bag was a nickel. A soda was a dime.

When the game was over, I had a dime left to take the trolley home. Some mornings, I saw Vin Scully get out of the Prospect Park station and I could walk to the stadium with him. Sometimes, I got penny postcards and gave them to Vin with my address and a stamp on them. He would put the cards into the players' coat pockets and the players would drop them in the mail.

Connie Mack III is a former United States congressman and the grandson of legendary Philadelphia A's manager Connie Mack.

One day, Branch Rickey came by to visit my grandfather during spring training. My brothers and I sat in the living room on the floor, listening to Rickey, our grandfather, and our father engaged in discussions about players and trades. My brother Dennis was a pitcher. Branch Rickey taught him how to throw a change-up curve. I was amazed at how one had to manipulate the ball. We moved to Ft. Myers when Dennis was about 13. They immediately warned him, you're too young to throw that pitch. And dad was always very careful that none of us would try to throw a curveball until after we were older.[39]

Forrest "Woody" Burgener is a retired pharmaceutical representative and a Revolutionary War historian:

In 1955, when I was 11 years old, I had a bet with Mr. Gallucci, the owner of the general store and ice cream fountain in Sparkill, New York. It was just two blocks from my house. The bet was if the Dodgers win, I get an ice cream soda consisting of vanilla ice cream with strawberry syrup. It cost about 15 cents, I believe. If the Yankees win, I sweep the store completely clean after the game is finished.

Game Seven was a day game. I watched on television as Johnny Podres pitched a gem. All my Dodger baseball cards were spread on the floor. My favorite was Gil Hodges. I loved Pee Wee Reese, Carl Furillo, Campy, and the Duke. When Berra hit a high fly ball to left field, my heart leapt into my throat. I crossed my fingers as they ball moved toward the fence. I saw Sandy Amoros sprint to his right, looking for the ball. He caught it! Ball game over! I hit the front porch in three strides, maybe two. My mom shouted, "Where are you going?" I shouted back, "To get my bet!" Mr. Galluci was laughing as I came through the front door about one minute later. He said, "Do you want it now? Or now!" Life was good![40]

Dr. Kenneth Prager is the Director of Clinical Ethics and Professor of Medicine at Columbia University Medical Center. He is also the father of Joshua Prager, author of *The Echoing Green: The Untold Story of Bobby Thomson, Ralph Branca, and the Shot Heard Round the World*.

I grew up at 2705 Kings Highway in the Midwood section of Brooklyn. For me, going to Ebbets Field was like going to the holy of holies. Some of the fondest memories of my childhood are my parents taking me to a Sunday doubleheader. My mother was a Dodgers fan. My father would give the ticket seller a buck for choice seats. The guy pulled out a pile of tickets and got us better seats. We had reserved seats, not box seats.

When we got to the seats, my mother unpacked the tuna fish sandwiches. We went over the statistics in the Sunday section of the *New York Times* and watched batting practice. Just the sight of the Dodgers wearing those white uniforms with red numbers on the front of their jerseys and playing in the green grass was the most wonderful possible sight that could be.

I remember my first night game was the day of Queen Elizabeth's coronation. My dad said that if I got a good grade in a class taught by Rabbi Mandelkorn, I could go to the game. The magic of the ballpark at night was the brightness of the lights contrasting with the blackness of the sky. We had seats on the third base side and the Dodgers lost to the Braves. I remember that we listened to news reports about the coronation on the ride home.

Greg DiGiovanna, son of Dodgers batboy Charlie DiGiovanna:

My dad got rheumatic fever after playing in the water from fire hydrants. It left him with a heart condition. While he recovered in the hospital, he wrote a letter to Leo Durocher, the Dodgers manager, asking for an autographed baseball. Durocher visited my dad, gave him the requested baseball, and, as he left, said, "Call me and I'll get you a job." When my dad got out of the hospital, he called the Brooklyn Dodgers offices and Durocher got him a job as a turnstile boy taking tickets. My dad was a workaholic. He died at 28. When the Dodgers

Yankees-Dodgers World Series match-ups became October rituals after World War II. Between 1947 and 1957, the teams met six times. Here, Steve Parlay (left) and Michael Cook sell accessories for fans during the 1953 World Series (Brooklyn Public Library—Brooklyn Collection).

won the World Series in 1955, they decided to give my dad a World Series ring, which I still have. It's my most valuable possession.[41]

John Giordano is a retired food industry professional. His family owned Giordano's Specialty Foods from 1947 to 1999.

There was a candy store near the corner of Avenue U and East First Street where we hung out. One day, Gil Hodges walks into the candy store. His hands were as big as baseball gloves! He stopped and talked to us for awhile. Back then, the players had a closer association to the fans because they lived in our neighborhoods. After the season ended, some players had jobs as salesmen.

When you watched a game at Ebbets Field, you felt like you were on top of the players. You could see every wrinkle in their faces. I was born and raised in Brooklyn, so I grew up loving the Dodgers. I lived in the Gravesend section. Joe Pignatano, Bob Aspromonte, and Sandy Koufax lived there, too. After the Dodgers left Brooklyn, I started collecting Dodger memorabilia. Now I have an entire room dedicated to the Brooklyn Dodgers![42]

Kenneth Roth is an attorney specializing in corporate, commercial, and transactional law:

I lived about three or four blocks from Ebbets Field until I was seven. We lived with my grandparents on Empire Boulevard, a few blocks down from the ballpark. My grandfather took me there two or three times. After he died in 1955, we moved to Clarendon Road. It was a different time. I could get on my bicycle and ride around with friends without my parents worrying. When the Dodgers had a home game, my friends and I would ride over to Ebbets Field, put our bicycles to the side, and wait on Bedford Avenue for a home run ball to come over the fence. If you caught a ball, they'd let you into the ballpark. We knew a ball was coming when we heard the roar of the crowd. Then there was a scramble for the ball.

Gil Hodges owned a bowling alley in Brooklyn. During the off-season, he was often there. For a little kid, it was a thrill just to see him in person. When people asked for autographs, he'd sometimes sign a bowling score sheet.

When the Dodgers announced they were moving at the end of the 1957 season, I was crushed. We had heard something about a possible move earlier, but I was too young to know anything about the politics between Robert Moses and Walter O'Malley. I remember my dad cursing O'Malley and telling me that the Dodgers were leaving Brooklyn and moving to Los Angeles and the Giants were moving to San Francisco.

At that point, I foreswore the Dodgers. I've rooted against them ever since. I became a Milwaukee Braves fan until the Mets came about because the Braves also had great players, for example, Hank Aaron, Eddie Mathews, Joe Adcock, Lew Burdette, Warren Spahn, and Red Schoendienst. I'm a National League guy, but I root for the American League team if the Dodgers are in the World Series. My exception is the Yankees. I couldn't go that far.

After the '57 season ended, a security guard let my friends and me into Ebbets Field and we ran around the bases. I took some infield dirt and put it in my pocket and then in an envelope. I still have it.[43]

Carl Erskine pitched for the Dodgers from 1948 to 1959:

Charlie DiGiovanna suffered from rheumatic fever and a heart condition. Leo Durocher offered him a job with the Dodgers. DiGiovanna worked as a ticket taker. He died at the age of 28 (Brooklyn Public Library—Brooklyn Collection).

There is a mystique about the Brooklyn Dodgers that's hard to explain. The Dodgers won occasionally, but it was not a consistent team until the Jackie Robinson era. From 1947 to 1956, the Dodgers won six National League championships. We only won the World Series once. I think those disappointments captured America. But I'm never sure if people outside Brooklyn were pulling for us or pulling against the Yankees.

We were part of the fabric of the community. The neighborhoods embraced us. Brooklyn had this open kind of attitude—you're one of us. We shared the bitter tears together. When I go back to Brooklyn, there are still people who remember us. I get a lot of mail from Brooklyn, not only from grandfathers, but also from the kids that learned about us. I get mail from soldiers overseas, guys in prison, and executives in large corporations. The variety is amazing.

Dr. Morris Steiner was the pediatrician for the Dodgers' kids. He was a marvelous man and a big Dodger fan. Several players and their families often had dinner with the Steiners at their home, which was above Dr. Mo's office on East 19th Street. During the off-season, Betty and I returned to Anderson, Indiana, with our kids. When one of the kids got sick, Betty didn't call a local doctor. She called Dr. Mo in Brooklyn. He was especially needed when Jimmy, our fourth child, was born with Down Syndrome. Dr. Mo was a great encourager.

I did not have a Hall of Fame career, but I had some Hall of Fame days. I pitched two no-hitters at Ebbets Field. One of those games was against our rivals—the Giants. I went 20–6 in 1953, which may have been the best year ever for the Dodgers in that era. I was scheduled for three starts in the World Series if it went seven games. I started in the first game, but Dressen took me out early. I had a bad first inning. The Yankees scored, but Dressen said, "You didn't throw a lot of pitches, so I'm starting you in the third game." I was even more motivated to win my next game.

I pitched against Vic Raschi, who was a tough pitcher. Casey Stengel said that he'd pick Raschi if he had to win a game. That day, the Yankees didn't hit me hard at all. Campanella hit a home run to give us a 3–2 lead. When I struck out Don Bollweg, that tied a World Series strikeout record of 13. Johnny Mize was the second hitter up in the top of the ninth inning. I struck him out. The crowd roared even louder. I didn't hear either announcement on the P.A. system. Then I got Joe Collins out. When I went inside, the writers crowded around me. Preacher Roe told me what happened, but it was so far out of my fantasy or expectations. I tell kids that failure can be a great motivator.

If you played bad, the fans got on you big time. But when you played good, they loved you. There was a big celebration on the street if we won. When I think about playing in Brooklyn, I don't just think about Ebbets Field. I think about the people. Our neighbors. Our babysitters. Abe Myerson owned a deli. He had a big family, maybe five or six kids. He would be at my door with two bags of groceries. Abe said, "You guys shouldn't pay rent. You shouldn't pay anything." Joe Rossi was our butcher. He couldn't do enough for us. Years after I retired, I would call and ask him to send me veal cutlets packed in dry ice. Today, if I go to Brooklyn and I don't call a couple of friends in the fire department, they get upset. They won't let me pay for anything. Captain Joe Dowd was a dispatcher at the Moran Towing Company. He was a huge fan. When we moved to Los Angeles, it really broke his heart.

Back then, we only had eight teams in each league, so you played every other National League team 22 times. But what really fanned the flames of the Giants-Dodgers rivalry was Leo Durocher going from the Dodgers to the Giants. That intensified everything. When Charlie Dressen came to manage the Dodgers, he had a passion about beating Leo because he had been Leo's first lieutenant.

I can't emphasize enough the feeling when we played the Giants. It was an intensity that didn't exist in games against other teams. No one was ever bitter off the field, but when you had those uniforms on, it was a high calling to beat the Giants. Brother, it was intense. Durocher played on the Yankees with Babe Ruth. There was a rumor that Durocher stole Ruth's watch. Don Newcombe would needle Durocher and say, "Hey Leo, go see what time it is on Babe Ruth's watch!" Leo would respond, then Jackie got into it. The most vicious profanity was between Jackie and Leo.

After the 1951 playoff against the Giants, we hurt more for our fans than we hurt for ourselves. Roe, Newcombe, and I pitched with short rest. When Lockman got his hit and put two men on base, they called the bullpen. Sukeforth told Dressen, "They're both ready." When Dressen asked who has the best stuff, Sukeforth said, "Erskine's bouncing his curveball." So they sent in Ralph Branca to replace Newcombe. We wouldn't have even made it to that 1951 playoff except for Jackie. It was a game against the Phillies. The Giants score had been posted during our game, so we need to beat the Phillies to tie the Giants for first place. That game went 14 innings. Jackie hit a home run to give us the victory.

We opened the 1958 season in San Francisco at Seals Stadium. The Giants-Dodgers rivalry bloomed again in California. I pitched the first home game in Los Angeles. The Los Angeles Memorial Coliseum slightly resembled the Polo Grounds. I was surprised Alston picked me because I hadn't had a real good spring. 80,000 people were in the stands, but they were quiet and curious. Ebbets Field was loud and boisterous.

I think the Brooklyn Dodgers represented the struggle for victory and that's why people related to it. We had great players, but we didn't always win. Life is like that. For a skinny kid from Anderson, Indiana, to get to play in that era with Jackie, Pee Wee, and Duke, it's a crowning honor to speak about this team.[44]

When the Dodgers returned to the World Series in 1956 to play the Yankees, they gave their fans another reason to hope for glory. Sadly, it was not to be. The Yankees prevailed, Don Larsen pitched the only perfect game in World Series history, and Brooklyn, once again, waited till next year.

It was the last World Series at Ebbets Field.

8th Inning: From Happy to Hollywood

"My best days in baseball had been at Ebbets Field. You know, I can almost smell it. Kids on Knothole Day. The celebrations after a win. When you try to describe it to somebody, they get this mysterious look in their face like, 'I don't know if I understand that.' They can't, if you hadn't been there."[1]—Carl Erskine

As dusk relieved the Sun of its duties during the New York City twilight of October 3, 1956, Paul Newman hustled through the stage entrance of the Mansfield Theatre, a Broadway institution on West 47th Street in Manhattan. Adrenaline pumping through his body, a natural reaction before a live performance, Newman navigated the Mansfield's backstage geography to his dressing room to prepare for his second performance of the day while the production crew scurried about the theatre testing lights, checking sound, and arranging the set.

Five years away from movie icon status with his role in *The Hustler*, the 31-year-old Newman began his acting career in legitimate theatre, complemented by roles in live television dramas during television's Paleolithic Age in the 1950s. On this October evening, however, Newman did not play a role; he played himself as a contestant on a live broadcast of *I've Got a Secret*, a hallmark of television's panel show genre.

I've Got a Secret featured Garry Moore as host and a panel of four celebrities trying to deduce the contestant's secret through questions and answers. Newman's secret—he paraded around Ebbets Field as a Harry M. Stevens vendor during Game 1 of the World Series between the Dodgers and Yankees earlier that afternoon and sold a hot dog to panelist Henry Morgan without Morgan realizing his identity. It was an elaborate scheme beautifully theorized, planned, and executed with the precision of a Swiss watch.

After Morgan surrendered his guessing, Moore encouraged Newman to go offstage. With a smile that could light up Broadway because of the prank's successful execution, Moore described the events leading up to Newman's appearance before the panel.

> Henry, we not only knew that you went to the World Series ball game this afternoon, we even contrived to have a friend call you up and invite you to go to the ball game. We knew what seats you were sitting in. We knew exactly where you were. Through the good offices of *Sports Illustrated*, we did have a photographer out there taking pictures from time to time. But you don't remember the occasion. Paul, are you ready? Maybe you'll recognize him better this way. Paul, come out![2]

Newman returned in his vendor garb and shouted a familiar ballpark refrain with heavy Brooklynese in his voice: "Get your hot franks here, ladies and gentlemen! Get your hot franks!"

Morgan replied, "I didn't know that you looked so ordinary!" He then certified Newman's Ebbets Field presence. "Weren't you the one that we had all the trouble with, you waited on like fifty people?"

"Yes," Newman answered.

"And we were screaming and yelling," Morgan continued.

"I understand that you were very irritated because you were very hungry and didn't have any breakfast," Newman revealed.

"You were there,"[3] confirmed Morgan.

Newman's working class vendor character could have been the American cousin of Eliza Doolittle, the cockney-accented, ignorant, and unrefined young woman transformed by Henry Higgins into a sophisticated lady of grace, goodness, and gentility in *My Fair Lady*—the smash hit musical had debuted earlier in 1956 at the Mark Hellinger Theatre, four blocks from the Mansfield.

Going incognito as an Ebbets Field vendor risked recognition. Newman's fame emerged in the 1950s with credits including a role as middleweight champion Rocky Graziano in *Somebody Up There Likes Me*, a film that premiered during the summer of 1956. Additionally, a week prior to the Ebbets Field charade, Newman starred in *The United States Steel Hour* television adaptation of *Bang the Drum Slowly*, the second book in Mark Harris' literary quartet of baseball fiction featuring major league baseball pitcher Henry Wiggen.

After the secret's revelation, Newman admitted that he was "terribly nervous" in carrying out the hoax. His commitment to the role would have made Thespis beam with pride—he sold dozens of hot dogs to unsuspecting fans!

The prank's success had a downside, though. It cost Newman an opportunity to enjoy a World Series extravaganza. Morgan remarked that Game 1 was "some game!" Newman exclaimed, "I didn't see any of the game!"

More is the pity.

It was a Dodgers-Yankees showdown for the ages. Brooklyn won the game, 6–3. Each team had nine hits as Gil Hodges belted a three-run home run and Jackie Robinson hit a solo homer for the Dodgers while Yankees stalwarts Mickey Mantle and Billy Martin each went yard with a two-run homer and solo homer, respectively.

Newman's Ebbets Field stunt illustrates the power of Muses—if one is inclined to believe in Muses. How else to explain the baseball fodder in our storytelling fiber? It must be the daughters of Zeus and Mnemosyne at work, inspiring storytellers, documentarians, and artists. Nowhere in the corridors of American culture—classical and popular—is there a richer beneficiary of the Muses' influence than the Brooklyn Dodgers baseball team. The Dodgers are represented in every artistic category.

Jackie Robinson, naturally, is a source for innumerable stories.

The 2013 movie 42 captures Robinson's challenges in breaking baseball's color line. Ebbets Field appears via computer-generated imagery, including advertisements for Schaefer Beer, Gem Razors, and Abe Stark—Brooklyn's leading clothier promising a free suit to any batter who hit his sign. The film also depicts the Ben Chapman episode—complete with the racial taunts—Rickey's interview of Robinson, and journalist Wendell Smith's shadowing Robinson at Rickey's behest. The film, while accurate, takes liberties for the sake of drama—Fritz Ostermueller never beaned Jackie Robinson. He did, however, hit Robinson in the arm.

The film 42 contrasts strongly with *The Jackie Robinson Story*, starring Robinson as himself. This 1950 film sugarcoats Robinson's obstacles, commits chronological errors, and discards history. Instead of playing for the Kansas City Monarchs, Robinson plays for the fictional Black Panthers of the Negro Leagues. When Clyde Sukeforth recruits Robinson, the Negro Leagues star thinks it's a joke. This misunderstanding never occurred. *The Court Martial of Jackie Robinson*, a 1990 TV movie made for TNT, showcases Robinson's courage during his court martial stemming from a refusal to sit in the back of a bus while he was an Army officer stationed in Texas. HBO's *Soul of the Game*, a 1996 TV movie, focuses on Rickey's desire to destroy baseball's racial barrier while balancing the pros and cons of selecting Josh Gibson, Satchel Paige, or Jackie Robinson. When Robinson meets Rickey, the circumstances are fictionalized—Robinson doesn't meet the scout responsible for assessing his skills until the meeting with Rickey, though he noticed the scout at Monarchs games because he's a "white guy following us around with a stopwatch." Also, the scout is named Pete Harmon, a portly fellow unlike the slender Sukeforth.

Branch is a one-man play featuring Branch Rickey talking to the audience, interspersed with recreations of conversations with Jackie Robinson and Charles Thomas. Written by Walt Vail, *Branch* spotlights the salient parts of the Rickey biography known from other media:

> The play is about racism, the basic American conflict. Rickey took a lot of the guilt about Charlie Thomas on himself. I see him as a typical American character. When he was acting on that, he was relieving his own pain. It's an inspiring story. Rickey is a good example of how people ought to behave. He did the right thing for himself and for everyone else. Shakespeare wrote about the kings of the past. Rickey is also an historical figure that we can learn a lot from. It took me quite awhile to write the play. I tried to write that hotel room scene after Thomas was refused registration. It wasn't going anywhere. Gradually, I decided that the best way to do it was with a one-man character and a variety of voices from offstage.[4]

Mr. Rickey Calls a Meeting showcases a summit between Branch Rickey, Paul Robeson, Joe Louis, Jackie Robinson, and Bill "Bojangles" Robinson. The play takes place in a hotel room, right before Rickey brings Robinson to the Dodgers in 1947. Rickey wants their approval. He leaves them to discuss the ramifications of Robinson joining the Dodgers.

Ed Schmidt wrote *Mr. Rickey Calls a Meeting*. It debuted in 1989 at the George Street Playhouse in New Brunswick, New Jersey; the West Coast premiere happened in 1992 at the Old Globe Theatre in San Diego. Schmidt's story revolves around a fictional event. "What led me to this specific idea was an autobiography ghostwritten for Joe Louis," says Schmidt. "There was a one-paragraph mention of a meeting in March 1947. When I researched it, I found that the meeting never took place."[5]

Mr. Rickey Calls a Meeting had a timely racial component—during rehearsals in San Diego, the Rodney King jury decided its verdict concerning the four Los Angeles police officers caught on videotape beating King:

> When I came back from lunch, the air in the theatre changed. These guys were all L.A. actors. They were livid and enraged. The depth of the rage was a complete surprise to me. I remember they were talking about grabbing bats and going to L.A. to crack heads. I was wise enough to sit there and listen and learn. Sheldon Epps said, "I'm as enraged as you are, but what we have in our hands is this play. This is our baseball bat. Let's create change with it."

What's really interesting to me is there aren't many playwrights who are white writing for black characters. By the end of our initial run, the audiences were integrated. Most audience members are upper middle class and mostly white. I think *Mr. Rickey Calls a Meeting* plays anywhere because of the universal themes.

Why should people study it? The story is largely about how one effectively brings about change. Is Rickey's measured approach a prudent one? Robeson advocates revolution. Rickey says that his job is to win baseball games. Robeson asks why Rickey doesn't hire all negro players. He wants to open the floodgates, but that's impractical. It's not unlike the Martin Luther King, Jr., vs. Malcolm X argument. Philosophically, it's important and it's a timeless debate. I think what I'm the most proud of in the play is that it presents everyone as right and wrong.[6]

Sheldon Epps directed *Mr. Rickey Calls a Meeting*. He remembers the story raising points of debate that went beyond social progress:

Ed's play was a debate as to whether it was a good idea to bring Jackie up. Some of the characters posited that integration would kill the Negro Leagues, which it did. Was Jackie Robinson the best player around? Rickey's point of view was that it took the right player temperamentally to endure the abuse.

The play examined the triumph but also some of the darker aspects and the economic aspects. It was a good business move.

My theory is that if the actors are good at playing the character of a real-life person, then he becomes that person for the audience. You don't want actors to become impressionists or mimics, but you try to cast actors with similar physical characteristics and you hope they'll come to some kind of understanding with an internal basis. If you do that successfully, then the actor begins to convince the person they are in fact that real life character, but not through mimicry.

What's important is to approach the role as a character, rather than a famous person. There's no difference between playing Jackie Robinson and Willy Loman. But the audience brings preconceived notions for a real-life person. That can be very difficult. As a director, I did research. I had a sense of the clothes and what the room should look like.[7]

The First, a Broadway musical, also depicts Jackie Robinson's breaking of the color line. It debuted on November 17, 1981, running less than a month. David Alan Grier played Jackie Robinson, Lonette McKee played Rachel Robinson, and David Huddleston played Branch Rickey:

I actually had to meet with Mrs. Robinson's approval before I was hired. She was at every audition. I have never had to go to as many callbacks as I did for that show. I auditioned at least six times. Four of the auditions were in L.A. and the final two were in NYC. I was waiting in a pub with David Alan Grier when the call came in that I won the role and remember him cockily bragging that "He already knew he was in" but that it was me "They weren't sure about."

Probably should have known that this was indicative of what working with him would be like. I flew back to L.A. to pack.

Once we opened, the reviews weren't good at all for the show, but much to my surprise, they were great for me! In fact, all the reviews were terrible for the production so much so that we didn't know if we would actually have a run. Of course, the certain kiss of death is a bad review in the *New York Times* and ours was definitely dismal. There were only three leads, me, Grier, and Huddleston. The few members of the ensemble who had befriended me asked if I knew anyone with clout who could help? I did have friends connected to politics, so we were able to get Jesse Jackson to do a press conference and talk about the fact that our show was one of the few black productions on Broadway and such an important chapter in American history deserved at least a shot at a run. But it did nothing to help us stay afloat.

We had major changes every night in the previews. And I do mean *major*. The entire cast was under tremendous pressure to learn new songs, new lines, new staging and choreography every day. They also started firing people left and right. At the last minute they even fired Darren McGavin who was originally cast as Branch Rickey, replacing him with David Huddleston just a few days before we opened. All theatrical pieces I've ever worked on are already set by the time you go into previews. I think the creative team knew they were in trouble and resorted to extremes in a last ditch effort to get the show on track.

By far the most humiliating moment (of many while doing that show) was when director Martin Charnin's assistant informed me that I had to darken myself with Egyptian pancake makeup because the producers thought David and I were too light-skinned. I'll never forget her rudely declaring, "You look like a white girl up on stage." My heritage is racially mixed. Mother is Swedish and Finnish. Dad is African American and Chippewa Indian. But they knew that when they hired me. I was always aware of racial issues and my parents openly talked with me about it when I was a child. But I somehow had the foolish notion that things had changed and that the entertainment industry was more open and tolerant.

In spite of the difficulties I had doing the show I'm still grateful to have been a part of it. I learned about all the firsts and Jackie Robinson's strength. God only knows privately what the Robinsons went through. Mrs. Robinson was understandably very particular about who would represent her in this piece. Yet for me Rachel Robinson was a highlight in an otherwise tough and generally unfriendly work environment. She was so very warm, magnanimous and supportive during the entire process. And I still believe that the play and any stories about Jackie Robinson and other trailblazers are important for all of us. After all ... how can we know who we are and where we're going until we know where we've been and who the heroes were that paved the way for us. The Robinsons are important civil and human rights leaders.[8]

Music, its name derived from the word Muses, is a cornerstone of baseball's history, more so in the annals of the Dodgers. Two Samuel 6:5

states, "And David and all the house of Israel played before the Lord on all manner of [instruments made of] fir wood, even on harps, and on psalteries, and on timbrels, and on cornets, and on cymbals." King David would have felt right at home in Section 8, Row 1, Seats 1–8 behind the Dodgers dugout at Ebbets Field. Those were the seats occupied by the Dodgers Sym-Phony Band, a group of musicians that played, among other songs, "Three Blind Mice" as a musical critique of an umpire's call. Frivolity reigned at Ebbets Field when the band played, especially during an event inspired by its sounds.

On August 13, 1951, the Dodgers held "Music Appreciation Night" at Ebbets Field and 2,426 musicians showed with their instruments—the definition of "musicians" being very generous for this particular event—and received complimentary attendance. The *Eagle* cited "magnus key harmonicas and fifes and clarinets and trumpets, bugles and guitars and banjos, trombones and French horns."[9] "Music Appreciation Night" responded to a potential silencing of the Dodgers Sym-Phony Band. "It was a Musicians' Union attempt to restrict the activities that led to the orchestral outburst,"[10] reported the *Eagle*. The band members did not play, rather, they basked in the support shown through musical notes, sometimes off-key.[11]

Patrons at Dodgers home games also enjoyed notes pounded on the organ keys by Gladys Gooding. Larry MacPhail hired Gooding after hearing her perform at Madison Square Garden in 1941. She stayed with the Dodgers till they left Brooklyn for Los Angeles after the 1957 season. Dodgers music reached the classical music genre with Annie Gosfield's composition "Brooklyn," October 5, 1941, a classical piano solo piece commemorating Mickey Owen dropping the third strike in the World Series. Marianne Moore's poem "Hometown Piece for Messrs." *Alston and Reese* appeared on the front page of the October 3, 1956, edition of the *New York Herald Tribune* to coincide with the first game of the 1956 World Series. A composition memorializing the 1955 World Champion Dodgers, *Hometown Piece* verses match the tune of *Hush, Little Baby*.

Moore initially pitched *Hometown Piece* to publications with literary pedigrees. She struck out. *The Hudson Review's* editorial director, Frederick Morgan, told Moore that the poem "is not quite up to your best."[12] *Life* rejected *Hometown Piece* because it didn't fit the format of poetry accompanying "a picture story."[13] The *New Yorker* passed because the 1956 National League pennant had not yet been decided when Moore submitted *Hometown Piece*. It could not secure publication until the end of September, an unwelcome scenario if the Braves won the National League pennant instead of the Dodgers.[14]

Moore developed a kinship with George Plimpton, a writer who found fodder in wacky sports ventures, like trying to pitch to the All-Stars of both leagues. This experience became the basis for Plimpton's 1961 book *Out of My League*. When the Dodgers played the Yankees in the 1963 World Series, Plimpton asked for the opportunity to watch a game with Moore at Yankee Stadium. "She had written some kind words about a baseball book I'd done a few years ago," wrote Plimpton in the 1964 article "The World Series with Marianne Moore" for *Harper's*.

> I wrote to thank her, and a correspondence had ensued—her letters typed, always with a network of footnotes, asterisks, additional comments, and then her name—these in ink and in a spidery hand as if touched on the paper by a Persian miniature painter with his brush of a cat-tail hair. You had to turn the letter around a few times to be sure there wasn't a line or so you'd missed.[15]

Plimpton conveyed the moment that baseball captured the fascination of Brooklyn's most famous baseball poet since Walt Whitman, who once wrote for the *Brooklyn Eagle*. It was a routine circumstance—a conference between pitcher and catcher. But for Moore, it was the gateway to the emotional nuances of baseball. The players involved were Roy Campanella and Karl Spooner.

The year was 1949, Campanella's rookie year. Plimpton wrote:

> He had stood there on the mound, resting the big catcher's mitt on his hip, the mask pushed back on the top of his head; and his earnest demeanor, his "zest"—as she put it—something of that moment, and how he imparted his encouragement with a pat to Spooner's rump as the pitcher turned back to the mound, caught her fancy, indeed made a baseball addict of her—this when she was sixty-six—incurably afflicted with what gets most people about the time they first come down with an attack of the mumps.[16]

Perhaps this experience sparked the appearance of Campanella three times in "Hometown Piece," more than any other Dodger.

"Take Me Out to the Ballgame" will likely be considered the ur-song for baseball's relationship with music. First published in 1904, it recounts the amusement of Katie Casey, who would rather be at the ballpark than on a date with her boyfriend. Beginning in the 1930s, the Brooklyn Dodgers inspired songwriters. The 1938 song "We're the Boys from Brooklyn" declares the title characters to be members of the "Flatbush Brigade" with unbridled enthusiasm for the Dodgers.[17] "The Brooklyn Dodgers" has no lyrics. Bennie Benjamin and George Weiss wrote this 1946 song. Roger

Segure arranged it for the guitar. The song's sheet music advises a swing tempo that's fairly bright.[18]

The year 1947 yielded two Dodgers songs, "The Dodger Polka" and "Follow the Dodgers." Sections of Brooklyn appeared in "The Dodger Polka" lyrics, including Flatbush, Greenpoint, Bay Ridge, Sands Street, and the Brooklyn Bridge.[19]

"Brooklyn Baseball Cantata," written by Michael Stratton and George Kleinsinger, also uses Brooklyn's neighborhoods in its lyrics. In addition to Flatbush and Greenpoint, Williamsburg makes an appearance.[20] C. G. Funk's *Flatbush Waltz* urges fans to root for the Dodgers,[21] while *Baseball Time in Brooklyn* hints at excitement when the Dodgers play.

Dan Beck wrote "I Used to Be a Brooklyn Dodger," recorded by Dion in 1978. Dripping with middle-aged lament for a time long past, the song honors the symbiotic relationship between the Brooklyn Dodgers and their fans:

> I had this idea that you can't go home again when I wrote *I Used to Be A Brooklyn Dodger*. I'm from Pittsburgh and the 1960 World Series got me into baseball. After going to college in Pittsburgh, I wound up in Nashville and then Brooklyn. Some friends of mine knew a guy named Tony, an actor who lived in Brooklyn. So when I moved to New York City, Tony and his family kind of adopted me. We hung out in Brooklyn a lot. He lived by the Verrazano Narrows Bridge, around Shore Road. His parents were on 66th Street.
>
> By spending time with them, I got a real sense of how Brooklyn is similar to a small town in western Pennsylvania. Everyone was warm and nice. Everyone had a nickname. So I started thinking of the analogy of the Dodgers can't go home anymore to the street dodgers hanging out and having a good time.
>
> This was the mid–1970s. I was an assistant to an artists manager who managed Dion Demucci. She saw the song and wanted to show it to Zack Glickman, part of Dion's inner circle. He loved it and wanted to show it to Dion. I didn't hear anything till almost a year later when Dion played the Bottom Line and Zack took me backstage. I didn't meet him, there were too many people.
>
> One day, I'm out to lunch and the receptionist, when I come back, says that a guy named Dion called eight times in the last hour. He wanted to see everything I've ever written. I finished the lyrics that night and faxed them over and within a day or two, Dion played me something over the phone. Dion did the song in his set for many years. I was told that Frank Sinatra considered recording the song, but he thought it was too sad, too remorseful.[22]

While Beck recalls an era with "I Used to Be a Brooklyn Dodger," Jim Gekas and Tony Calderisi mourn the passing of baseball's glory years in "Mr. Robinson." Mickey Mantle, Willie Mays, Joe DiMaggio and, of course, Jackie Robinson appear in the lyrics.[23]

Jackie Robinson inspired a rhetorical musical inquiry in 1949—"Did You See Jackie Robinson Hit That Ball?" Originally recorded by Buddy Johnson, the song attracted Count Basie to record it. It's the Count Basie version that's better known. "In that era, baseball players served as topics for song writers, including Mickey Mantle, Joe DiMaggio, and Willie Mays," says Dr. Hugo Keesing, a cultural historian and retired adjunct associate professor at the University of Maryland. "But recordings went beyond music. I had a 78 rpm of "Slugger at the Bat," a Columbia ten-inch record for kids. It's a tale of doing the right thing. It featured Pee Wee Reese and Jackie Robinson."[24]

Two songs with Dodgers references have lists rather than lyrics. Dave Frishberg honored Van Lingle Mungo, a Dodgers pitcher from 1931 to 1941, with an eponymous song reciteing the names of players from the past, including Roy Campanella.[25] Billy Joel used Campanella's name in "We Didn't Start the Fire," a song cataloging people, events, and icons from 1949 to 1989. The 1955 World Series championship team is also mentioned.[26]

"I'm in Love with the Dodgers" proclaims adoration linked with pride. True to its title, it summarizes the feeling that radiated from Ebbets Field to every street corner, stoop, and schoolyard."[27]

Fans are at the heart of the Brooklyn Dodgers legacy; their appearances in Dodgers fiction convey unbreakable devotion to the team. Willard Mullin created the "bum" emblem in the 1930s as a result of a conversation with a cab driver. Mullin's obituary in the *New York Times* revealed, "After a game at Ebbets Field, Mullin took a cab back to his office and the driver asked, 'What did our bums do today?'"[28]

It was an epiphany.

If Willard Mullin's bum is the emblem of the Brooklyn Dodgers, then Aloysius "Taxi" Potts is the team's ur-fan in popular culture. Played by William Bendix in the 1943 World War II film *Guadalcanal Diary*, Potts dreams about being thousands of miles away from the South Pacific. Ebbets Field, to be precise. He wants to see his "beautiful bums" play baseball. When the Cardinals and Yankees meet for the 1942 World Series, the Marines try to listen to the game on the radio. Potts shows no loyalty to the National League, preferring to root for a New York team.[29] Bendix's portrayal in *Guadalcanal Diary* mirrors his performance as tough-talking Aloysius K. Randall in *Wake Island*, another 1942 movie set in World War II. Bendix played Chester A. Riley in *The Life of Riley* on radio and television. He also starred in "The Time Element," an episode that Rod Serling used as a pilot for *The Twilight Zone*.

151

There must be some higher connection between the name Aloysius and the Dodgers. In the 1954 movie *Roogie's Bump*, the ghost of fictional Hall of Fame pitcher Aloyisus "Red" O'Malley exerts supernatural influence on Remington Rigsby, self-nicknamed "Roogie" because he doesn't like the name Remington. Transplanted from Ohio with his widowed mother, aunt, and grandmother, Roogie suffers new kid syndrome—the neighborhood kids won't let Roogie play with them. His father died of pneumonia.

When Roogie meets Red's ghost in the park, Red creates a supernatural right arm for Roogie. After "Roogie" writes Dodgers manager Doug Boxi about his arm, Boxi dismisses the letter as the dreams of a child and sends him two tickets. When a foul ball down the third base line comes to Roogie, he throws it back with such force that it knocks Roy Campanella into a backwards somersault, landing him in the dugout. The Dodgers sign their new sensation, but the magic fades, eventually. O'Malley's ghost admits to overstepping his boundaries in trying to help Roogie.

The film's climax has the kids who once shunned Roogie, then embraced him because of his fame, shunning him again when they play football. When the ball reaches O'Malley's ghost, he throws it to Roogie, who punts it beyond a distance that a regular punt would go.[30] A similar ending happened in a 1965 episode of *The Munsters* revolving around Herman Munster trying out for the Los Angeles Dodgers.

Whistling in Brooklyn is the third and last installment in Red Skelton's film trilogy revolving around the adventures of fictional radio star Wally Benton. This 1943 film features Benton, writer and star of a show revolving around a character named The Fox, trying to clear his name after the police mistake him for a serial murderer. Amateur sleuth Benton deduces the real killer's identity. Ebbets Field, Leo Durocher, and the Brooklyn Dodgers appear in a rather long baseball sequence, where Benton masquerades as a member of the opposing Beavers in an exhibition against the Dodgers. Durocher delivers his lines with the roughness that made him a beloved figure in Brooklyn.

In Jay Neugeboren's short story "Ebbets Field," the Brooklyn Dodgers provide the background to a friendship between Howie and Eddie. Eddie, a Jew from an Orthodox family, moves to Howie's Brooklyn neighborhood in the fall of 1955. Both are students in P.S. 92's eighth grade class and rabid Dodgers fans, playing hooky to go to a game at Ebbets Field. But the 6'2" Eddie is more than a fan; he's an outstanding ballplayer who won a Roy Campanella autographed baseball on *Happy Felton's Knothole Gang*. That's a ticket to stardom on the playgrounds in Brooklyn. When Eddie switches to Erasmus High School with his sights on a college scholarship, his future seems bright. He reveals that a heart problem will prevent him from playing sports at Erasmus, thereby cancelling his sports plans.

The bonds of friendship loosen a little when Howie goes to NYU. Home on a spring vacation during his junior year, Howie discovers that Eddie bought a half-interest in Mr. Klein's kosher butcher shop on Rogers Avenue. They reconnect and Eddie discloses that a draft physical revealed no heart problem. Seemingly, his family members did not like the thought of Eddie immersing himself in sports, so they arranged with a doctor to tell Eddie that there was something wrong with his heart. Howie is crestfallen at the thought of what Eddie missed out on. Eddie, not so much. He's made peace with his life trajectory.

Their bond appears weakened.

> Eddie and I tried to get up a conversation about the old ballplayers and what they were doing then—Hodges managing the Senators, the Duke still hanging on as a pinch hitter, poor Campy in a wheelchair since his crash, conducting interviews on TV between Yankee doubleheaders—but our hearts weren't in it anymore and there were a lot of long silences.[31]

An invitation to a three-on-three Saturday morning basketball game at the schoolyard punctuates the silence because the school was the geographic epicenter of the friendship. Being in its presence recaptures the feeling of safety, friendship, and wonder that can only happen in schoolyards.

Murder is the focal point of two novels and a comic book about the Brooklyn Dodgers. Donald Honig's 1992 novel *The Plot to Kill Jackie Robinson* spotlights *New York Daily News* reporter Joe Tinker as the hero unearthing the 1946–1947 mystery that gives the book its title. A Marine with three years tenure in World War II's Pacific Theatre, Tinker is in bed with his girlfriend Sally, a society writer at the *Daily News*, when pistol shots ring out on Christopher Street. The victim—Harry Wilson, a dedicated NYPD cop and a New York City sports legend.

Tinker, a decorated World War II veteran with a Purple Heart and a Bronze Star, tires of the sporting beat. He blows off Games 6 and 7 of the 1946 World Series for a romp in a hotel room with a gorgeous woman who happens to be a senator's wife "starved for sex." His reporter's instinct leads to uncovering Wilson's murder and plans for an assassination of Robinson in plain sight on Opening Day at Ebbets Field.[32] Honig continued Tinker's involvement with the Brooklyn Dodgers in a second novel, *Last Man Out*.

Robert B. Parker's 2004 novel *Double Play* gives Robinson a body-guard for 1947—a burned-out World War II veteran named Joseph Burke, who uncovers a complex murder plot involving a gangster. Parker weaves personal reminiscences about the Dodgers between the chapters. "Normally on Sundays teams played a doubleheader, so all the slow summer afternoon I would hear Red Barber's play-by-play with Connie Desmond, until the sound of it became the lullaby of summer, a song sung in unison with my father. I saw Ebbets Field in my imagination long before I ever saw the bricks and mortar."[33]

Troy Soos created the Mickey Rawlings murder mystery series, set between 1912 and 1922. Rawlings, a utility baseball player, solves murders when he's not deciphering the next pitch. *Murder at Ebbets Field* draws Rawlings into solving the murder of Florence Hampton, a Ziegfeld Follies chorus girl who married William Daley, a showman and a part-owner of the Dodgers. Hampton, also a silent film actress, inherits Daley's portion of the team after he dies. Then, she is murdered. Rawlings finds her body on the Coney Island beach outside the Sea Dip Hotel, "on the border between the respectable and disreputable sections of Coney Island."[34]

With supporting roles by John McGraw and Casey Stengel, *Murder at Ebbets Field* also illustrates the Brooklyn–New York rivalry through the eyes of Rawlings, the narrator. "I explained to him that the rivalry between Brooklyn and New York baseball teams was already a fierce one when my grandfather saw the Brooklyn Atlantics play the New York Mutuals in the 1850s. Landfors still looked lost. Then I mentioned that the Manhattan clubs were made up of gentlemen and the Brooklyn clubs of mechanics and firemen."[35]

Murder at the World Series appears in the November-December 1946 issue of the comic book *True Sport Picture Stories*. Though the story does not mention the Brooklyn Dodgers, hallmarks abound in this fictional yarn. The iconic Brooklyn "B" adorns the cap of the pitcher on the comic book's cover, for example. Narrated by Dopey Dillock, the cover's pitcher, the story's dialogue indicates Brooklyn as the setting. "Wal, meanwhile at the park th' game was already late 'n' Leo our M.G.R. was arguin' with Big George, the ump." Logic points to Leo Durocher and George Magerkurth as the "Leo" and "George" in the dialogue.[36]

Dillock, a former star pitcher, recounts the story of pitching ace Pete Chance fainting after a storm forces the team's plane to land at a small emergency field. On their way back from Boston with a 3–2 lead in the World Series, the team takes refuge at a restaurant in the airport; Dillock took the train instead of joining the team. The waiter, also the local sheriff, deduces that Chance is dead because of "froth aroun' his lips." Cause of death—poison. Dillock, the team's only pitcher at the park, replaces Chance on a hodgepodge of a team. The radio announcer, an homage to Red Barber, exclaims, "'N' here they come! An' I swear! This old Red-Head's never seen the likes of it!! A catcher is playin' third ... an outfielder second. An' old cripple arm, Dopey Dillock is pitching!! Will his soft stuff be able to hold these Bosox hitters? We'll see."[37]

Dillock reclaims his star status, pitching a perfect game. Then, in a surprise ending, he reveals the murderer's identity.

Writers pounded out stories about the Dodgers, either in game reports, columns, or books. Shirley Povich had an eight-decade career at the *Washington Post*. To say that he saw it all is an understatement.

David Povich, a Washington, D.C., attorney, recalls his dad's legendary journalism:

What my dad liked the least was segregation. He was one of the first proponents to integrate. He demanded that Sam Lacey, a black reporter from Baltimore, be in the press box. He was the first president of the BBWA and then he integrated that. He wrote every Monday about the Redskins not having black players and, for example, would write that "Jim Brown integrated the Redskin end zone three times today."

He started writing in the 20s when the Senators won the pennant. And he read everything. He thought that integration was inevitable. He always claimed that players on the Washington Negro League team were good enough to play in the major leagues. I think in his heart he rooted for the underdog, because it made a better story. Integrity, ability, and story are the three things I associate with him. He dictated his column because he had a rhythm and he wanted to hear it. He wouldn't let anyone change a word because then you change the rhythm.[38]

Terence Smith followed in his father Red's footsteps, becoming a journalist:

My family moved to Malvern on Long Island in 1946 when I was seven years old. We stayed there until Summer of 1952 when we moved to Stamford, Connecticut. That's the period of my greatest exposure to the Dodgers as an enthusiast of the team and culture. And that was really Dodger country in Nassau County. It was part of the air. I suppose there were some Yankee fans allowed to live on the North Shore, but Malvern, Lynbrook, Hempstead was all Dodger country. The Yankees were the overdogs and everyone else were underdogs.

I would usually go to Ebbets Field with my father and participate in *Happy*

Felton's Knothole Gang. He would have about ten kids who were fodder for his show, so we would get to go on the field at least an hour and a half before the game.

In Green Bay, my dad was known as Brick because of the color of his hair. Then the nickname became Red. He got one reply after writing to 50 newspapers. It was the *New York Times* and it was no. So, he went to the *Milwaukee Journal.* He started as a junior reporter. Then, he learned there was a job at the *St. Louis Star-Times* and he worked there. He met and married my mother. Then, he went to the *Philadelphia Record*, where he worked for ten years. Stanley Woodward hired him immediately after World War II for the *New York Herald Tribune.* His rhythm was to get up, read the papers, and offer a running commentary on what he was reading. He called his study a sweatshop. He went there around 1:00 p.m. and began writing. Originally, he took the copy to Western Union. By 5:00, 5:30, he had the column finished. Later, he dictated the column by telephone. Abe Rosenthal hired him for the *New York Times*, where he won the Pulitzer Prize. He continued to write the column until his death in 1982. My father spoke of himself as a reporter.

His dream was to play the Palace, the Big Apple. Grantland Rice was his hero became a great mentor. He also admired Frank Graham from Journal American and W.C. Heinz, John Lardner, and Roger Kahn. He thought Jimmy Cannon was mostly about Jimmy Cannon, though he was a terrific sports writer but not a great fan. The reporters' clubhouse was Toots Shor's. When you entered Shor's, you walked across a hard wood floor and a raised circular bar, Come in and angle right about forty degrees. Turn left into the rather large dining room. Table 1 was immediately on left, Table 2 immediately on right. And then the dining room, drinks were good, company couldn't be improved upon. Gather after a big game or a fight. You had a crowd that was made up of politicians, sports figures, actors. I remember being in there one time agog when Joe D walked in with Marilyn Monroe and wore an illustrious camel hair coat. There was an aura.[39]

Happy Felton's Knothole Gang **was a television show featuring children showcasing their baseball skills with a Dodger player judging their abilities (Brooklyn Public Library—Brooklyn Collection).**

Ed Linn became the go-to scribe for autobiographies, accompanying Bill Veeck for *Veeck as in Wreck*, Leo Durocher for *Nice Guys Finish Last*, and Sandy Koufax for *Koufax*. His résumé encompasses 17 books. Hildy Angius, Linn's daughter, remembers her father as a dedicated writer who loved the craft of sports writing, earned respect from his peers, and escaped fate by turning down a job offer:

> My dad went to school on the GI Bill at Boston University. He saw a writing class being taught be a guest lecturer that he respected. It was the daughter of the dean of the journalism school. She mentors him and he writes a story called "The Kitten" that she submits to the *Saturday Evening Post* behind his back in the late 1940s.
>
> He started writing sports articles and he moved to NYC and was an editor for *Sport* magazine for awhile and doing freelance articles. Sports writing led to the books. He wrote Leo Durocher's autobiography but his favorite was *Veeck as in Wreck*. He struck up a friendship with Mike Todd, who asked him to write his autobiography but he had previous commitments. The writer he hired went down in the plane crash—Art Cohn.[40]

Norman Rockwell portrayed an Ebbets Field scene in his painting "Tough Call," appearing on the cover of the April 23, 1949, edition of the *Saturday Evening Post*. It was steeped in controversy. Rockwell, famous for his art depicting Americana, researched Ebbets Field during the 1948 baseball season with a photographer to assemble "reference images" of life at the ballpark, including players and umpires. Wintering in California, he relied on the photographs as a platform for "Tough Call," a scene illustrating three umpires—Larry Goetz, Beans Reardon, and Lou Jorda—deciding whether the rain is sufficient to stop a Dodgers vs. Pirates game while Clyde Sukeforth apparently teases Pirates manager Bill Meyer that the rain is minimal. If the umpires call the game, the Pirates win because they're leading the Dodgers 1–0 in the bottom of the sixth inning. Once a game completes 4½ innings, it's official.

To Rockwell's ire, somebody touched up the painting submitted to the *Saturday Evening Post*. That somebody was William H. Rapp, a Philadelphia artist directed by *Post* art editor Ken Stuart "to adjust details of other artists' illustrations including size, signature placement, changing real advertising signs to imagined ones, eliminating brand names, and other minutiae required of the editors."[41]

Rockwell took action, complaining after Rapp "adjusted" three other *Post* covers of his in 1948 and 1949. In a letter to Stuart, Rockwell wrote, "I cannot go on painting with any strength or conviction with the threat of such changes to my work constantly hanging over my head."[42] The *Post* changed its policy, tasking editor-in-chief Ben Hibbs and managing editor Robert Fuoss to "review Rockwell's work on arrival, and afterward consult with the artist about possible changes."[43]

Baseball is the connective tissue binding successive generations of the Schneider clan in *The Brooklyn Nine* by Alan Gratz. Alexander Cartwright, John Kieran of the *New York Times*, Patsy Donovan, and King Kelly make cameo appearances. The Great New York City Fire of 1845, the Civil War, World War II, and the Dodgers leaving Brooklyn provide background for the characters.

Babe Herman's hit that led to three men on base in 1926 is recounted in "The Fifth Inning: The Numbers Game." In this chapter, John Kieran of the *New York Times* explains why he likes the Brooklyn Robins and Ebbets Field over the New York Yankees and Yankee Stadium. "Oh, it's very fancy," Kieran explains. "And Lou Gehrig, Tony Lazzeri, Babe Ruth—they hit a great many home runs and win a great many ball games, if you like that sort of thing. But a foolish consistency is the hobgoblin of little minds. I much prefer the capricious Brooklyn Robins. You never know what's going to happen next."[44]

A baseball created from twine and leather is an *objet d'art* for Felix Schneider in 1845. The baseball's connection to the Schneider family seems unbreakable until an act of generosity during wartime forces its separation, only to reappear at the book's end in a surprising and heartwarming way.

Linda Sue Park's *Keeping Score* features an 11-year-old girl named Maggie as the main character. Befriended by a neighborhood fireman named Jim, she learns the value of friendship across enemy lines—Jim is a Giants fan! Maggie's father used to be a fireman until an accident forced him out of active duty. He operates in an administrative capacity and hires Jim.

Keeping Score takes place in the early 1950s, concurrent with the Korean War. When Jim is drafted, he and Maggie exchange letters. But when the letters stop coming, Maggie is concerned, then angry. She learns that Jim is incapable of communicating because of trauma. He witnessed civilians being killed by friendly fire, including a South Korean boy that his unit adopted. Maggie saves her money to take family and friends to Ebbets Field for a Dodgers game. But Jim doesn't show up. The story has a heartwarming conclusion showing a glimmer of hope for Jim's recovery.

Park describes a Dodgers fan's intangible connection to the team, a connection stronger than concrete.

There was something else about keeping score—and Maggie loved this most of all. Like every other Dodger fan she knew, she felt almost like part of the team, like she herself was one of the Bums. It was as if cheering for them, supporting them, listening to the games, talking about them, somehow helped them play better.

Maggie knew that this didn't really make any sense. It wasn't like Jackie and Campy and Pee Wee *knew* that her radio was turned on, or played worse if it wasn't. But there were times when it felt as though the strength of her w ishes, combined with those of thousands of other fans all over Brooklyn, pulled the player or the bat or the ball in the right direction—for a stolen base or a hit or a strikeout, exactly when it was needed most.[45]

In the Year of the Boar and Jackie Robinson, a Chinese girl faces challenges assimilating into American society—specifically, Brooklyn. Bette Bao Lord drew on her personal experience to write the heartwarming tale of Shirley Temple Wong, a ten-year-old immigrant who doesn't speak English but transforms into a bright-eyed student immersed in the ups and downs of the 1947 Brooklyn Dodgers. Shirley meets her idol, Jackie Robinson, at a P.S. 8 class assembly where she presents him with a key to the school.

Once a shy girl unaware of American customs, Shirley corrects Robinson when he offers the promise of America, where anyone can be President of the United States. Maybe Shirley, he suggests. Affirming her assimilation, Shirley responds, "No sir. Mrs. Rappaport taught us that the Constitution of the United States clearly states that the President must be born in America, and I was born in China. But, Mr. Robinson, my brother who is not born yet, he can be President someday. He can!"[46]

Assimilation. That's the Brooklyn way.

In *Brooklyn Boy*, a memoir masquerading as a novel, Alan Lelchuk uses a school assignment about Brooklyn history as the platform for describing Brooklyn. His alter ego, Aaron Schlossberg, illustrates Brooklyn for the reader. Schlossberg grows up in Brownsville.

But Brooklyn, my Brooklyn, is really best known for its collection of odd and mangy characters (and happenings?) through the years, characters with cock-eyed accents and cocky ways. As much for gangsters like Bugsy and Louie in Brownsville as for great Hassidic rebbes who immigrated to Williamsburg; as much for tommy guns and barbershop murders as for payess curls and an eighteenth-century Polish village relocated. As much for the dropped syllables and rat-tat-tat rhythm of speech, throwing a nasty curve into the language, as for its museums or libraries. For a baseball team that was infamous for its major calamities, such as dropping third strikes in World Series games or sending two men home at once to score, only to get two outs at once.[47]

Ebbets Field's demise prompts Lelchuck to write, "And Brooklyn's never been the same since, without Ebbets Field. After all, would Paris be the same without the Cathedral of Notre Dame, Leningrad without its Hermitage, Rome without the Vatican?"[48]

Gary David Goldberg created the television show *Brooklyn Bridge* about the fictional Silver family living at 6706 21st Street in the Benson-hurst section of Brooklyn.[49] Airing on CBS from 1991 to 1993, *Brooklyn Bridge* revolves around the Silver boys—12-year-old Alan and 8-year-old Nathaniel. It takes place in 1956–1957, with the last episode, "No Time Like the Future," centering on the 1957 World Series and the Cold War concerns about Russia's Sputnik satellite. Many episodes incorporate the boys' devotion to the Dodgers.

"When Irish Eyes Are Smiling," the series premiere, features Jeffrey Nordling as Gil Hodges making a personal appearance at the Brooklyn Union Savings Bank. Jules, the Silver boys' maternal grandfather, fabricates a tale for Nathaniel's amusement—he played baseball against Hodges in Russia with the Bears team before emigrating to the United States. Nathaniel is enthralled, unable to detect the nuances in an elder's voice categorizing a tale as enhancement, exaggeration, or fantasy.

Nathaniel and his friend, Nicholas Scamparelli—accompanied by Nathaniel's grandmother, Sophie—go to the bank. When Jules meets them there, his charade approaches a flashpoint. Hodges diffuses what could be an embarrassing situation for Jules.

"That's my grandpa, Jules Berger. You played against him in Russia," explains Nathaniel.
"I did?" responds Hodges.
"He played for the Russian Bears," says Sophie. "Maybe you forgot," says Sophie.
"Hello, Mr. Hodges. Jules Berger," Jules says, shaking Hodges' hand.
"Yeah, I understand we played against each other in Russia," says Hodges, faking recognition for the sake of Nathaniel.
"Oh, no, no," Jules responds. "You wouldn't remember."
"I remember," says Hodges, playing along with Jules' fabrication.
"You do?" asks Jules, surprised at Hodges' recognition.
"Of course," says Hodges. "You played for the Bears, right?"
"Right!" exclaims Jules as a wave of relief washes over him.
They share a laugh.
"It's good to see you again," says Hodges.
"Wonderful to see you! Do you speak Yiddish?" inquires Jules.
"Ah, no," responds Hodges.
"Well, you should know what a mensch is, because that's you," states Jules.[50]

Goldberg's depiction of the personal connection between the Dodgers and children of 1950s Brooklyn benefits from first-hand experience combined with a television auteur's dramatic license. Stan Goldberg says that the emotions in the show were truthful.

> My brother mixed and matched stories for *Brooklyn Bridge*, but the sentiment is absolutely real. My mom took us to see Gil Hodges at an A&S in downtown Brooklyn. We probably found out about the appearance through a newspaper advertisement and I clearly remember my brother and I pleading, "We've gotta go! We've gotta go!" Hodges signed a baseball that I unfortunately used in a park. I hit it into the woods and I lost it![51]

The episode's mention of the grandfather playing for the fictional Bears team is also drawn from a real-life experience, as was the character of George Silver.

> Being from Russia, my grandfather never played baseball as a child. One day, after a Little League game, Gary and I implored him to give it a try. "Come on, Grandpa! Play with us!" He managed to hit the ball and we cheered him. He joked, "Yes, I played baseball for the Bears in Russia!" The father in Gary's show had a couple of similarities to our father. Both were named George. Both worked at the Post Office. Our dad was an amazing student of the game. He played baseball for Boys High in Brooklyn. When Gary and I were growing up, you really had to use your imagination because radio was the prominent medium. So you had to think things through in your mind. That thought process also occurred in the early days of television because you didn't have the benefit of instant replays. Today, announcers don't just dissect every play. They dissect every pitch. So, some of the romance and forced thinking are removed.[52]

In the episode "Where Have You Gone, Jackie Robinson?," the Silver boys and their friends mourn the Dodgers' trade of Jackie Robinson to the rival Giants. Nate wonders, "I don't understand. If Jackie plays for Brooklyn, and we're Brooklyn, then how can they trade him without asking us." When Alan explains the realities of a team owner doing what he wants because he owns the team and pays the players, Nate asks, "They get paid?"[53]

Alan lets Nate pinch-hit for him in a stickball game in the episode "Boys of Summer." Alan's friend and the opposing pitcher, Warren Butcher—the only Giants fan in Alan's circle of friends—voices his opposition to Nate's batting. "But this counts. If he makes an out, it's an out for you guys." Alan's response typifies what any self-respecting Dodgers fan would say in that moment. "What a jerk. No wonder you're a Giants fan."[54]

"Boys of Summer" also depicts Alan getting picked for *Happy Felton's Knothole Gang*, with a recreation of Ebbets Field's iconic right field wall.

Alan plays for the Royals of the Coney Island League, sponsored by Cardini's Market. He competes against Barry Connors from the Cadets of the CYO League and Anthony Gambuzza from the Apex Machine Company Panthers of the Parade Grounds League. Pee Wee Reese selects Anthony as the winner.[55]

Alan faces a dilemma in the episode "Death in Brooklyn." When Uncle Ira dies, Alan gets selected to be the tenth man at a minyan—a Jewish prayer requiring ten people—during Ira's shiva call. The death of Ira, whom nobody liked, demands Alan's attention rather than the Dodgers game that conflicts with the shiva call—a game which would be Alan's first date with Katie Monahan. Alan saved up 50 ice cream wrappers to trade them for Dodgers tickets, a trademark offer for kids in Brooklyn's neighborhoods. Alan succumbs to guilt, lets Warren take Katie to the game, and receives updates from Nate, who gets the information from people listening to radios outside.[56]

At the end of "Death in Brooklyn," Alan's grandmother, Sophie, explains that Ira was the first member of the family to emigrate from the old country. He sent money so the rest of the family could come to America.

The "Plaza Sweet" episode depicts the experience of witnessing Dodgers in Brooklyn's neighborhoods. Benny Belinsky convinces Alan that he knows the address of Duke Snider's apartment building. Initially wary, Alan accompanies Benny on a stakeout. Their reward is a sighting of Snider with other Dodgers, including Carl Furillo and Gil Hodges.

Benny exclaims, "It's a Chevy full of Dodgers!"

Alan responds, "There's over 400 RBIs in that car!"

Initially wary of Benny's information regarding Snider's address but fulfilled by the experience, Alan surrenders doubt. "Three and a half days of waiting," he says.

"It was worth it," responds Benny.

"Yeah," says Alan.[57]

Marty Adler described the thrill of seeing Brooklyn's heroes around the borough, an experience mirroring the events of *Plaza Sweet*:

> Ebbets Field was special. Yankee Stadium is like the King James version of Westminster Abbey. You could see Joe DiMaggio smiling. But at Ebbets Field, you saw Pee Wee Reese sweating. The Dodgers gave Brooklyn an identity. And we knew the statistics of the players from the previous seasons as well as the current season. One time, we saw Hodges, Campanella, and Snider in a car. We said, "There goes 422 RBI's."
>
> When we wanted to induct Pete Reiser into the Brooklyn Dodger Hall of Fame, I called his widow in Woodland Hills, California. I said, "By the way,

your area code is 343, the average that your husband had when he won the batting championship. The next four numbers added together is the sum of runs scored, RBIs, and at bats." She asked how I knew that. I said, "There are 10,000 of us who know it!"[58]

H. Allen Smith's 1946 novel *Rhubarb* revolves around the New York Loons, a professional baseball team inherited by a cat from its deceased owner. Its zaniness inspired the 1951 movie of the same name, but the team's name was changed to the Brooklyn Loons. To give the story a dash of verisimilitude, Smith references the Brooklyn Dodgers and other baseball hallmarks, including Bob Feller, Yankee Stadium, and the World Series.

Brooklyn, Colm Tóibín's 2009 love story about an Irish immigrant girl and a Brooklyn plumber, introduces the Dodgers as an element of life in the borough. Antonio "Tony" Giuseppe Fiorelle has a deep passion for the Dodgers and an instant love for Ellis Lacey. It inspires him to declare, "You know what I really want? I want our kids to be Dodgers fans."[59]

It Happened in Flatbush depicts a year in the life of a Brooklyn ballclub, though it does not mention the Dodgers by name nor does it show the part of Ebbets Field's façade including the stadium's name. Still, the stadium's identity is revealed by baseball scenes and a shot of the entrance to Ebbets Field's rotunda. Frank McGuire, nicknamed "Butterfingers" by sportswriter Danny Mitchell for costing Brooklyn a pennant seven years earlier, receives a chance at redemption from Mrs. McAvoy, the Brooklyn ballclub's owner. McGuire, presently the manager of the Clovertown Spartons, a team that is either in the minor leagues or the semi-pro leagues—the film does not clarify this point—remains doubtful, remembering the treatment generated by his error. "Dear old Brooklyn. Born in it, raised in it, and knifed in it."[60]

McAvoy remains hopeful that she has a chance to redeem her firing of McGuire because of the pressure from fans and the press. McGuire agrees to return to his homeland. "Why do you think I've stayed in baseball all these years, playing in these cowtowns, hopping buses instead of the streamliner? I've been hanging around for just one thing, a chance to go back and make those monkeys eat their words."[61]

On the day McGuire returns, Mrs. McAvoy dies. Her death triggers a distribution of the team's stock with a majority going to her niece, Kathryn Baker. Other relatives are also stockholders. A love story develops between the refined Kathryn and the blunt well-meaning McGuire. And, of course, Brooklyn wins the pennant.

Perhaps the best example of popular culture's depiction of the love affair between Brooklyn and the Dodgers takes place in the 1960s television series *McHale's Navy*. Set during World War II, *McHale's Navy* follows the comic adventures of PT-73 Captain Quinton McHale and his crew, including Torpedoman Lester Gruber from Brooklyn. Ernest Borgnine plays McHale and veteran comic actor Carl Ballantine plays Gruber. In the episode "The Day the War Stood Still," Gruber exclaims, "Skip, forward my mail to Ebbets Field! Brooklyn, here I come!"[62] Gruber's plea is natural—Brooklynites considered Ebbets Field to be their second home.

For nearly 40 years, Dan Parker splashed tongue-in-cheek poetry amongst witticisms, analysis, and commentary in his column for the *New York Daily Mirror*. A standard bearer for sports scribes, Parker used humor to inform, illuminate, and inspire his readers in Brooklynese lingo. For example, "them" became "dem" in this dialect. On September 28, 1941, Parker's column showcased a poem entitled "Dem Bums." Credited to "Harried Schoolmaster," "Dem Bums" highlighted the upcoming World Series pitting the Brooklyn Dodgers against the New York Yankees.[63]

Credited to Harold Hirsh, "Ducky on Da Bench" appeared in Parker's column on April 18, 1942, to lament the benching of left fielder Joe Medwick. A postscript explained the poem's Brooklynese dialect: "P.S. Brooklynites don't really talk like dis but it's de only way youse Giant fans could understand us."[64]

Nothing, according to Parker, compared with the beauty of baseball at Ebbets Field. Timed to coincide with the beginning of the baseball season, "When It's Springtime Out in Flatbush!" appeared in the April 1, 1942, edition of the *New York Daily Mirror*. Once again, Parker scribed in Brooklynese. The last paragraph balanced the beauty of Brooklyn against other destinations:

> Some people rave of England when it's April in de air.
> Some like da heart of Texas, dough I hear it's quite deep dere,
> And some may go for Paris which I poiss'nally tink's a fraud,
> But I'll take Spring in Brooklyn at da ball game wit' me broad![65]

The Muses embraced the Dodgers. Across the country, even people with a tangential interest in baseball knew the names of Jackie Robinson, Roy Campanella, and Leo Durocher. The Brooklyn Dodgers were a brand, indeed. Within Brooklyn, fans revered the Dodgers. Baseball, an imperfect game in an imperfect world, seemed different at Ebbets Field. In *Double Play*, Robert B. Parker wrote, "It was a night game with the Braves. Burke was where he always sat near the dugout. Barber and Desmond were in the broadcast booth. The Dodger Sym-Phony was marching back and forth. Hilda Chester was ringing her cowbell. Eddie Bataan was blowing his whistle. *Everything's in place,* Burke thought, *all the way it should be.*"[66]

Parker's words reflect the feeling of permanence surrounding Ebbets Field. It would last forever.

Not exactly.

9th Inning:
A Ravine of Gold

*I covered a team that no longer exists in a demolished
ballpark for a newspaper that is dead.* —Roger Kahn[1]

To be the president of the Brooklyn Dodgers in the 1950s was to be
a politician.

Walter Francis O'Malley was up to the task. And then some. With
affability honed by instinct, O'Malley would have been running a city, a
state, or the Democratic National Committee if he were not running the
Dodgers. During his formative years, O'Malley revealed his potential as
a bespectacled cadet at the Culver Military Academy in Culver, Indiana.
His 1922 yearbook caption states, "A pleasing personality is perhaps his
greatest asset, and with it he has won himself many friends. His next greatest feature is his home town, and although there may be many people in
it, he is sure to come to the front before long."[2]

Poker was an O'Malley hobby that served him in business. A 1957
editorial in the *New York Times* states, "Walter Francis O'Malley is a man
of many accomplishments. A good game of poker is not the least of them.
His reputation on this score at times has misled the unwary. Just when a
bluff seems most likely, he often will lay down a fistful of aces."[3] O'Malley
the poker player kept his cards close to his vest, indeed, much like
O'Malley the businessman.

A 1978 profile in the *Los Angeles Times* revealed,

Of course, he also is wearing the O'Malley mask, a veil of charm so beguiling
it becomes hard to remember he is a tough, tenacious man who is, above all,
pragmatic. He rarely shows anger. And it has always been his style to cover up
the tenacity, the ambition—the same way he covers his competiveness on the
golf course by playing practical "jokes" like blowing smoke and coughing when
his opponents are hitting.

O'Malley loves poker. As in life, he doesn't play his cards. He gauges the people, and bets accordingly.[4]

O'Malley's actions regarding a new stadium for the Dodgers, seen as a bluff in some, if not most, corners of Brooklyn, warranted concern. Could the Dodgers really move from Brooklyn? It was not feasible in the minds of Dodgers fans, despite precedent—the Braves moved from Boston to Milwaukee in 1953, the Athletics, the year after. Once a Philadelphia institution, the Athletics belonged to Kansas City till they moved again in 1968, to Oakland.

After O'Malley's machinations forced Rickey out the doors of 215 Montague Street in 1950, Arch Murray wrote a profile of O'Malley for the *New York Post*. Murray found a businessman dedicated to rising at 6:00 a.m. "no matter what hour he hits the sack" and being "the first man at his desk in the morning."[5] O'Malley was fond of mirth, too. He wanted to remake the Dodgers experience, which, in his eyes, Rickey had based on statistics rather than emotion. Analysis rather than instinct. "The 47-year-old O'Malley," Murray wrote, "with the lilt of Irish laughter in his eyes and on his lips, is a man of multifold facets. He combines the warmth and gregariousness of the born mixer with the shrewd hard head of the successful business man. It is his plan to retouch the cold and efficient canvas painted by Rickey with a splash of the color and glamour of the old boisterous Dodgers."[6]

O'Malley, ever the homebody, preferred the company of friends to nightclubs. His gregariousness did not extend to working a room, shaking hands with his right hand and toasting with his left. Friendship fueled him, not popularity. "He likes having his friends around and the hum of happy voices is sweet music to his ears. Wallflowers and sour dispositions are barred at the door when O'Malley is playing host."[7]

Catering to the fans was an O'Malley priority. In a post–Rickey regime, as Milton Gross noted in a May 1954 article titled "The Artful O'Malley and the Dodgers" in *True* magazine, O'Malley jettisoned double admissions for twi-night doubleheaders. While it impacted revenue, a single admission price for both games rewarded fans with value for their loyalty. In addition, Gross noted, O'Malley restructured ticket sales, resulting in 12,000 available seats for sale on game days. He expanded the Dodgers' fan base to women. "Ladies Days were increased and baseball clinics were set up at department stores where the female fan could learn more about the game."[8] Harold Parrott said, "He's wrapped up the Dodger rooters and their heroes in one emotional sandwich."[9]

Even when fans turned against him, O'Malley saw opportunity, or at least a challenge, where others saw a waste of time. When Bobby Thomson's home run destroyed Brooklyn's soul, two men numbed their sorrows in an Amityville bar. Then, they searched out Amityville resident O'Malley. "Let's go see O'Malley and make him get rid of Dressen for calling in Branca to throw that home-run pitch to Thomson."[10] While the duo searched for O'Malley's home, the bartender called the police. By the time the police got to O'Malley's, the two troublemakers were "sipping Scotch, being hypnotized by O'Malley and agreeing that Dressen was blameless for the pennant loss."[11]

Ambition fueled O'Malley, whose oratory may have seemed bestowed by the Blarney Stone. As a young lawyer, O'Malley struggled until a chance phone call from a priest changed his course. Thinking that O'Malley's name was as Irish as Dublin, Father Barrett reached out to his fellow Irishman for assistance concerning a parishioner's will, which is to say, the parishioner did not have a will. Because the parishioner was dying, rapidity was a essential. Father Barrett had leaned on his pastor for legal assistance, but the pastor recently died, leaving the priest with a dilemma that only a lawyer could solve. And if that lawyer was a member of St. Patrick's tribe, all the better.[12]

O'Malley originally thought that Father Barrett said "wells" instead of "wills," but he adjusted out of necessity for keeping his law practice afloat. "I was getting desperate," he explained. "I didn't understand the caller but I'd have dug a well or written a will."[13] O'Malley's law practice blossomed because of the client, who owned "several mortgage bonds in default."[14] With mortgage reorganization law a "relatively unexplored legal field,"[15] O'Malley saw a hole and widened it into a canyon that he dominated. Influence came with the territory.

> In collaboration with George Brower, a judge of the Supreme Court and the State Superintendent of Insurance, O'Malley prepared a program of new legislation and the laws were passed. Thus, from an attorney who would take any case, he became one who commanded legal fees as high as $100,000 for a single case. At one time his practice was so vast O'Malley represented nine large banks.[16]

Banking law led to baseball for the powerhouse lawyer. With the Dodgers in debt to the Brooklyn Trust Company, the bank president, George V. McLaughlin, turned to O'Malley for legal counsel. "In 1943 when Rickey replaced MacPhail, McLaughlin arranged for O'Malley to replace Wendell Wilkie [sic] as the Dodgers' attorney."[17] O'Malley, prosperous in law, benefited from his status as Brooklyn Trust's attorney by having a pipeline to information involving Dodgers management. "In 1944 the Edward J. McKeever Estate advised the Brooklyn Trust Company it wished to sell half of its 50 percent interest in the Dodgers. McLaughlin counseled O'Malley to take an option on the stock. He did, forming a syndicate for its purchase at close to $300,000."[18]

O'Malley expanded his asset in 1945 when his syndicate consisting of himself, Rickey, and Pfizer Chemical Company president John Smith bought the Ebbets 50 percent ownership of the Dodgers for $850,000. Each partner owned 25 percent, till O'Malley maneuvered Rickey out of the Dodgers' inner sanctum. By buying Rickey's share and, after Smith died, Mrs. Smith's inherited share, O'Malley had a majority ownership of 75 percent with Frank McKeever's heir, Mrs. James A. Mulvey, controlling the remaining 25 percent.[19]

Then, O'Malley saw a rainbow beginning at Ebbets Field and ending in a pot of gold 3,000 miles away. A ravine of gold, actually.

Terrific scholarship has been produced concerning the battle to keep the Dodgers in Brooklyn. In *The Dodgers Move West*, Neil J. Sullivan analyzes the politics of New York City and Los Angeles that provided the foundation for the move to Los Angeles—"O'Malley as villain may offer some emotional satisfaction, but it is poor history."[20] Michael D'Antonio takes a pro–O'Malley thesis in *Forever Blue: The True Story of Walter O'Malley, Baseball's Most Controversial Owner, and the Dodgers of Brooklyn and Los Angeles*. "Given the effort he devoted to the stadium issue, O'Malley clearly wanted to stay in Brooklyn,"[21] writes D'Antonio.

Longtime Dodgers executive Fresco Thompson wrote in his 1964 autobiography *Every Diamond Doesn't Sparkle*, "The last thing Walter O'Malley wanted to do was to leave Brooklyn. But a fear haunted him—fear that Brooklyn was becoming a decadent borough."[22] O'Malley also saw the suburban phenomenon that began in Levittown, Long Island, siphoning the Dodgers' fan base. With only 700 parking spaces and mass transit not readily available for transplanted Brooklynites, Ebbets Field sprinted toward oblivion in a post-war culture craving automobile travel.

O'Malley had another problem—the current fan base. Generosity, camaraderie, and togetherness no longer governed Ebbets Field, its aura stained by the acts of patrons no longer shouting "Dem Bums" in affection, but rather, acting like the moniker. Thompson explains,

> Ebbets Field had a double-decked grandstand, and to sit safely in the lower portion it was almost necessary to wear raincoats on a day when the sun was shining brightest. Rowdies cascaded beer, ice cream, peanut shells, etc., onto

the heads and clothing of those seated below. Cash boxes were repeatedly stolen from public telephones. Urinals were even pried from the men's lavatories and carried home, for what purpose no one could guess.[23]

Revolutionary when it debuted in 1913, Ebbets Field was destined for the stadium scrap heap. To resolve the situation, O'Malley turned to Emil Praeger, a civil engineer and architect involved in the design for the Phoenix, a concrete breakwater creating an artificial harbor for boats during the Normandy invasion. O'Malley's October 14, 1946, missive to Praeger invited him to begin thinking about alternatives to the present state of Ebbets Field.[24]

Like moths to a flame, real estate brokers and investors launched a flurry of inquiries to 215 Montague Street. Almost exactly a year after his letter to Praeger, for example, O'Malley received an inquiry from George J. Pidgeon on letterhead belonging to John H. Ward of Waterfront Investments. Pidgeon talked with George McLaughlin's office, which sent him to O'Malley.

Pidgeon represented an owner with "an ideal property proposition" for O'Malley to build a new stadium. "The property is the last large vacant tract in Brooklyn in single ownership and comprises 225 acres. It is situated at the Belt Parkway and is only two short blocks from the Subway. A Bus Terminal is also at the property."[25] Pidgeon also referred to the Brooklyn Battery Tunnel, in construction, being 20 minutes from the site and tens of thousands of automobiles having access to parking.

Gilliam & McVay Real Estate offered a lease of "the former site of Luna Park at Coney Island."[26]

Norman Bel Geddes, industrial designer, wrote to Branch Rickey on December 17, 1947, about a designing breakthrough. O'Malley had $5,500 appropriated for Bel Geddes.[27]

Sidney H. Bingham, chairman of the Board of Transportation of the City of New York, expressed concerns about the transportation in downtown Brooklyn on game days. He suggested an area in East New York accessible by mass transit and automobiles."[28]

John Bellew of George C. Johnston, Jr. Real Estate offered 1,000,000 square feet in the Rego Park section of Queens at $1 per square foot.[29]

No idea seemed practical to the situation. O'Malley had a different idea—a dome in another area of Brooklyn yet to be identified. He expressed this vision to Frank Schroth, publisher of the *Brooklyn Eagle*, in a letter on June 17, 1952.[30]

Two months later, O'Malley further emphasized the dome idea in another letter to Schroth. Promoting a story written by Tom Meany for the September 26 issue of *Collier's*, O'Malley talked about a "two page color spread" documenting his vision. When completed, the structure would be "the largest covered convention hall in the world."[31]

O'Malley also wanted a retractable roof for his geodesic dome. It seemed like a perfect solution to avoid rainouts. But he needed a power hitter, the political equivalent of Duke Snider. George McLaughlin, naturally. O'Malley wrote McLaughlin a letter on June 18, 1953, and sent it to his office at the Manufacturers Trust Company at 177 Montague Street, a baseball toss away from the Dodgers' base of operations—Manufacturers Trust had merged with Brooklyn Trust.

Admittedly, O'Malley needed the government's help in condemning land if he wanted to own the new stadium privately.[32] In New York City, Robert Moses was the government. O'Malley may have loved poker but Robert Moses played with a stacked deck that he alone shuffled and dealt. Never elected to a political office, Moses held power for decades as the head of various agencies, including the Triborough Bridge Authority. Moses designed the Long Island Expressway in addition to tunnels, bridges, and highways connecting New Yorkers to each other. With the Triborough Bridge Authority making money every time a driver plunked a coin into the toll, Moses had power backed by money. And he knew how to use it.

For O'Malley to get a new stadium site in Brooklyn, which he was vocal about paying for with private funds, he needed Moses to condemn land under Title 1 of the 1949 Federal Housing Act. Under Title 1, Moses had the authority to re-designate land under the guise of slum clearance. The re-designation had to be for a public purpose, though. A stadium, in the Moses paradigm, did not qualify.

Moses described his position in a letter to Schroth dated October 16, 1953. He sent O'Malley a copy of the letter[33] and followed up with a personal letter on October 20 emphasizing the same points.[34]

Further, Moses did not oppose O'Malley building a new stadium. In fact, he condoned the idea of improving surrounding areas for a site that O'Malley might buy, including the street system, a new school, and a playground. Moses also dismissed Praeger's suggestions because, in the Moses paradigm, a new stadium did not fall under the umbrella of a public purpose.[35]

Concerning the finance part, O'Malley wrote NO in a handwritten notation. He wanted to finance the stadium privately, but he needed Moses' help in condemning the land so he could buy it at an affordable price. O'Malley countered with a parking garage plan to satisfy the public purpose requirement.[36] In a letter dated October 28, 1953, O'Malley tried to clarify his position to Moses,[37] who responded, "It is true that there is existing law which permits the acquisition of property for public garage purposes, but in this instance it is obvious that the garage is financially incidental to the stadium and that the real purpose is to build a new Dodger Stadium."[38]

Bel Geddes offered solace on December 31, 1953, expressing confidence that O'Malley would achieve his goal because New York City needed a new stadium for the Dodgers.[39]

O'Malley considered alternatives, but ultimately, they fell short. His letter to Schroth on February 11, 1954, indicated an offer to build a new stadium in Long Island City. While O'Malley found the prospect "interesting for a number of reasons," he was concerned about Brooklyn's loss of identity should the Dodgers move from the borough. O'Malley also expressed his preference of Long Island City over Los Angeles, so the idea of a West Coast move was, at the very least, brewing in O'Malley's mind in 1954—three years before he decided to leave Brooklyn."[40] O'Malley persevered, pleading on deaf ears, blind eyes, and a closed mind. Moses rebuffed him, not caring much whether the Dodgers stayed in Brooklyn or left as long as the decision didn't interfere with his vision for New York City's transportation arteries.

Frank Schroth observed this tale from the other foundation offering a common thread throughout the borough—the *Brooklyn Daily Eagle*. Soon to perish in 1955, the *Eagle* enjoyed a history dating back to 1841. Quoting Brooklyn borough president John Cashmore, Schroth said, "Brooklyn without the *Eagle* would be an oddity, without a newspaper voice of its own, and without a champion of its best public interest. Such a state of affairs would be unthinkable."[41]

So, Schroth shared O'Malley's plight, to a degree. O'Malley was not in danger of losing the Dodgers, only in finding a home for the team, hopefully within the boundaries of Brooklyn. Schroth felt the same way about the Dodgers as he did about his newspaper. In a letter to O'Malley dated February 12, 1954, Schroth wrote that moving the Dodgers from Brooklyn would have a "tragic" effect.[42]

Moses held the line, refusing to budge one millimeter from his footing. He would not bend to O'Malley's will, the Dodgers' emotional gravity in the borough notwithstanding. Moses responded to Schroth, again emphasizing his unwillingness to use eminent domain powers for an Ebbets Field successor.[43]

Robert Grannis echoed Schroth's sentiments in the May 2, 1954, edition of the *Eagle*, responding to O'Malley's warning that a 5 percent amusement tax might affect the Dodgers looking at other cities for a home base. "The Dodgers are as much a part of our town as the Brooklyn Bridge, as dear to the heart of the masses as Coney Island and as indispensable as hot dogs and beer. There is no better baseball town than Brooklyn anywhere in the United States, no more loyal fans, nor no equally feverish interest."[44]

Meanwhile, O'Malley continued deflecting ideas for stadium sites, including those from the press. Mike Lee, sports editor of the *Long Island Daily Press*, lobbied for a site in Queens that had a transportation benefit. Lee's site offered proximity—a couple of miles—to the stations at Eighth Avenue and the BMT and IRT at 74th Street in Jackson Heights.[45]

So much a fixture in the borough since George Taylor's vision of a professional baseball team, the Dodgers in another city seemed incongruous. O'Malley had the backing of Mayor Robert Wagner, Brooklyn Borough President John Cashmore, and the Rockefellers, probably the most influential family in New York City. But their cards, however played, could not overcome those of Robert Moses.

O'Malley did not rebuff all alternate sites to his desired target, the intersection of Atlantic Avenue and Flatbush Avenue. He mentioned to Colonel Sidney H. Bingham, executive director and general manager of the New York City Transit Authority, the possibility of a site at Horace Harding Boulevard and Junction Avenue, Queens.[46] O'Malley wanted Bingham's counsel regarding mass transit's sufficiency in the area. Bingham presented a glimmer of hope for O'Malley should the Dodgers owner plan to move to Queens, praising the value of mass transit in addition to the borough's growth.[47]

Still, O'Malley persisted in his quest for a geodesic dome in downtown Brooklyn. He asked MIT's Eero Saarinen for "photographs or technical articles" regarding Saarinen's "architectural study for the MIT auditorium."[48] O'Malley also inquired of Harold Boeschenstein, president of Owens-Corning Fiberglass Corporation, about his opinions regarding a translucent shell with a diameter of 700 feet to cover the field.[49]

Frank M. McCurdy Real Estate, located in the same building as the Dodgers offices, described the former Luna Park area in Coney Island as a possible site for a stadium. Transportation was a key factor in the suggestion—transit lines at Stillwell Avenue and Surf Avenue in addition to the Shore Parkway.[50]

O'Malley shot down this idea because it lacked an area for sufficient parking, a mandatory item for a new stadium.[51] After reading "The Dymaxion World of Buckminster Fuller," an article in the Spring 1953 issue of *American Fabrics*, O'Malley consulted visionary architect Fuller about the dome possibility.[52]

With a new stadium site in limbo, Brooklynites saw red when O'Malley announced that the Dodgers would play seven games in Jersey City during the 1956 season. "If Jersey wants a baseball team, let them get their own team. The Dodgers belong in Brooklyn,"[53] stated Bill Murray of 681 Lafayette Street.

Theresa Pearl, a legal stenographer, analogized other cities that lost teams. "They should make every effort to keep the Dodgers here. I'll bet St. Louis is sorry it lost the Browns and Philadelphia the Athletics. Things like that are bad for business."[54]

Alfred Kushin, an insurance agent, acknowledged the business aspect of baseball. "It's a foolish move, I think. But baseball's a business and you can understand it. What we really need is a larger ball park in Brooklyn. Ebbets Field is too small and there isn't enough space to park."[55]

Barney Haller, a Dodgers season ticket holder, emphasized that Dodgers loyalty had its boundaries. "You won't catch me taking that long haul to Jersey City. When the Dodgers play there, they won't be the Dodgers to me."[56]

On August 19, 1955, Giants owner Horace Stoneham sent a warning cry upon O'Malley's meeting with Mayor Wagner, Moses, and Cashmore. Needing a new stadium, too, Stoneham floated the idea of a stadium owned by the city for the Giants and the Yankees. It would be located near the Whitestone Bridge in the East Bronx. Stoneham's suggestion surprised George Weiss, general manager of the Yankees. "We're very happy with Yankee Stadium. It's probably the best stadium in the country and we wouldn't consider moving. Not unless someone built one just as good and offered it to us rent-free,"[57] said Weiss.

Moses referenced Brooklyn's passion for the Dodgers in his 1955 commencement address at Pratt Institute.[58] But his actions did not consider the psychic value that the Dodgers added to Brooklyn life.

Again, Moses wrote to O'Malley, underscoring the unavailability of Title 1 for a new stadium. He repeated his suggestion that O'Malley buy land privately rather than have the government condemn land for him.[59]

Two days later, O'Malley made the Jersey City announcement.[60]

Moses had the law on his side, not to mention the power that extended into every corner of New York City. Charles M. Richardson believed that Moses was the point man for the Dodgers' decision-making. He sent a letter on August 22, 1955, asking Moses to consider the Flushing Airport in Queens within the boundaries of the Whitestone Parkway, Linden Street, 130th Street, and 20th Avenue. Richardson's idea was to develop the approximately 262 acres for park and amusement use. The city was in the process of acquiring title, thereby rendering legal maneuvers, including Moses' classic use of condemnation, irrelevant.

Moses responded on September 1, 1955, clarifying that he has no responsibility regarding the Brooklyn Dodgers. He also mentioned that the area described by Richardson lacked eligibility for Title I redevelopment.[61] He emphasized that the stadium site was incidental to the Atlantic and Flatbush area, despite the contrary framing by O'Malley and other advocates for a new stadium.[62]

As Brooklyn reveled in the glow of the 1955 World Series victory over the Yankees, O'Malley pushed ahead. The New York Water Service Corporation offered approximately 63 acres in Nassau County, specifically, Massapequa, Long Island. The land, "zoned for industrial use," offered a stop on the Long Island Railroad in addition to automobile access—Sunrise Highway and Carman Road.

Although O'Malley dismissed alternate sites for the Dodgers and Moses dismissed O'Malley, a codification of efforts to maintain the Dodgers' Brooklyn status took place in Albany on April 21, 1956, when Governor Averell Harriman signed Assembly Bill, Introductory Number 2180, Print Number 2274 at Brooklyn's Borough Hall: the Brooklyn Sports Center Authority Act.

The Act created the Brooklyn Sports Center Authority, its members to be selected by Robert Wagner. Mayor Wagner endorsed the bill in a letter dated March 30, 1956, arguing that a sports center satisfied the public purpose requirement.[63]

The members of the Brooklyn Sports Center Authority were Robert E. Blum and Chester A. Allen. Charles J. Mylod was chairman.[64] Meanwhile, O'Malley considered other stadia as comparables, asking J. G. Taylor Spink, publisher of *The Sporting News*, for a list of municipally owned stadia.[65] Spink responded with a list broken down by Organized Baseball (AA and higher), Stadia Used for Other Sports, and Baseball Parks Built By Private Capital (A and higher).[66]

Chester Allen, president of the Kings County Trust Company, saw the value in a renovated area at Flatbush and Atlantic. On February 6, 1956, Allen wrote to O'Malley about his family's loyalty to the Dodgers, whose migration could drastically impact the area's financial health if development remained static.[67]

When the Sports Authority delivered its report, Moses declared his thoughts about it to Mayor Wagner, emphasizing the importance of private financing for a stadium while ignoring the Long Island Railroad Terminal's possibilities in a renovated state."[68]

O'Malley realized that keeping the Dodgers in Brooklyn was akin to climbing a block of ice with your hands dipped in oil. He wrote to Frank Schroth on December 27, 1956, apologizing for his actions leading to this point. After selling the real estate for the Brooklyn Dodgers and Montreal Royals stadiums, O'Malley had $4,000,000. But a looming disbanding of the Sports Authority would move O'Malley in a westerly direction."[69]

In 1957, the Dodgers' chances of staying in Brooklyn looked bleak. Desperate, even. In the song "Let's Keep the Dodgers in Brooklyn," Phil Foster urged his fellow Brooklynites to rally around the team. With a voice that sounded like he gargled with gravel, Foster emblemized the Brooklyn dialect in a noble attempt. In a memorandum dated February 6, 1957, O'Malley expressed concern about the likelihood of a solution.[70]

A couple of weeks later, O'Malley signaled the West Coast as a destination—he bought the Los Angeles Angels of the Pacific Coast League and Wrigley Field in Los Angeles from Cubs owner Phil Wrigley. The deal included $3,000,000 for the territorial rights for Los Angeles. O'Malley masked the purchase as "investing baseball dollars into baseball. There is an element of protection in the future of this action."[71] He admitted, however, "Our long-range plan has caused us to take these steps to accumulate enough of our dollars with which to build a new Dodger stadium, preferably in Brooklyn."[72]

It wasn't as if a move of this caliber came without warning. Ten days prior, O'Malley said, "Unless something is done within six months, I will have to make other arrangements. There is still a short time left before we could be forced to take an irrevocable step to commit the Dodgers elsewhere."[73]

Ever the poker player, O'Malley began to show his cards. "If it becomes necessary for us to play any place other than Brooklyn, I think the final location is obvious. Then it would become a matter of picking the place with the greatest future."[74] The Wrigley deal also included Brooklyn's Fort Worth team in the Texas League, with the Dodgers' "limited working agreement" with Portland in the Pacific Coast League going to Wrigley.[75]

No *deus ex machina* arose with any realism for the Brooklyn Dodgers remaining the Brooklyn Dodgers.

Circle Realty Company of Brooklyn suggested "the easterly or westerly side of Pennsylvania Avenue, south of Fairfield Avenue (Flatlands Avenue) and north of the Belt Parkway."[76] It was not viable for O'Malley. Ed Sullivan's "Little Old New York" column in the *New York Daily News* on April 15, 1957, mentioned an interview that Mayor Wagner gave to John Cameron Swayze in which Wagner "held out little hope for a new Dodger stadium."[77]

The City Fusion Party suggested the area surrounding the East New York Station of the Long Island Railroad, offering mass transit possibilities in addition to proximity to the Belt Parkway and the Interborough Parkway for suburban fans.[78] Meanwhile, the Brooklyn Sports Center Authority, tasked with investigating the possibilities of a new sports arena in Brooklyn, fizzled much like the Edsel that Ford produced in the late 1950s. By the fall, Horace Stoneham announced his decision to transplant the Giants to San Francisco.

The knockout blow may have been a memorandum from the corporation counsel to Dr. John J. Theobald, chairman of the Mayor's Committee regarding the Redevelopment of Downtown Brooklyn Business Section. "It is my opinion that the Sports Center Authority is not empowered to acquire property merely for the purpose of immediate resale."[79]

O'Malley courted the Los Angeles power structure for a new Dodgers home. And vice versa, while Brooklyn's power structure tried to maintain the Dodgers' link in Brooklyn. Taking the Dodgers out of Brooklyn was like separating salt from the ocean. It wasn't feasible to a Brooklynite, no matter the political, financial, or real estate challenges. Moses had offered O'Malley a site in Flushing Meadows; it later became the site for Shea Stadium, home of the New York Mets. On September 8, 1957, Brooklyn Borough President John Cashmore sent a Western Union telegram to Walter O'Malley requesting a stay of execution should O'Malley decide to move the Dodgers out of Brooklyn.[80]

A handwritten note, probably a draft of a response, says, "Glad to have a pinch hitter. Anymore at home like you?"[81]

Offers continued to reach O'Malley's desk at 215 Montague Street.

Mayor Robert Baldwin of South Plainfield, New Jersey, offered property. "SO WE SAY TO YOU—GO WEST DODGER—but only across the Hudson to South Plainfield, New Jersey. You have the Team, Rockafeller [*sic*] has the money, and we have the land."[82]

Construction mogul Samuel Lefrak proposed his services to build a new stadium for cost.[83]

Meanwhile, Los Angeles made overtures to the Dodgers in the persons of Rosalind Wyman and Kenneth Hahn. Already a mecca for the entertainment industry because of weather that allowed film and television studios to produce on location year-round, Los Angeles had the Angels and the Hollywood Stars for baseball. A major league team could enhance the Los Angeles brand.

So, Walter O'Malley went west, where the Los Angeles political structure gave him Chavez Ravine gratis for a new stadium site. An unsigned statement read, "In view of the action of the Los Angeles City Council yesterday and in accordance with the resolution of the National League made Oct. 1, the stockholders and directors of the Brooklyn Baseball Club have today met and unanimously agreed that necessary steps be taken to draft the Los Angeles territory."[84]

O'Malley had received a reprieve from the National League clubs in the form of a two-week extension past the October 1 deadline. He needed only one. In his lead for the *New York Mirror* on October 9, Gus Steiger summarized the feeling of loss surrounding Brooklyn: "Walter F. O'Malley has completed his mission. He killed the Brooklyn Dodgers yesterday, a club that has operated in the National League continuously since 1890."[85] In the *New York Herald Tribune*, Tommy Holmes honored the fans: "Through the lean years, the faith and the hope of the Brooklyn fan was proverbial."[86]

While Brooklyn mourned, Los Angeles rejoiced. A luncheon at the Statler Hotel on October 28 boasted more than 1,100 people in attendance. O'Malley said, "The next time you will be asked to stand will be when your own Duke Snider hits the first home run for your Dodgers here."[87] Snider, a native of southern California, had misgivings about the move.

> The people of Brooklyn had become more than just neighbors. They were like family, and the thought of leaving them was a sad one. We'd be leaving so many terrific people who meant so much to us, people we'd known and grown to love as long as I had been a Brooklyn Dodger. The thought of leaving these people made us heartsick. No more Bay Ridge? No more McKinneys or Steiners or Barwoods or Baumans for neighbors? No more living close to the Erskines, Reeses, and Walkers? No more taking the subway into New York on Saturday night? No cop telling me he hates baseball while he gives me a speeding ticket? No more Vinnie's Meat Market for club steak when I'm in a slump? And no more "Duke of Flatbush"?

Worst of all, there would be no more Ebbets Field. No more Hilda and her cowbell. No more Sym-Phony playing Dixieland music. No more Happy Felton and his Knothole gang, or Tex Rickard announcing that "a little boy has been found lost" or telling the fans along the bleacher railing to remove their clothes. No more fans screaming at us as "dem Bums" and calling my roommate "Oisk" and me "Dook."[88]

At the Statler luncheon, Master of Ceremonies Joe E. Brown read a telegram: "Here's hoping it rains every day in Los Angeles from April to October." It was signed, "an ex–Brooklyn fan."[89]

When Dodgers fans awoke on September 24, 1957, trauma stifled the borough of Brooklyn with a tension that could make Cupid doubt love. That evening, the Brooklyn Dodgers were scheduled to play the Pittsburgh Pirates in the last Dodgers game at Ebbets Field. The unthinkable had happened. Nothing was official, though all indications pointed 3,000 miles west to a massive hole in the ground that the City of Los Angeles offered to Walter O'Malley as the site of a new Dodgers home. It would be modern. It would be fan-friendly with a good view from every seat. And it would have sufficient room for parking, a primary reason that O'Malley abandoned Ebbets Field and a necessary requirement in the car culture dominating southern California. Thank you, Mr. Goodyear. Thank you, Mr. Firestone.

In 1957, the world changed beyond the demise of the Brooklyn Dodgers. Rapidly.

American Bandstand targeted the teenage market with a show geared to the recent phenomenon of rock-and-roll. The new Interstate Highway System connecting states and regions would be a boon for travelers, vacationers, and automobile and tire companies. Jack Kerouac popularized the Beat Generation in his autobiographical novel *On the Road*, while Ayn Rand critiqued the potentially disastrous effect of government regulations on business, science, and society in her novel *Atlas Shrugged*.

Ford introduced the Edsel. The Russians launched Sputnik. And United States Marine Major and future astronaut John Glenn broke a transcontinental flight record when he flew an F8U supersonic jet from California to New York in 3 hours, 23 minutes, and 8 seconds.

World events fulfilled a Chinese proverb—"May you live in interesting times."

They were merely raindrops compared to the storm of betrayal soaking Dodgers fans.

On the same autumn day that President Eisenhower sent federal troops to Little Rock's Central High School to ensure the safety of nine black students enrolling in the school, Ebbets Field faced its mortality. And so did Brooklyn.

For the 6,702 fans who went to Ebbets Field one last time and for thousands of others mourning across the borough, a bond once thought unbreakable had shattered. It was impossible. And yet, it was happening.

As they opened their newspapers to the sports pages, Dodgers fans wondered, "What's next? Will they sell the Soldiers' and Sailors' Arch in Grand Army Plaza?" Readers of the *New York Times* would find a glowing piece about Red Schoendienst being the key to the Milwaukee Braves winning the National League pennant after being traded to the Braves from the New York Giants in June.

As the game time of 7:55 p.m. approached, they tuned their Philcos, Zeniths, and Emersons to WOR to see Danny McDevitt pitch against the Pirates. After a few minutes, the pain of watching the last Dodgers game at Ebbets Field might have inspired a switch to WCBS at 8:00 p.m. for comedic distraction courtesy of *The Phil Silvers Show*.

McDevitt's two-hit shutout provided little solace for a borough steeped in disbelief. Other teams had left their cities. But it couldn't happen in Brooklyn. Could it? Who really cared if the Braves left Boston for Milwaukee, the Athletics left Philadelphia for Kansas City, or the Browns left St. Louis to become the Baltimore Orioles? The section of the scoreboard dedicated to promoting the next Dodgers home game remained blank. No opponent would play the Dodgers at Ebbets Field in the future. Not in 1957. Not in 1958. Not ever.

The day after Pirates third baseman Gene Baker made the last out of the last game by flying to Dodgers right fielder Elmer Valo on a 2–2 pitch, synagogues began the Jewish New Year at sundown—Rosh Hashanah. A mainstay of Brooklyn's populace, Jews undoubtedly prayed silently for the Dodgers to stay in Brooklyn as cantors sang the ancient Hebrew prayers from the Torah and the horn-like sound of the shofar bounced off the synagogues' walls. The Dodgers were a God-given entity, after all. Brooklyn was their homeland, like Israel for the Jews. Prayer was futile, however.

The shofar sounded more like a wail than a call to arms.

Walter O'Malley. Visionary or villain? Depends on who you ask. "If you were a board member of the Dodgers in those days, you'd think O'Malley should be in the Hall of Fame to see that future and to move the team west," said Carl Erskine in the HBO documentary *The Ghosts of Flatbush*. "You can't convince that to a Brooklyn fan. And I don't ever try."[90]

Friends were not the only ones mourning the loss of Brooklyn's team. Foes mourned, too. Billy Crystal, for example, has pinstriped loyalty in his blood. An actor, writer, director, and comedian, Crystal is a deep-rooted Yankees loyalist; he is fond of saying that Mickey Mantle's Oklahoma drawl inspired his Bar Mitzvah speech. Crystal showcased his passion for the Yankees in the HBO TV-movie *61, highlighting the 1961 home run battle between Roger Maris and Mickey Mantle to surpass Babe Ruth's record of 60 home runs in a single season. Despite his affinity for the Yankees, the loss of the Dodgers represented confusion, angst, and sorrow to Crystal.

> It was baseball. When the Brooklyn Dodgers would up and leave to Los Angeles, which seemed like, "Why don't you go to Borneo?" You know, the only time I had seen L.A. was *The Mickey Mouse Club* would show "Disneyland is under construction." And it looked like the Amazon. Where'd they go? Why here, it's so far away and it was a mountaintop they're preparing for a ballpark? In a mountaintop? No, in the city next to the dry cleaners so you could talk about it when you pick up your suit that had a mustard stain from the game before. Where's the corner bar? Where's the arguments? You know, where's the trolley? Where's the subway? How do you get there? Where'd they go? Palm trees? What's Cary Grant and Doris Day doing at a game? You know, where's Al Shmenglowitz who should sit there? Where's the band? What's gonna happen to that band that was in right field? That crazy band? You know, what's gonna happen?[91]

The Dodgers went Hollywood, increasing their notice across the country by appearing on television shows, becoming entrenched in Los Angeles culture, and easing the transition from "Brooklyn" to "Los Angeles" in the baseball vernacular. Tommy Davis, Don Drysdale, and Sandy Koufax sang on the October 25, 1963, episode of *Bob Hope Presents the Chrysler Theatre: Bob Hope Variety Special*. They also traded barbs with the legendary comedian, a baseball fan who, at one time, owned a percentage of the Cleveland Indians.

Moose Skowron, Tommy Davis, Don Drysdale, Ron Perranoski, and Frank Howard sang a parody of "High Hopes" on the May 2, 1964, episode of *The Joey Bishop Show*, though Howard, teased by Bishop, could hardly keep a straight face during the chorus. Drysdale, dressed to the nines in a tuxedo, led the uniformed Dodgers in lyrics recounting the 1963 season, including the Dodgers' World Series victory against the Yankees. At the emphatic "ker-plop" lyric, Skowron attempted to substitute smashing a blown-up paper bag for the word "plop." Staged for comedic and dramatic effect, Skowron failed once, but succeeded on the second try.[92]

The Dodgers also ventured into situation comedies. Don Drysdale appeared as himself on *The Donna Reed Show* and *The Brady Bunch*. Leo Durocher—back in a Dodgers uniform as a coach—tried to recruit Herman Munster for the Dodgers in the episode *Herman the Rookie* on *The Munsters*. While talking with reporter Charlie Hodges, Durocher gets knocked on the head by a baseball hit from several blocks away. He discovers that Herman Munster hit the ball.

Eager for a brand-new discovery, Durocher arranges for Herman to have a formal tryout with the Dodgers. Undoubtedly, Herman's physical strength is the tool that will propel the Dodgers to the National League pennant and the World Series. Literally crushing the ball out of the park, Herman could single-handedly win every game.

With every asset comes liability. When Herman hits a ground ball, it goes under ground and destroys the infield. When Herman hits a home run, the ball knocks over the scoreboard. Durocher exclaims that he doesn't know whether to sign Herman or send him to Vietnam! Herman's baseball dreams evaporate when he learns that the Dodgers won't sign him because of expenses. Walter O'Malley, the Dodgers owner, would have to spend $75,000 after each game to repair Dodger Stadium.[93]

The episode's tag—the scene before the final credits—repeats the opening scene's circumstances. When former Los Angeles Rams player and current Rams executive Elroy "Crazylegs" Hirsch discovers a football kicked from several blocks away, much farther than the length of a football field, Hodges advises him to forget about identifying the kicker and signing him to the Rams.

Durocher also tries to recruit Jethro on *The Beverly Hillbillies* in the episode "The Clampetts and the Dodgers." Jethro can make a baseball dance in the air when he throws it—an amazing skill for a pitcher—but Durocher discovers that Jethro's ability stems from a substance on the ball that umpires would deem illegal. Wally Cassell plays Buzzie Bavasi in the episode.[94]

According to America's favorite talking horse, the Dodgers won the 1963 National League pennant thanks to his advice in "Leo Durocher Meets Mr. Ed," another television episode featuring Durocher. This *Mr. Ed* episode opens with the title horse surrounded by pictures of Dodgers in his barn as he watches Vin Scully announce a televised Dodgers-Giants twilight doubleheader at Candlestick Park. Wearing a Dodgers cap, Mr. Ed laments that Moose Skowron drops his right shoulder in the batter's box. Frustrated, Mr. Ed exclaims, "Those bums should have stayed in Brooklyn."[95]

Left to right: Buzzie Bavasi, Walter O'Malley and Fresco Thompson formed the power structure of the Dodgers organization. Actor Wally Cassell played Bavasi in an episode of *The Beverly Hillbillies* (Brooklyn Public Library—Brooklyn Collection).

When Mr. Ed suggests that he could advise the Dodgers before the second game of the doubleheader, his owner, Wilbur Post, responds with humor, "What does a horse know about baseball? I know, I know. You played in the Pony League."[96]

Claiming Wilbur's identity, Mr. Ed calls Candlestick Park to share his insights about Skowron with Leo Durocher in the dugout. He leaves his number with Durocher—POplar-91769, an example of the two-letter, five-number telephone exchange that preceded all-number calling. Durocher, in disbelief, changes his mind when he notices that Skowron, indeed, drops his shoulder. When Durocher calls the Post home to offer gratitude—the advice helped the Dodgers win the second game of the doubleheader—he asks Wilbur to visit Dodger Stadium to offer more tips.

Wilbur declines, unfortunately, because of a Palm Springs trip his wife Carol planned with their neighbors, the Addisons. When he confesses that his wife is not a Dodgers fan, so she would not enjoy a trip to the ballpark instead of Palm Springs, Durocher exclaims, "She's not a Dodger fan? That guy's got grounds for divorce."[97]

Mr. Ed tries to trick Wilbur into believing that Palm Springs is soaked with rain, thus unsuitable for a vacation. Wilbur, keen to Mr. Ed's tricks, calls the auto club for a weather forecast and leaves his number. Mr. Ed then calls the Post home from the barn—presumably, the Posts have two lines as Wilbur leaves the same POplar-91769 number with the auto club—disguises himself as an auto club representative when Carol answers, and warns that Palm Springs is enduring flash floods. Wilbur gets a reprieve and heads to Dodger Stadium with Mr. Ed; moments later, Kay Addison informs Carol that the weather in Palm Springs is fine, as the Addisons were listening to a golf championship on the radio.

Wilbur and Mr. Ed concoct a scheme in which Mr. Ed will use sign language to inform Wilbur of insights into the players' bad habits for Durocher. Wilbur will also read Mr. Ed's lips. Willie Davis, John Roseboro, Moose Skowron, and Sandy Koufax make cameo appearances in the episode. Frustrated at Wilbur getting the glory, Mr. Ed grabs a bat and steps into the batter's box. Initially against it, Durocher succumbs when Willie Davis suggests the scenario would make a great publicity shot. The scene is the episode's climax—Mr. Ed's inside-the-park home run against Sandy Koufax during practice, galloping around the bases, and a slide home. Carol, of course, disbelieves Wilbur's story about meeting the Dodgers, only to be shocked when Durocher appears at the Post home to offer Wilbur "some season passes" to Dodger Stadium.[98]

The episode's tag shows Mr. Ed reading the *Los Angeles Chronicle* front page story about the Dodgers clinching the pennant. Mr. Ed inquires, "I can hit and I can run and I can field, right?"

Wilbur responds, "So?"

Mr. Ed inquires, "Do you think the Dodgers would sign me up as a player?"

Wilbur says, "A horse on the Dodgers?"

Mr. Ed reasons, "Oh why not? They already got a moose!"[99]

Beyond television, music venerated the Los Angeles Dodgers. After winning the 1959 World Series against the Chicago White Sox, the Dodgers enjoyed two additions to the roster of songs honoring them—"You Ought to See the Dodgers" and "Dodgers Charge" 1960. Further, Danny Kaye recorded "D-O-D-G-E-R-S Song (Oh, Really? No, O'Malley")" in 1962, offering a play-by-play of a Dodgers-Giants game

The Dodgers belonged to Los Angeles and the Brooklyn Dodgers belonged to history. In 1956, the Dodgers traded Jackie Robinson to the rival Giants, but Robinson retired, never having to wear the dreaded black and orange. In 1958, Roy Campanella struck a telephone pole on a drive home in the middle of the night. Campanella, who emblemized strength, boyishness, and skill, suffered paralysis of his body, but not his spirit. His autobiography is titled *It's Good to Be Alive*. "There is a gallantry about Roy Campanella's *It's Good to Be Alive* that is almost beyond understanding," wrote Charles Poore in his review for the *New York Times*. "But it is the very humanity in these pages that makes us see that he and others who have gone through what he has gone through create the highest standards of the human spirit."[100] Paul Winfield stars as Campanella in the eponymous 1974 TV movie based on the book.

Mela Cassvan, a Brooklynite born on Montague Street, remembers, "I wouldn't trade Brooklyn for any other place. I went from Montague to Hunts Lane to Montague to Atlantic Avenue. My whole life is contained in a five-block radius. After the Dodgers left, it was devastating. I wasn't a baseball fan after that."[101] Lou Silverman, owner of a chain of movie theaters in Pennsylvania and New York state, rooted for the Dodgers even though he grew up in Altoona, Pennsylvania. "My brother and I always liked underdogs. And the Dodgers were bad in some of my formative years. I was born in 1935; my brother, in 1933. We took some trips to Ebbets Field. And we hated to see them leave Brooklyn."[102]

The Brooklyn Dodgers returned to their homeland, in a sense, when four entrepreneurs opened up the Brooklyn Dodger Sports Bar and Restaurant in the late 1980s. The Los Angeles Dodgers and Major League Baseball sued, claiming trademark infringement. David vs. Goliath revised. David won. Judge Constance Baker Motley of the United States District Court for the Southern District of New York ruled that no infringement occurred. "However, at no time during their consideration of the 'Brooklyn Dodger' name did the individual defendants have any reason to believe that 'The Brooklyn Dodger' mark was being used by Los Angeles, and certainly not for restaurant or tavern services."[103]

Destroyed in 1960, Ebbets Field's legacy continues in homages through art, documentaries, films, biographies, non-fiction, fiction, and even real estate. Ebbets Field Estates in Edwardsville, Illinois, stands in the middle of "Cardinals Nation" because of developer Robert Plummer's affinity for the Dodgers. Little Ebbets Field stands in Amesbury, Massachusetts, as a field for wiffle ball games.

When the Dodgers voyaged to Los Angeles in 1958, southern Californians were no less passionate than their "fancestors," those who embraced George Taylor's vision of professional baseball in Brooklyn; crowded both incarnations of Washington Park; basked in Ebbets Field's aura of camaraderie; adored Charles Byrne, Charles Ebbets, and Steve McKeever; rooted for Zack Wheat, suffered through Leo Durocher's suspension; cheered Jackie Robinson's revolution of social change; prostrated from Bobby Thomson's "Shot Heard Round the World"; celebrated the Dodgers' 1955 World Series championship; and mourned the loss of a civic institution.

Still, one edict remains.

You can take the Dodgers out of Brooklyn, but you'll never take Brooklyn out of the Dodgers.

Epilogue:
Vincit Qui Patitur

People ask me what I do in winter when there's no baseball.
I'll tell you what I do. I stare out the window and
wait for spring. —Rogers Hornsby[1]

October 15, 1978. Sunday morning. Springfield, New Jersey.

The night before, I remarked to my mother, "I'm just not interested in the World Series this year. I'm not following it at all." For the third consecutive year, the Yankees were in the World Series. They lost in 1976 to the Cincinnati Reds in four straight games. Facing the Los Angeles Dodgers, the Yankees won the 1977 World Series.

The year 1978 was more of the same to me. Another World Series. Another Dodgers-Yankees matchup. Another season of Phil Rizzuto's exclamations. If he wasn't shouting "Holy Cow!" when a Yankee made a spectacular play, he was shooting another television commercial for The Money Store, an alternative lending institution for people who did not want to deal with traditional banks. Rizzuto's commercials for The Money Store were ubiquitous in the New York City metropolitan area during the 1970s and the 1980s.

Then, the telephone rang. History repeated itself as my father and I received an invitation from a family friend to go to Yankee Stadium that afternoon and see Game 5 of the World Series. My mother had barely conveyed the message when I shouted, "Yes!!!!"

"But you told me you weren't interested in the World Series this year," she said.

"That's different! I didn't know that I could actually go to a World Series game!" I explained, leaving my mother to comprehend, to no avail, the logic of an 11-year-old boy.

My father worked harder than anyone I ever knew. From a home office, he cranked out real estate appraisals like a McDonald's assembly line produces Big Macs. An 80-hour work week was the norm, in addition to a reading diet of five books a week, thanks to his speed-reading ability. When he took a break, which wasn't often, he watched a rerun of a cop show. *Ironside, Dan August,* and *Kojak* were favorites along with whatever John Wayne or Humphrey Bogart offering was on WOR's *Million Dollar Movie.* A World War II buff, he knew every battle in the Pacific and European Theatres. Undoubtedly, he could have passed any requirements for a Ph.D. in history if he had chosen an academic route for his career.

Tired from work, often exhausted, he never complained about the pressure. His mantra was the Latin code for success: *Vincit Qui Patitur.* He conquers who endures.

On this October day, I prayed that neither work nor exhaustion would interfere with this gift from the baseball gods. My father donned his Armor School jacket, a rarely seen accessory from his service in the Army reserves. It made cameo appearances throughout my childhood, usually on Sunday morning journeys to Taylor Park in Millburn, a neighboring town, with me and my sister, Staci. It was a weekly event that I later deduced was a method employed to let my mother rest in a quiet house absent a husband and two kids after being the CEO of the Krell household during the week.

Our journey to Yankee Stadium began at the house of the family friend—Mark Goldman, a self-made businessman who started his career as an accountant. Mark's wife, Connie, and my mother first met when they worked as legal secretaries at the same Newark law firm while my father and Mark were launching their respective careers.

Mark acquired World Series tickets through his company, which owned Sports Phone, a pay-per-call service that thrived in the 1970s and the 1980s, before the Internet commandeered information by the millisecond.

In 1972, someone came to me and my partners with the idea of Sports Phone. "Quicker than the ticker" was the slogan. We were the guy's sales representatives, but he had no money. In less than a month, he left and we took over the business. Information about sports, time, and weather was accessible for a fee that we charged on a per call basis. Gamblers called several times a day during college football weekends.

We promoted the Yankees heavily. I was a Yankee fan from the time I was born. I grew up in Hillside, New Jersey, on Schley Street. One of our neighbors was Phil Rizzuto, who played stickball with us. Yogi Berra was always around, too. I was at Yankee Stadium the night that Reggie Jackson hit three home runs in one game in the 1977 World Series. My brother and I were at the game in

1956 when Mickey Mantle nearly hit a home run out of Yankee Stadium. The ball hit the façade.[2]

At the Goldman house, a limousine awaited us. We piled in with Mark and members of his family. When we got to Yankee Stadium, the crowd engaged in a moment of silence for Junior Gilliam, the 1953 Rookie of the Year and Dodgers coach who passed away a week earlier. Bob Hope threw out the first ball, his celebrity spanning three generations as a result of movies, radio, and NBC television specials that became as identifiable with the network as its peacock logo. When the Yankees took the field after the National Anthem, the crowd erupted with a vocal upsurge containing enough energy to power ConEd for at least three of the city's five boroughs.

Preaching behavioral conservatism like a priest sermonizing on Sunday morning, my father warned me never to aim to be the center of attention and always to be mindful of how comportment matters in public and private. Acts of generosity happened quietly, too; he sought no recognition for benevolence. One example occurred on a family vacation to Miami Beach in the late 1970s. From a couch whose primary days probably occurred during the Kennedy administration, a long-retired prizefighter sold ties, his inventory surrounded by poorly framed photos of himself in his prime with celebrities, including Frank Sinatra.

My father engaged the fighter in about 15 minutes of conversation soaked with nostalgia about great fighters of the 1950s. A couple of times, my father asked the fighter about his strategy against certain opponents. The once legendary pug, now frail with slight tremors, expressed appreciation through his eyes, formerly sad but presently bright because someone took time to show him respect for his accomplishments in the ring. He was, for a moment, not forgotten.

Generosity boosted to a different orbit. My father bought three ties, a shocking development for two reasons: (1) My mother had veto power on all clothes in the Krell household, (2) These ties were beyond ugly. My finger painting projects at the Happy Days Nursery School had better patterns.

"Let's go put these ties in the room. Then, we'll go to the pool," he said.

As we approached the elevators, I needed to demystify what just happened. Before I could launch my inquiry, my father said, "Later, when he's not looking, I'm going to put the ties back."

Quiet no more, the generous tie buyer became a shouting member of the Yankee Stadium denizens. His black, wavy hair had thinned, his face had achieved a roundness resulting from a couple of dozen extra pounds, and his energy had lowered a couple of notches owing to waking before dawn to draft appraisals headed for the redwell folders that lined his home office floor like planes on a runway awaiting the go-ahead signal—each folder bore a typed label marked with the law firm that ordered the appraisal, the address of the property, and the property's owner. "I'm trying to keep all the plates spinning, David," he often said, recalling performers who revolved plates atop poles without letting them hit the ground during performances on *The Ed Sullivan Show*.

The middle-aged man disappeared. In his place, a teenaged boy emerged—the boy who sat among elders at a Dodgers-Yankees World Series game a quarter-century prior, enveloped in Ebbets Field's carnival atmosphere that Don Drysdale described.

Playing catch in the backyard after dinner became a regular occurrence during my Little League years, but mostly, my father's interest in sports reduced to a time-killer requiring scant attention while giving a few moments of recreation from the mundane chores of life. Once in awhile, we'd watch a Yankees game at night on WPIX for a couple of innings, but his tangential interest in present-day sports elevated on that October day to showcase a dimension of enthusiasm that I did not see again and had not seen before.

I cannot remember if he was cheering for the Yankees or the Dodgers, but I'm gambling that it was the former—a testament to the paradigm of doing as the Romans do when you're in Rome. I like to think he also cheered for a World Series memory etched with the sharpness of the knives my mother used to slice brisket for holiday dinners.

Boredom outpaced enthusiasm as the Yankees pummeled the Dodgers with 18 hits leading to a 12–2 victory, a blowout holding as much suspense as an episode of *The Love Boat*. Ross Newhan used a Broadway analogy in the *Los Angeles Times*: "The Dodgers continued to perform Sunday as if they belonged farther off Broadway than the Bronx.

"Even New Haven wouldn't be far enough.

"Taking stock of this company, the Dodgers would seem to belong back in Vero Beach for a cram course in all phases of their art."[3]

Scott Ostler of the *Los Angeles Times* also used a Broadway parallel: "Suffice it to say the Dodgers made the biggest hit on Broadway since King Kong's half-gainer off the Empire State Building."[4]

Ostler quoted the Dodgers' Rick Monday expressing perplexity at the rough-and-tumble world of the Big Apple. "I don't like the park, I don't like the town, I don't understand their way of life here. How can you continuously be rude, profane and hostile? I'm not just talking about this series, I'm talking about this series, I'm talking about five years playing here when I was in the American League."[5]

Monday's "stranger in a strange land" narrative continued, regarding Yankees fans showering the Dodgers with objects along with verbal assaults. "What objects? You name it," Monday said. "Start with the first letter of the alphabet and I'm sure they threw something that starts with that. Did I throw anything back? Why? You think I want to give 'em a second chance?"[6]

The Yankees beat the Dodgers in 1978 for their second consecutive World Series championship; Game 5 is an experience that lasts with the permanence of granite, conquering the inferno of sadness ignited by my father's passing in 1999. Though memories cannot fill his absence entirely, their endurance makes the pain of loss tolerable.

After deciding to start his own real estate appraisal business in the late 1960s, my father bumped into Elmer Schwartz—chairman and founder of Archie Schwartz Company, a commercial and industrial real estate brokerage company on Broad Street in downtown Newark. It was their second meeting. The first took place when my mother introduced my father to Elmer. She knew Elmer from her legal secretary days—he was a client of the firm where she had worked. Elmer told my father, "You always have a desk here." That law firm is also where my father first met my mother; he went there to discuss a business matter with the firm's attorneys.

Upon the second meeting with Elmer—which happened because of fate, if one has a bit of stardust in the eyes—my father took him up on his offer. The kinship born from that meeting lasted 30 years. Carl Krell was the only non-broker in the offices of Archie Schwartz Company, which had moved to East Orange around 1970. But he had a desk, a secretary to answer the phone and take messages, and, when he wasn't writing appraisals in his home office, a place to both gather and give information about real estate. Always enlightening but never condescending, my father vocalized insights about history, current events, and everyday life, in addition to real estate. Elmer proudly dubbed him "a certified genius." And my father never forgot Elmer's generosity.

In the late 1980s, he joined dozens of other real estate professionals for a testimonial honoring Elmer Schwartz, who proved invaluable to their careers, especially my father's.

The testimonial was a night of laughter as people rose to excavate stories—some long forgotten—about Elmer's powerful influence on their careers, psyches, and personal lives. The master of ceremonies bestowed the label "our resident historian" on my father, who described Elmer as a parallel to Vince Lombardi, the legendary coach of the Green Bay Packers dynasty in the 1960s.

> He set the example, in terms of leadership, in terms of hard work, in terms of there's no easy way to do it. A lot of us really owe whatever we are today to him. He took an amorphous mass, which all of us were. Winning is what it's all about and that's the most important thing that he taught us. There is no substitute for winning. Second place is ridiculous. Losing is ridiculous. Losing with grace is stupid. There is no substitute for winning and for victory.
>
> And the most important lesson, I think, that he taught us is that you're going to bounce back. If you make a deal that fouls up, if you do an appraisal that fouls up, you lose a case, whatever it is. In life, the ability to bounce back is really critical. He took that amorphous mass of people, some of whom I knew, and really he made us into what we are.
>
> A lot of people couldn't stand the test. And a lot of people aren't here tonight. It was a crucible. The people that lasted, they became something. The people that couldn't take the heat, what happened was they fell by the wayside, which is as it should be. But I think the people who are here tonight, who worked for him or who worked with him, all owe him a standing ovation for making them what they are today. And I'd like to lead that applause.[7]

Vincit qui patitur.

If I could resurrect my father, even for only 15 minutes, I would grab two gloves and a baseball, implore him for another catch in the backyard, and ask him to tell me, once again, about the time he saw Mickey Mantle hit a grand slam in the 1953 World Series.

Chapter Notes

Prologue

1. John Drebinger, "Yankees' 4 Homes Beat Dodgers, 11–7 for 3–2 Series Edge," *New York Times*, October 5, 1953.
2. Red Smith, "Views of Sport: Tale of One Pitch," *New York Herald Tribune*, October 5, 1953.
3. Leonard Lewin, "Told Mantle to 'Punch' to Left—Case; Brooks 2d-Guess Brooks," *New York Daily Mirror*, October 5, 1953.
4. Roscoe McGowen, "Mantle Connected on Meyer's 'Best Pitch,' Unhappy Brooklyn Hurler Says," *New York Times*, October 5, 1953.
5. Carl Erskine, Telephone Interview with author, November 3, 2014.
6. Rud Rennie, "Mantle Hit Grand Slam with 'Frozen' Hand, Leg," *New York Herald Tribune*, October 5, 1953.
7. Linda Forgosh, *Jews of Weequahic*, Images of America (Charleston: Arcadia Publishing), 8.
8. Joseph Lilly, "Assorted Metropolitan Crowds: Ebbets Field Baseball Fans Rabid Rooters and Caustic Critics," pt. 3, *New York World-Telegram*, July 7, 1932.

1st Inning

1. Leo Durocher with Ed Linn, *Nice Guys Finish Last* (New York: Simon & Schuster, 1975), 285–286.
2. Don Drysdale with Bob Verdi, *Once a Bum, Always a Dodger: My Life in Baseball from Brooklyn to Los Angeles* (New York: St. Martin's Press, 1990), 8.
3. Sandy Koufax with Ed Linn (New York: Viking Press, 1966), 122.
4. Nicholas Kostis, telephone interview with author, April 21, 2013.

5. Joshua Prager, "Was the '51 Giants Comeback a Miracle, or Did They Simply Steal the Pennant?" *The Wall Street Journal*, January 31, 2001, http://www.wsj.com/articles/SB980896446829227925.
6. Joshua Prager, *The Echoing Green* (New York: Pantheon Books, 2006), 340.
7. Ian O'Connor, "Branca-Thomson Bond as Strong as in '51," *USA Today*, September 28, 2001, http://usatoday30.usatoday.com/sports/baseball/stories/2001-09-28-shot.htm.
8. Marty Adler, telephone interview with author, June 27, 2011.
9. David Krell, "Stealing Home: Major League Baseball Properties, Inc. v. Sed Non Olet Denarius, Ltd. and the Glory, Heartbreak, and Nostalgia of the Brooklyn Dodgers," *New York State Bar Association's Entertainment, Arts, and Sports Law Journal* 22, no. 1 (Spring 2011): 197–198 quoting Telephone Interview with David Krell, January 4, 2011.
10. Don Drysdale, *Once a Bum*, 79.
11. http://www.youtube.com/watch?v=xQs0S_a-KvA.
12. David Krell, "Stealing Home," 198.
13. Arnie Korfine, telephone interview with author, December 30, 2013.
14. Arthur Ritz, telephone Interview with author, December 6, 2011.
15. David Krell, "Stealing Home," 197.
16. David Krell, "Stealing Home," 196.
17. Ron Schweiger, telephone interview with author, June 14, 2011.
18. David Ritz, *The Man Who Brought the Dodgers Back to Brooklyn* (New York: Simon and Schuster, 1981), 174–175.
19. *Ibid.* at 188.
20. Ed Fitzgerald, ed., *Sport Magazine's Book of Major League Baseball Clubs: The National League* (New York: Grosset & Dunlap Publishers, 1955), 6.
21. *Ibid.*

2nd Inning

1. Duke Snider with Bill Gilbert, *The Duke of Flatbush* (New York: Zebra Books, 1988), 64.

2. Charles H. Ebbets, Thomas S. Rice, ed., "History of Baseball in Brooklyn," Chapter 7, *Brooklyn Daily Eagle*, January 18, 1913.

3. Ronald G. Shafer, *When the Dodgers Were Bridegrooms: Gunner McGunnigle and Brooklyn's Back-to-Back Pennants of 1889 and 1890* (Jefferson, NC: McFarland, 2011), 7.

4. *Ibid.*

5. *Ibid.* at 10.

6. "The Yale Nine Defeats the Alaskas of Brooklyn—Other Games," *New York Times*, May 10, 1883.

7. Sports and Pastimes: Baseball, *Brooklyn Daily Eagle*, May 10, 1883.

8. *Ibid.*

9. "Brooklyn at the Bat: Defeating the Trenton Team on the New Baseball Grounds," *Brooklyn Daily Eagle*, May 13, 1883.

10. Frank Graham, *The Brooklyn Dodgers: An Informal History*, Writing Baseball series ed. (Carbondale and Edwardsville, Illinois: Southern Illionis University Press, 2002), Facsimile of 1st ed. (New York: G.P. Putman's Sons), 6–7.

11. "Ebbets Dead; Was Victim of Heart Disease," *Brooklyn Daily Eagle*, April 18, 1925.

12. *Ibid.*, 7.

13. http://www.milb.com/content/page.jsp?sid=t547&ymd=20081210&content_id=486270&vkey=team2.

14. Ronald G. Shafer, *When the Dodgers Were Bridegrooms*, 60–61.

15. *Ibid.*, 61.

16. *Ibid.*

17. *Ibid.*

18. "Bothered About the Mets: Day Says They Have Forfeited New-York," *New York Times*, March 8, 1888.

19. *Ibid.*

20. "Met Defeat," *Brooklyn Daily Eagle*, April 6, 1888.

21. *The Sporting Life* April 11, 1888.

22. Bob McGee, *The Greatest Ballpark Ever: Ebbets Field and the Story of the Brooklyn Dodgers* (New Brunswick, New Jersey: Rivergate Books, An imprint of Rutgers University Press, 2005), Third paperback printing, 30.

23. *Ibid.*

24. "Charles H. Byrne," *Brooklyn Daily Eagle*, January 5, 1898.

25. *Ibid.*, 33.

26. Bob McGee, *The Greatest Ballpark Ever*, 34.

27. "It Is a Real Estate Speculation: G.W. Chauncey Explains the Motive Behind Consolidation Plans," *Brooklyn Daily Eagle*, March 15, 1893.

28. "Greater New York" in *The Brooklyn Daily Eagle Almanac*, 135, reprinted at http://books.google.com/books?id=acEWAAAAY AAJ&printsec=frontcover&source=gbs_ge_summary_r&cad=0#v=onepage&q&f=false.

29. *Ibid.*

30. *Ibid.*

31. *Ibid.*

32. *Ibid.*

33. *Ibid.*

34. *Ibid.*

35. *Ibid.*

36. "Brooklyn or New York East?: Another Assortment of Opinions in the Eagle's Canvass," *Brooklyn Daily Eagle*, May 22, 1897.

37. "Brooklyn's Last Days," *Brooklyn Daily Eagle*, October 19, 1897.

38. "Annexation of Brooklyn to New York!," *Brooklyn Daily Eagle*, August 25, 1845.

39. "Farewell to City, Hail to Borough: Brooklyn Citizens of Every Class Attend the Observance," *Brooklyn Daily Eagle*, January 2, 1898.

40. Burt Solomon, *Where They Ain't: The Fabled Life and Untimely Death of the Original Baltimore Orioles, the Team That Gave Birth to Modern Baseball* (New York: Doubleday, 1999), 40.

41. Bob McGee, *The Greatest Ballpark Ever*, 36–37.

42. "Hanlon Reads Ebbets Out of the Management: Springs a Surprise on the Party in Power in the Brooklyn Baseball Club," *Brooklyn Daily Eagle*, November 13, 1906, citing Corporation Act of New Jersey.

43. *Ibid.* "If such report be not so made and filed, all of the directors of any such corporation, who shall willfully refuse to comply with the provisions hereof, and who shall be in office during the default, shall, at the time appointed for the next annual election and for a period of one year thereafter, be thereby rendered ineligible for election, or appointment, to any office in the company, as directors, or otherwise." *Ibid.*, quoting Corporation Act of New Jersey.

44. "Brooklyn Loses Another Game, but Wins a Legal Point," *Brooklyn Daily Eagle*, April 30, 1907.

45. Burt Solomon, *Where They Ain't*, 252.
46. "His Faith in the Baseball Patron Has Carried Him to the Top of the Heap," *New York Times*, January 21, 1912.
47. Ed Fitzgerald, ed., *Sport Magazine's Book of Major League Baseball Clubs*, 14–15.
48. "Chas. H. Ebbets, Brooklyn Ball Club Head, Dies: Succumbs to Heart Disease While Asleep in Waldorf Suite; Ill There Since Return from South," *New York Herald Tribune*.
49. "His Faith in the Baseball Patron Has Carried Him to the Top of the Heap," *New York Times*, January 21, 1912).
50. *Ibid.*
51. "Why I Am Building a Baseball Stadium," *Leslie's Weekly*, April 4, 1912.
52. Frederick Boyd Stevenson, "Ebbets, for 38 Years in Baseball, Tells of the Great American Game," *Brooklyn Daily Eagle*, October 3, 1920.
53. Arthur Daley, "Sports of the Times," *New York Times*, August 19, 1955.
54. "Dirt Flies in New Brooklyn Ball Park: President Ebbets Turns the First Spadeful and Borough President Speers Makes Speech," *New York Times*, March 5, 1912.
55. Ed Fitzgerald, ed., *Sport Magazine's Book of Major League Baseball Clubs*, 19.
56. *Ibid.*

3rd Inning

1. Brooklyn National League Baseball Club, Newspaper Advertisement, 1936.
2. "Crowded Ball Park Mars Opening Game: Mayor Gaynor, in Crush at Washington Park, Orders Out City Police," *New York Times*, April 12, 1912.
3. http://losangeles.dodgers.mlb.com/la/history/year_by_year_results.jsp.
4. Lyle Spatz and Steve Steinberg, *1921: The Yankees, the Giants, & the Battle for Baseball Supremacy in New York* (Lincoln and London, Nebraska: University of Nebraska Press, 2010), 109.
5. Jack Kavanagh & Norman Macht, *Uncle Robbie* (Cleveland: Society for American Baseball Research, 1999), 59.
6. http://www.baseball-reference.com/players/d/dahlebi01.shtml.
7. "Baseball Axe Cuts off Bill Dahlen: Deposed as Manager of the Brooklyn Team After Four Years," *New York Tribune*, November 18, 1913.
8. http://www.baseball-reference.com/players/d/daubeja01.shtml.
9. Jack Kavanagh & Norman Macht, *Uncle Robbie*, 73.
10. Harold Rosenthal, "Old Legend Out with Dodgers—Casey Didn't Drop Grapefruit: Woman Flyer Forgot to Bring Baseball, Tossed Substitute," *New York Herald Tribune*, December 4, 1957.
11. Jack Kavanagh & Norman Macht, *Uncle Robbie*, 74.
12. Harold Rosenthal, "Old Legend Out with Dodgers—Casey Didn't Drop Grapefruit: Woman Flyer Forgot to Bring Baseball, Tossed Substitute," *New York Herald Tribune*, December 4, 1957.
13. "Ray Chapman Dies; Mays Exonerated," *New York Times*, August 18, 1920.
14. Lyle Spats and Steve Steinberg, *1921*, 81.
15. Thomas S. Rice, "Superbas in 26 Inning Tie," *Brooklyn Daily Eagle*, May 2, 1920.
16. "Baseball Leaders Won't Let White Sox Return to the Game," *New York Times*, August 4, 1921.
17. http://www.baseball-almanac.com/legendary/lispit.shtml.
18. http://baseballhall.org/hof/grimes-burleigh.
19. Joe Niese, *Burleigh Grimes: Baseball's Last Legal Spitballer* (Jefferson, North Carolina: McFarland & Company, Inc., 2013), 72, citing Interview with Charles Clark, Clear Lake, WI, August 14, 2011.
20. *Ibid.*, 66.
21. "Ebbets Relapses; Condition Critical: Son and Daughter of Brooklyn Baseball President Called to Bedside at Waldorf," *New York Times*, April 18, 1925.
22. "Chas. H. Ebbets, Brooklyn Baseball Club Head, Dies: Succumbs to Heart Disease While Asleep in Waldorf Suite; Ill There Since Return from South," *New York Herald Tribune*, April 19, 1925.
23. *Ibid.*
24. "C.H. Ebbets Dies of Heart Disease: Confined to Room Since Return from Brooklyn Camp 2 Weeks Ago," *New York Times*, April 19, 1925.
25. *Ibid.*
26. "The Death of Charles H. Ebbets," *The Reach Official American League Guide*, 1926.
27. "Giants Beat Robins Before 25,000 by 7–1: Capture the Opening Game of Series as Hostile Fans Jeer at Ebbets Field," *New York Times*, April 19, 1925.

28. "Tuesday Games Off in National League: Contests Are Postponed by Heydler on Day of Funeral of Charles H. Ebbets," *New York Times*, April 19, 1925.

29. "Organized Baseball Pays Tribute to Charles H. Ebbets, *New York Herald Tribune*, April 22, 1925.

30. *Ibid.*

31. "Thousands at Rites for Chas. H. Ebbets: Throngs Line the Streets as Funeral Cortege Passes and Overflow the Church," *New York Times*, April 22, 1925.

32. http://losangeles.dodgers.mlb.com/la/history/owners.jsp.

33. Uncredited Press Release, *Wilbert Robinson—Newly Elected President of the Brooklyn Ball Club*, June 14, 1925.

34. *Ibid.*

35. http://www.baseball-reference.com/players/w/wheatza01.shtml.

36. F.C. Lane, "Razzing Uncle Robbie: Wilbert Robinson Isn't Inclined to Worry and His Philosophy of Life Has Inured Him to Hard Knocks. This is Fortunate for Robbie Has Encountered Enough Unmerited Abuse This Spring to Sour the Most Genial Disposition," *Baseball*, September, 1931, 437.

37. Thomas Holmes, "Brooklyn Baseball Club Will Officially Nickname Them 'Dodgers:' Ebbets Field Leaves It to Writers, Who Choose Old 'Handle,' *Brooklyn Daily Eagle*, January 23, 1932.

38. *Ibid.*

39. "Many Tributes Paid as Widespread Grief Is Voiced Over Death of Former Manager of the Dodgers—Directors of Brooklyn Club Adopt Resolution of Confidence," *New York Times*, August 10, 1934.

40. *Ibid.*

41. *Ibid.*

42. Damon Runyon, "The Mornin's Mornin," *New York American*, September 19, 1915.

43. http://www.baseball-reference.com/minors/player.cgi?id=hanley001t—

44. Damon Runyon, "The Mornin's Mornin," *New York American*, September 19, 1915.

45. *Ibid.*

46. Rud Rennie, "Terry Predicts Giants Finish Among First 3: Declares Pirates, Cards and Cubs Are the Teams to Beat; Schumacher Signs," *New York Herald Tribune*, January 25, 1934.

47. http://www.baseball-reference.com/players/s/stengca01.shtml

48. "Ebbets Had to Bid High for Stengel," *The New York Times*, January 26, 1915.

49. "When More Dodgers Are on Third Than on the Bench Someone's Bound to Score, Declares Casey Stengel," *New York World-Telegram*, October 2, 1934.

50. *Ibid.*

51. *Sports Interview*, #79, Rebroadcast, Armed Forces Radio Service.

52. John Lardner, "What About It?," *Boston Globe*, May 14, 1936.

53. Brooklyn National League Baseball Club, Newspaper Advertisement, 1936.

54. "Judge M'Keever, Dodger Chief, Dies," *Brooklyn Daily Eagle*, March 7, 1938.

55. *Ibid.*

56. Robert Lewis Taylor, "Borough Defender-Part 1," *New Yorker*, July 12, 1941, 20.

57. *Ibid.*

58. "1 Slain, Diamond's Son Shot in Barroom Row," *Brooklyn Daily Eagle*, July 13, 1938.

59. *Ibid.*

60. *Ibid.*

61. *Ibid.*

62. *Ibid.*

63. *Ibid.*

64. *Ibid.*

65. Arthur Ritz, telephone interview with author, December, 6, 2011.

66. Roscoe McGowen, "Fan Fells Umpire in Fist Fight After Dodgers Lose to Reds, 4–3," *New York Times*, September 17, 1940.

67. *Ibid.*

68. "Draftee Rooter to See Series If Flock Wins," *New York Journal-American*, September 19, 1941.

69. *Ibid.*

70. http://www.usar.army.mil/ourstory/History/Documents/Chiefs%20of%20the%20Army%20Reserve.pdf.

71. Al Sharp, "'It's Wonderful What Dem Bums Will Do for a Guy!," *The Atlanta Constitution*, September 27, 1941.

72. "Aurora Borealis Gives City a Show as Sun Spots Disorganize Radio," *New York Times*, September 19, 1941.

73. Robert Lewis Taylor, "Borough Defender-Part 2," *The New Yorker*, July 19, 1941, 30.

74. Letter from Major League Baseball Commissioner Kenesaw Mountain Landis, 14 January 1942 to President Franklin Delano Roosevelt.

75. Letter from President Franklin Delano Roosevelt, 15 January 1942, to Major League Baseball Commissioner Kenesaw Mountain Landis.

76. "Baseball Owners, Lampooned at Writers Dinner, Forget Troubles Temporarily," *New York Times*, February 2, 1942.

77. *Ibid.*, Frank Graham, *The Brooklyn Dodgers*, 216.

78. Graham, 216–217.

79. *Ibid.*, 229.

80. Robert Lewis Taylor, "Borough Defender-Part 1," *The New Yorker*, July 12, 1941, 20.

81. Graham, 230.

82. Roscoe McGowen, "Dodgers Down Braves in 11th and Keep Alive Faint Hope of Staying in Race," *New York Times*, September 26, 1942.

4th Inning

1. Arthur Daley, "Opening Day at Ebbets Field," *Sports of the Times*, *New York Times*, April 16, 1947.

2. "Rickey Genius Lifts Cards from Doldrums to Pinnacle: Ohioan Creates 'Chain Store' System That Sends Constant Stream of Talent to St. Louis," *Cleveland Plain Dealer*, February 14, 1932.

3. Agreement for services as General Manager of Brooklyn National League Baseball Club, Inc. and of Ebbets-McKeever Exhibition Company, Inc., signed by Branch Rickey and Joseph A. Gilleaudeau, Vice President, Brooklyn National League Baseball Club, Inc., October 28, 1942, Branch Rickey Papers, Box 33, Folder 10, Baseball File, Brooklyn Dodgers, Contracts of Rickey, 1942, 1948, Library of Congress.

4. Harold Parrott, "Meet Mr. Rickey: 'The Brain' Is Perfect Frame for Brooklyn Baseball Scene," First in a series of five articles about Branch Rickey, *Brooklyn Daily Eagle*, October 30, 1942.

5. Harold Parrott, "Rickey Is Real Cutie as a Trader: 'You Outsmart Branch If You Keep Your Watch!' Says Stengel," Fifth in a series of five articles about Branch Rickey, *Brooklyn Daily Eagle*, November 3, 1942.

6. Barrett Branch Rickey, telephone interview with author, January 4, 2012.

7. George Howard Williams to Alice Rickey, 23 September 1918, George Howard Williams Papers, Box 10, Folder 1, Missouri History Museum.

8. J. Roy Stockton, *The Gashouse Gang and a Couple of Other Guys*, 6th Printing (New York: A.S. Barnes & Company, November 1947; 1945), 20.

9. Edward Seckler, in discussion with author, December 29, 2011.

10. Branch Rickey to Sue Rickey, 3 January 1938, Branch Rickey Papers, Box 1, Folder 1, Family Papers, Correspondence, Adams, Sue Rickey and Steve, 1938–1951, Library of Congress.

11. *Ibid.*

12. Los Angeles Dodgers, http://losangeles.dodgers.mlb.com/la/history/walter_omalley.jsp

13. *Ibid.*

14. "Powell Suspended for Radio Remark: Landis Imposes Ten-Day Ban on Yankee Player After Protest by Negroes," *New York Times*, July 31, 1938.

15. *Ibid.*

16. Chris Lamb, "Public Slur in 1938 Laid Bare a Game's Racism," July 27, 2008.

17. "Bias Bill Assailed by State Chamber: Ives-Quinn Measure Seen as Incitement to Race Riots and Intolerant Groups," *New York Times*, February 12, 1945.

18. "Bias Bill Assailed by State Chamber," *New York Times*, February 12, 1945.

19. Leo Egan, "Anti-Racial Bill Signed by Dewey: It Sets Up a Special Commission to Deal with Discrimination in Employment," *New York Times*, March 13, 1945.

20. Barrett Branch Rickey, telephone interview with author, January 4, 2012.

21. Kevin Bender, Dana Atchley, Interview with Red Barber, *Baseball's Voices of Summer* (1989; Balltalk Productions: 2007), DVD.

22. Arthur Mann, *Branch Rickey: American in Action* (Boston: Houghton Mifflin Company, Cambridge: The Riverside Press, 1957), 219–220.

23. Clyde Sukeforth, telephone interview with Jim Kreuz, November 28, 1993, Jim Kreuz, "Tom Greenwade," http://sabr.org/bioproj/person/9fb19ce0.

24. Jim Kreuz, "Tom Greenwade," http://sabr.org/bioproj/person/9fb19ce0.

25. John Thorn and Jules Tygiel, "The Signing of Jackie Robinson: The Untold Story," *Sport*, June 1988, 69.

26. Branch Rickey to Arthur Mann, 7 October 1945, Arthur Mann Papers, Box 1, Folder 1, General Correspondence, 1901 May 8 – 1946 Dec. 27, Library of Congress.

27. Arthur Mann to Christopher LaFarge, 6 April 1946, Branch Rickey Papers, Box 18,

Folder 5, Correspondence, Mann, Arthur, 1942–1949, Library of Congress.

28. Branch Rickey to Arthur Mann, 12 April 1946, Branch Rickey Papers, Box 18, Folder 5, Correspondence, Mann, Arthur, 1942–1949, Library of Congress.

29. "Negro Ball Prexy, Frick May Confer," *Brooklyn Daily Eagle*, October 27, 1945.

30. Michael Gaven, "Monarchs Protest Loss of Robinson," *New York Journal-American*, October 24, 1945.

31. *Ibid.*

32. *Ibid.*

33. "Closer Relations Between Big Leagues, Negroes Seen as Robinson Sequel," *Brooklyn Daily Eagle*, October 25, 1945.

34. Milt Smith, "Robinson Confident He'll Make Dodgers," *Brooklyn Daily Eagle*, October 25, 1945.

35. *Ibid.*

36. "Montreal Signs Negro Shortstop: Robinson Joins Dodger Farm from Kansas City Monarchs to Establish a Precedent," *New York Times*, October 24, 1945.

37. Dan Burley, "Bklyn Dodgers Hire Negro Star: Color Line in Baseball Crumbles as Shortsop Jackie Robinson Signs," *New York Amsterdam News*, October 27, 1945.

38. Jackie Robinson to Branch Rickey, 13 July 1946, Branch Rickey Papers, Box 24, Folder 12, Correspondence, Robinson, Jackie, 1945–49, Library of Congress.

39. Roger Kahn, *Lines on the Transpontine Madness*, Foreword to *The Boys of Summer* (New York: Harper Perennial Modern Classics 2006; repr., New York: Harper & Row Publishers, Inc., 1972), xvii. Citations refer to the Harper Perennial edition. *The Boys of Summer* was published in March 1972, though magazine excerpts appeared in 1971." Roger Kahn, in discussion with author (December 28, 2010).

40. Interview with Rachel Robinson, National Visionary Leadership Project, http://www.youtube.com/watch?v=SJcTuIS6fUk&feature=related.

41. "Negroes in The Majors," *Atlanta Daily Journal*, October 28, 1945.

42. Fay Young, "End of Baseball's Jim Crow Seen with Signing of Jackie Robinson," *The Chicago Defender*, November 3, 1945.

43. "A Crack in Baseball Jim Crow," *New York Amsterdam News*, November 3, 1945.

44. Wendell Smith, "Rickey Tells Courier Why He Signed Jackie Robinson: Major League Owner Sees Nothing Unusual in Sign-ing Robinson, *The Pittsburgh Courier*, November 3, 1945.

45. Memorandum of Conversation Between Mr. Rickey and Mr. Sukeforth, Monday, January 16, 1950, Arthur Mann Papers, Box 4, Folder 2, Subject File, Memorandum of Conversation Between Branch Rickey and Mr. Sukeforth, 1950 Jan. 16, Library of Congress.

46. *Ibid.*

47. Marilyn Kaemmerle, "Lincoln's Job Half-Done…," *The Flat Hat*, College of William and Mary, Williamsburg, Virginia, February 7, 1945.

48. Richard Stradling, "At W&M, The Column Before The Storm: Student's Editorial Created Stir in '45," *Daily Press*, http://articles.dailypress.com/1995-02-20/news/9502200073_1_student-editorial-william-and-mary-college-s-student-newspaper.

49. *Ibid.*

50. *The Ghosts of Flatbush*, HBO, July 11, 2007.

51. Gerald Stern, telephone interview with author, January 6, 2012.

52. *Ibid.*

53. Hunter Atkins, "Rabbi Expands Tributes to Robinson Beyond the Major Leagues," *New York Times*, April 15, 2013.

54. Memorandum of Conversation Between Mr. Rickey and Mr. Sukeforth, Monday, January 16, 1950.

55. Arnold Rampersad, *Jackie Robinson: A Biography* (New York: Alfred A. Knopf, 1997), 164.

56. Carl T. Rowan with Jackie Robinson, *Wait Till Next Year: The Life Story of Jackie Robinson* (New York: Random House, 1960), 175.

57. Harold Parrott, *The Lords of Baseball*, 260.

58. Leo Durocher with Ed Linn, *Nice Guys Finish Last*, 203–205.

59. Carl T. Rowan with Jackie Robinson, *Wait Till Next Year*, 176.

60. Harold C. Burr, "Brooklyn's Man of the Week: Dixie Walker's More than Man-of-Week to Brooklyn," *Brooklyn Daily Eagle*, July 7, 1946.

61. "'Not Worried About Robinson, He's Not with Us'—Walker," *Brooklyn Daily Eagle*, October 24, 1945.

62. Memorandum of Conversation Between Mr. Rickey and Mrs. Sukeforth, Monday, January 16, 1950.

63. Ira Berkow, "Sports of the Times: Dixie Walker Remembers," *New York Times*, December 10, 1981.

64. *Ibid.*

65. Roger Kahn, *The Era: 1947–1957, When the Yankees, the Giants, and the Dodgers Ruled the World* with a new afterword by the author (Lincoln and London, Nebraska: University of Nebraska Press, 2002; repr., New York: Houghton Mifflin, 1993), 35, fn. 2. Citations refer to the University of Nebraska edition.

66. Arthur Daley, "Sports of the Times: Exit for the Peepul's Cherce," *New York Times*, December 10, 1947.

67. Ira Berkow, "Sports of the Times: Dixie Walker Remembers," *New York Times*, December 10, 1981.

68. Louis Effrat, "Dodgers Purchase Robinson, First Negro in Modern Major League Baseball," *New York Times*, April 11, 1947.

5th Inning

1. Pee Wee Reese with Tim Cohane, "14 Years a Bum...," *Look*, March 9, 1954.

2. Louis Effrat, "Chandler Bars Durocher for 1947 Baseball Season, *New York Times*, April 10, 1947.

3. John Drebinger, "Dressen Top Aide to Bombers' Pilot," *New York Times*, November 6, 1946.

4. "Durocher Had Bid to Pilot Yankees," *New York Times*, November 17, 1946.

5. Roscoe McGowen, "Durocher Signs with Dodgers for Year as Highest Paid Pilot in Baseball," *New York Times*, November 26, 1946.

6. *Ibid.*

7. "MacPhail Claims Signing of Harris Was Delayed as Favor to Durocher," *New York Times*, November 27, 1947.

8. *Ibid.*, 52.

9. "Catholics Quit Dodgers Knothole Club in Protest Over the Conduct of Durocher," *New York Times*, March 1, 1947.

10. Mann, *Baseball Confidential, Baseball Confidential: Secret History of the War Among Chandler, Durocher, MacPhail and Rickey* (New York: David McKay Company, Inc., 1951), 74.

11. Arthur Mann, *Baseball Confidential*, 39.

12. Leo Durocher, "Durocher Says," *Brooklyn Daily Eagle*, March 3, 1947.

13. Harold C. Burr, "Ban Durocher 1 Year: Dressen Also Out 30 Days," *Brooklyn Daily Eagle*, April 9, 1947.

14. Arthur Mann, *Baseball Confidential*, 100.

15. Louis Effrat, "Chandler Bars Durocher for 1947 Baseball Season," *New York Times*, April 10, 1947.

16. Arthur Daley, "Sports of the Times: Chandler Flexes His Muscles," *New York Times*, April 10, 1947.

17. Tommy Holmes, "Three Iimpressions of Leo's Farewell," *Brooklyn Daily Eagle*, April 11, 1947.

18. "Dodger Fans Howl Blue Murder at News of Lippy's Suspension," *Brooklyn Daily Eagle*, April 9, 1947.

19. "Leo Durocher Held in Assault on Critical Fan at Ebbets Field," *New York Herald Tribune*, June 11, 1945.

20. "Durocher Wins Jury's Verdict in 38 Minutes," *New York Herald Tribune*, April 26, 1946.

21. *Ibid.*

22. *Ibid.*

23. *Ibid.*

24. Rud Rennie, "Chandler Suspends Durocher and Calls Hearing for Tuesday," *New York Herald Tribune*, April 30, 1949.

25. *Ibid.*

26. Walter White, "People, Politics and Places, *The Chicago Defender*, April 26, 1947.

27. "Let's Restrain Ourselves!," *The Pittsburgh Courier*, April 26, 1947.

28. Wendell Smith, "Fans Swamp Jackie; Public Affairs Out," *The Pittsburgh Courier*, April 26, 1947.

29. "Baseball's Color Bar Broken," *Christian Century*, April 23, 1947.

30. http://www.baseball-reference.com/players/w/walkefl01.shtml.

31. http://mlb.mlb.com/mlb/history/mlb_negro_leagues_profile.jsp?player=walker_fleetwood.

32. Nat Trammell, *Colored Baseball & Sports Monthly*, Volume 1, Number 1, September 1934.

33. William Hageman, "Chicago's 55-year-old secret: Jackie Robinson's tryout with the White Sox," *Chicago Tribune*, March 26, 1997.

34. Jerome Holtzman, "How Wendell Smith Helped Robinson's Cause, *The Chicago Tribune*, http://articles.chicagotribune.com/1997–03–31/sports/9703310169_1_clyde-sukeforth-jackie-robinson-kansas-city-monarchs, March 31, 1997.

35. Wendell Smith to Edward Collins, 27 April 1945. Wendell Smith Papers, National Baseball Hall of Fame and Museum, Box 1, Folder 5, Clippings, Correspondence, BL-5302.97.

36. Edward T. Collins to Wendell Smith, May 11, 1945. Wendell Smith Papers, National Baseball Hall of Fame and Museum, Box 1, Folder 5, Clippings, Correspondence, BL-5302.97.

37. Jack Robinson to Wendell Smith, October 31, 1945, Wendell Smith Papers, National Baseball Hall of Fame and Museum, Box 1, Folder 5, Clippings, Correspondence, BL-5302.97.

38. Wendell Smith to Branch Rickey, November 27, 1946, Wendell Smith Papers, National Baseball Hall of Fame and Museum, Box 1, Folder 2, Correspondence, 1945–1949, BL-5302.97.

39. *Ibid.*

40. *The Ghosts of Flatbush*, HBO, 2007.

41. Carl T. Rowan with Jackie Robinson, *Wait Till Next Year*, 183.

42. Jackie Robinson as told to Alfred Duckett, *I Never Had It Made* (New York: G. P. Putnam's Sons, 1972; repr., HarperCollins Publishers, 1995), 60. Citations refer to the HarperCollins edition.

43. Harold Parrott, *the Lords of Baseball*, 268.

44. Dan Parker, "U.S. Soccer Attendance Mark About to Be Broken," *New York Daily Mirror*, April 27, 1947.

45. Jackie Robinson as told to Alfred Duckett, *I Never Had It Made*, 62.

46. Jackie Robinson as told to Wendell Smith, *Jackie Robinson: My Own Story* (Whitefish, Montana: Kessinger Legacy Reprints, 2007), Facsimile of 1st ed. (New York: Greenberg, 1948), 128. Citations refer to Kessinger edition.

47. Jackie Robinson, "Jackie Robinson Says;," *The Pittsburgh Courier*, May 3, 1947.

48. Jackie Robinson, "Jackie Robinson Says;," *The Pittsburgh Courier*, May 17, 1947.

49. Wendell Smith, "'Stop Race Baiting'—Chandler," *The Pittsburgh Courier*, May 10, 1947.

50. *Ibid.*

51. Stanley Woodward, "National League Averts Strike of Cardinals Against Robinson's Presence in Baseball," *New York Herald Tribune*, May 9, 1947.

52. *Ibid.*

53. Peter Golenbock, *The Spirit of St. Louis: A History of the St. Louis Cardinals and Browns*, 1st ed. (New York: Spike, 2000), Paperback ed. (New York: It Books, 2001), 382. Citations refer to the It Books edition.

54. *Ibid.*

55. Bill Roeder, *Jackie Robinson*, 137.

56. *What's My Line*, Syndicated, November 20, 1969.

57. *Ibid.*

58. "Vintage WGN interview: Branch Rickey tells Brickhouse he deserves no credit," http://wgntv.com/2013/04/15/branch-rickey-i-deserve-no-credit-for-jackie-robinson/.

59. "Big" Ed Stevens, *The Other Side of Jackie Robinson* (Mustang, Oklahoma: Tate Publishing & Enterprises, LLC, 2009), 47.

60. Marty Adler, telephone interview with author, June 27, 2011.

61. Dave Anderson, *A Flame Grew in Brooklyn*, *New York Times*, December 5, 1971, S5.

62. Bill Roeder, *Jackie Robinson*, Most Valuable Player Series (New York: A.S. Barnes and Company, 1950), 138.

63. Roscoe McGowen, "He's Biggest 'Little Man' of Majors," *The Sporting News*, December 26, 1956.

64. Wendell Smith, "Noticeable Change in the Team," The Sports Beat, *The Pittsburgh Courier*, June 28, 1947.

65. William Nack, "Dodgertown," *Sports Illustrated*, March 14, 1983, 52.

66. Kahn, *The Era*, 127.

67. http://www.baseball-reference.com/players/g/gionfal01.shtml.

68. *The Ghosts of Flatbush*, HBO, July 11, 2007.

69. Red Smith, "Views of Sport: Casey Didn't Say Anything," *New York Herald Tribune*, September 9, 1949.

70. *Ibid.*

71. "Reese Thumbed Out of 1,000th Tilt," *Brooklyn Eagle*, May 5, 1950.

72. "John Galbreath, 90, a Sportsman and Real Estate Developer, Dies," *New York Times*, July 21, 1988.

73. Lee Lowenfish, *Branch Rickey*, 492–493.

74. http://losangeles.dodgers.mlb.com/la/history/walter_omalley.jsp.

75. Jackie Robinson to Branch Rickey, 1950 (Undated), Branch Rickey Papers, Box 24, Folder 13, Correspondence, Robinson, Jackie, 1950–1951, Library of Congress.

76. *Ibid.*

6th Inning

1. *The Ghosts of Flatbush*, HBO, July 11, 2007.

2. Andrew Goldblatt, *The Giants and the*

Dodgers: Four Cities, Two Teams, One Rivalry (Jefferson, North Carolina: McFarland & Company, Inc., 2003), 6.

3. "One Game for Brooklyn," *New York Times*, October 19, 1889.

4. Harold Parrott, *The Lords of Baseball*, 39.

5. Leo Durocher, *Nice Guys Finish Last*, 279.

6. *Ibid.*, 280.

7. *Ibid.*, 14.

8. *Ibid.*

9. *Ibid.*

10. *Ibid.*, 284.

11. Joseph Wilkinson, "Flock's Rooters View Giants with Quiet Disdain," *Brooklyn Daily Eagle*, October 3, 1951, 3.

12. Bobby Thomson with Lee Heiman and Bill Gutman, *"The Giants Win the Pennant! the Giants Win the Pennant!": The Amazing 1951 National League Season and the Home Run That Won It All* (New York: Zebra Books, 1991), 241.

13. John Thorn, ed., *The Glory Days: New York Baseball, 1947–1957* (New York: Collins, 2007), 158.

14. Shirley Povich, "This Morning," *The Washington Post*, October 4, 1951.

15. Red Smith, "Views of Sport: Last Chapter," *New York Herald Tribune*, October 4, 1951.

16. Rud Rennie, "Giants Win Pennant in 9th, 5–4, on Thomson's 3-Run Homer, *New York Herald Tribune*.

17. Jimmy Cannon, "Jimmy Cannon Says," *Newsday*, October 4, 1951.

18. Harold C. Burr, "Victory Just Wasn't in Books for Us," *Brooklyn Daily Eagle*, October 4, 1951.

19. Hal Burton, "Change of Pace," *Newsday*, October 4, 1951.

20. Carl Lundquist, "Thomson's HR Caps Giant Comeback," *Newsday*, October 4, 1951.

21. "No Acceptable Excuse Found to Ease Defeat," *Brooklyn Daily Eagle*, October 4, 1951.

22. "It Just Wasn't Meant for Dodgers to Win," *Brooklyn Daily Eagle*, October 4, 1951.

23. Bill Lee, "With Malice Toward None," *The Hartford Courant*, October 4, 1951.

24. Jack Altshul, "Head and Tales: Tony Won't Talk Baseball," *Newsday*, October 4, 1951.

25. Bobby Thomson with Lee Heiman and Bill Gutman, *"The Giants Win the Pennant! the Giants Win the Pennant!,"* 256.

26. *The Ghosts of Flatbush*, HBO, July 11, 2007.

27. Stuart Greenwald, telephone interview with author, January 6, 2012.

28. Ronnie Klein, telephone interview with author, August 22, 2013.

29. I. Kaufman and Sid Frigand, "Dodger, Giant Rooters Jam Stands Early," *Brooklyn Daily Eagle*, October 3, 1951.

30. "She Said It, and She Does," *Brooklyn Daily Eagle*, October 4, 1951.

31. *The Ghosts of Flatbush*, HBO, July 11, 2007.

32. Sal Maglie with Dick Schaap, "I Always Three Bean Balls," *Cavalier*, September 1959.

33. Rud Rennie, "Giants Win Pennant in 9th, 5–4, on Thomson's 3-Run Homer, *New York Herald Tribune*.

34. *Ibid.*

35. Doris Kearns Goodwin, *Wait Till Next Year: A Memoir* (New York: Simon & Schuster, 1997; Paperback ed., Simon & Schuster, 1997), 146. Citations refer to the paperback edition.

36. *Ibid.* 154.

37. Roscoe McGowen, "Dodgers' Pennant Failure Finds Players Despondent but Dressen Unshaken," *New York Times*, October 4, 1951.

38. "1951 Brooklyn Dodgers—New York Giants National League Playoff," an episode in *The Way It Was*, KCET, October 3, 1974.

39. Roscoe McGowen, "Dodgers' Pennant Failure Finds Players Despondent, but Dressen Unshaken," *New York Times*, October 4, 1951.

40. Bobby Thomson with Lee Heiman and Bill Gutman, *"The Giants Win the Pennant! The Giants Win the Pennant!"* 263.

41. *Ibid.*, 263.

42. Joshua Prager, Author's Note to *The Echoing Green: The Untold Story of Bobby Thomson, Ralph Branca and the Shot Heard Round the World* (New York: Pantheon Books, 2006; Paperback ed., New York: Vintage Books, 2008), 351. Citations refer to the paperback edition.

43. Bill Veeck with Ed Linn, *Veeck as in Wreck*, repr. ed. (New York: Putnam, 1962; Chicago: University of Chicago Press, 2001), 161. Citations refer to the University of Chicago edition.

44. Dave Hanson, "Bright not bitter: Blow helped clean up sports," *Des Moines Register*, November 13, 1980.

45. Darlene Greene, telephone interview with author, January 31, 2012.

46. *Ibid.*

47. Scott Vandehey, Introduction, *Verboort:*

A Priest & His People (Forest Grove, Oregon: Wildwood Publishers, 2010), 4.

48. "Not According to Script," *Brooklyn Daily Eagle*, October 24, 1951.

49. Arthur Mann to Branch Rickey, memorandum, 10 March 1948, Arthur Mann Papers, Box 1, Folder 2, General Correspondence, 1947 Jan. 29–1948 Mar. 10, Library of Congress.

50. Kevin Bender, Dana Atchley, Interview with Red Barber, *Baseball's Voices of Summer* (1989; Balltalk Productions: 2007), DVD.

51. Debra Sifen, telephone interview with author, February 22, 2012.

52. Steve Goldberg, telephone interview with author, April 1, 2012.

53. Debra Sifen, telephone interview with author, February 22, 2012.

54. John Drebinger, *Giants Capture Pennant, Beating Dodgers 5–4 in 9th on Thomson's 3-Run Homer*, October 4, 1951.

55. "Telephone Traffic Heavy After the Ball Game," *New York Times*, October 4, 1951.

56. Tommy Holmes, "It Just Wasn't Meant for Dodgers to Win," *Brooklyn Daily Eagle*, October 4, 1951.

57. John Lee Smith to National Baseball Hall of Fame, Undated, Robert Brown Thomson File, National Baseball Hall of Fame and Museum.

58. *Ibid.*

7th Inning

1. Roger Kahn, "An Epilogue for the 1990s and the Millennium," epilogue to *The Boys of Summer*, 447.

2. Irving Rudd and Stan Fischler, *The Sporting Life: The Duke and Jackie, Pee Wee, Razor Phil, Ali, Mushky Jackson and Me* (New York: St. Martin's Press, 1990), 85–86.

3. Rex Lardner, "Talk of the Town: Incidental Music," *The New Yorker*, September 3, 1949, 18.

4. *Ibid.*

5. *Ibid.*

6. Anne Berlin, e-mail message to author, November 13, 2013.

7. Walter Alston with Si Burick, *Alston and the Dodgers* (Garden City, New York: Doubleday & Company, Inc., 1966), 79.

8. Thomas Oliphant, *Praying for Gil Hodges: A Memoir of the 1955 World Series and One Family's Love of the Brooklyn Dodgers* (New York: Thomas Dunne Books, 2005; Paperback ed. (New York: St. Martin's Press, 2006), 256. Citations refer to the paperback edition.

9. *Ibid.*, 36.

10. Tom Clavin and Danny Peary, *Gil Hodges: The Brooklyn Bums, the Miracle Mets, and the Extraordinary Life of a Baseball Legend* (London: New American Library, 2012), 109.

11. *The Ghosts of Flatbush*, HBO, July 11, 2007.

12. Joe Williams, "Everything's Just Lovely in Brooklyn, U.S.A.," *New York World-Telegram and the Sun*, October 5, 1955.

13. Bill Roeder, Podres Life of Party, Too," *New York World-Telegram and the Sun*, October 6, 1955.

14. Chuck Dressen, "Taking Byrne Out the Key," *New York World-Telegram and the Sun*, October 6, 1955.

15. Joe Williams, "When Indians Stole Sign to Beat Bums," *New York World-Telegram and the Sun*, October 6, 1955.

16. Tommy Holmes, *Dodger Daze and Knights: Enough of a Ball Club's History to Explain Its Reputation* (New York: David McKay Company, Inc., 1953), 11.

17. Nicholas Kostis, telephone interview with author, April 21, 2013.

18. Charles Babcock, telephone interview with author, December 20, 2011.

19. Bob Greene, telephone interview with author, March 8, 2012.

20. Branch Rickey III, telephone interview with author, January 4, 2012.

21. Dawna Amino, telephone interview with author, October 1, 2013.

22. Gerald Stern, telephone interview with author, January 6, 2012.

23. Ken Mailender, telephone interview with author, March 21, 2012.

24. Mark Cane, telephone interview with author, May 9, 2012.

25. Marty Appel, telephone interview with author, March 8, 2012.

26. Jerry Wiskin, telephone interview with author, July 14, 2014.

27. Ralph Hunter, interview with author, March 5, 2012.

28. Ron Bittel, telephone interview with author, January 29, 2012.

29. Ron Schweiger, telephone interview with author, June 14, 2011.

30. Ronnie Klein, telephone interview with author, August 22, 2013.

31. Samuel Roberts, telephone interview with author, March 6, 2012.

32. Scott Andes, telephone interview with author, March 4, 2012.

33. Stan Goldberg, telephone interview with author, July 1, 2011.

34. Robert Garfinkel, telephone interview with author, July 24, 2014.

35. Howard McCormack, telephone interview with author, July 14, 2014.

36. Paul Parker, interview with author, August 1, 2014.

37. Stuart Greenwald, telephone interview with author, January 6, 2012.

38. Ted Hollembeak, telephone interview with author, February 22, 2013.

39. Connie Mack III, telephone interview with author, February 23, 2012.

40. Woody Burgener, e-mail message to author, August 2, 2014.

41. Greg DiGiovanna, telephone interview with author, January 29, 2014.

42. John Giordano, telephone interview with author, October 30, 2014.

43. Kenneth Roth, Telephone Interview with author, October 27, 2014.

44. Carl Erskine, Telephone Interview with author, November 1, 2014.

8th Inning

1. *The Ghosts of Flatbush*, HBO, July 11, 2007.

2. *I've Got a Secret*, CBS, October 3, 1956.

3. *Ibid.*

4. Walt Vail, telephone interview with author, February 24, 2012.

5. Ed Schmidt, telephone interview with author, February 24, 2012.

6. *Ibid.*

7. Sheldon Epps, telephone interview with author, March 8, 2012.

8. Lonette McKee, telephone interview with author, February 25, 2012.

9. "Hey, There, Toscanini—Dodgerville's Music Appreciation Night' Produces a Symphony of 2,426 Pieces," *Brooklyn Eagle*, August 14, 1951.

10. *Ibid.*

11. *Ibid.*

12. Frederick Morgan to Marianne Moore, 31 August 1956. Marianne Moore Papers, Hudson Review, Correspondence with Marianne Moore, V:29:33, Rosenbach Museum & Library.

13. Tom Prideaux to Marianne Moore, 19 September 1956, Marianne Moore Papers, Life, Correspondence with Marianne Moore, V:36:20, Rosenbach Museum & Library.

14. Howard Moss to Marianne Moore, 12 September 1956, Marianne Moore Papers, New Yorker, Correspondence with Marianne Moore, V:45:20, Rosenbach Museum & Library.

15. George Plimpton, "The World Series with Marianne Moore," *Harper's Magazine*, October 1964, 51.

16. *Ibid.* at 53.

17. Moe Jaffe, *We're the Boys from Brooklyn (Brooklyn Dodgers)* (New York: Mills Music Inc., 1938).

18. Bennie Benjamin and George Weiss, *The Brooklyn Dodgers* (New York: Leeds Music Corporation, 1946).

19. Bernard Francis Martin, *The Dodger Polka* (Brooklyn: Bernard Francis Martin, 1947).

20. Michael Stratton and George Kleinsinger, *Brooklyn Baseball Cantata* (New York: Mills Music, Inc., 1949).

21. C.G. Funk, *Flatbush Waltz* (C.G. Funk, 1951).

22. Dan Beck, telephone interview with author, May 8, 2013.

23. Jim Gekas and Tony Calderisi, *Mr. Robinson* (2010).

24. Hugo Keesing, telephone interview with author, February 24, 2012.

25. Dave Frishberg, *Van Lingle Mungo* (New York: Red Day Music, 1969).

26. Billy Joel, *We Didn't Start the Fire* (New York: Columbia Records, 1989).

27. Robert Sylvester, Billy Hickey, and Murray Tannen, *I'm in Love with the Dodgers* (Brooklyn: Jo Golden, 1952).

28. William N. Wallace, "Willard Mullin Dies; Cartoonist Created 'Bums,'" *New York Times*, December 22, 1978.

29. *Guadalcanal Diary*, directed by Lewis Seiler (1943; Beverly Hills, CA: Twentieth Century Fox Home Entertainment, Inc., 2002), DVD.

30. *Roogie's Bump*, directed by Harold Young (1954; Burbank, CA: Warner Home Video, 1996), VHS.

31. Jay Neugeboren, "Ebbets Field," *On the Diamond: A Treasury of Baseball Stories*, ed. Martin H. Greenberg (New York: Bonanza Books, 1987), 327. Reprinted by permission of the author.

32. Donald Honig, *The Plot to Kill Jackie Robinson* (New York: Dutton, 1992).

33. Robert B. Parker, *Double Play* (New York: G.P. Putnam's Sons, 2004).

34. Troy Soos, *Murder at Ebbets Field* (New York: Kensington Publishing Corp. 1995; Paperback ed., New York: Kensington Publishing Corp. 2013), 41. Citations refer to the paperback edition.

35. *Ibid.*, 74.

36. "Murder at the World Series," *True Sport Picture Stories*, Volume 3, No. 10 (Nov.-Dec. 1946).

37. *Ibid.*

38. David Povich, telephone interview with author, March 22, 2012.

39. Terence Smith, telephone interview with author, February 24, 2012.

40. Hildy Angius, telephone interview with author, April 3, 2013.

41. http://www.rockwell-center.org/exploring-illustration/game-called-because-of-rain/.

42. *Ibid.*

43. *Ibid.*

44. Alan Gratz, *The Brooklyn Nine: A Novel in Nine Innings* (New York: Scholastic Inc.), 151.

45. Linda Sue Park, *Keeping Score: A Story About Life, Faith, and America's Favorite Pastime, Baseball* (New York: Sandpiper, 2008), 35.

46. Bette Bao Lord, *In the Year of the Boar and Jackie Robinson* (New York: Harper & Row, 1984; Revised Edition, New York: HarperTrophy, 2003), 168. Citations refer to the HarperTrophy edition.

47. Alan Lelchuck, *Brooklyn Boy* (New York: McGraw-Hill Publishing Company, 1990; repr., Madison, Wisconsin: University of Wisconsin Press, 2003), 12–13. Citations refer to the University of Wisconsin Press edition.

48. *Ibid.*, 90.

49. Where Have You Gone, Jackie Robinson?" an episode of *Brooklyn Bridge*, CBS, December 11, 1991.

50. "When Irish Eyes Are Smiling," an episode of *Brooklyn Bridge*, CBS, September 20, 1991.

51. Stan Goldberg, telephone interview with author, July 1, 2011.

52. Stan Goldberg, telephone interview with author, June 11, 2014.

53. "Where Have You Gone, Jackie Robinson?"

54. "Boys of Summer," an episode of *Brooklyn Bridge*, CBS, October 4, 1991.

55. *Ibid.*

56. "Death in Brooklyn," an episode of *Brooklyn Bridge*, CBS, September 27, 1991.

57. "Plaza Sweet," an episode of *Brooklyn Bridge*, CBS, September 19, 1992.

58. Marty Adler, telephone interview with author, June 27, 2011.

59. Colm Tóibín, *Brooklyn* (New York: Scribner, 2009), 148.

60. *It Happened in Flatbush* (20th Century Fox DVD screened by author under restrictions mandated by 20th Century Fox Home Video, 1942).

61. *Ibid.*

62. "The Day the War Stood Still," an episode of *Mchale's Navy*, ABC, September 16, 1963.

63. Dan Parker, "Yanks in Six is My Series Guess," *New York Daily Mirror*, September 28, 1941.

64. Dan Parker, "Flatbush Demands Its Ducky Wucky," *New York Daily Mirror*, April 18, 1942.

65. Dan Parker, "When It's Springtime Out in Flatbush!" *New York Daily Mirror*, April 1, 1942.

66. Robert B. Parker, *Double Play* (New York: G.P. Putnam's Sons, 2004), 284.

9th Inning

1. Roger Kahn, *The Boys of Summer*, xix.

2. *Roll Call* (Culver Military Academy, 1922), p. 118.

3. "A Sound Poker Player," *New York Times*, February 22, 1957.

4. Penelope McMillan, "L.A. Ravine: Fertile Soil for O'Malley," *Los Angeles Times*, June 4, 1978.

5. Arch Murray, "O'Malley Loves Dem Bums," *New York Post*, November 5, 1950.

6. *Ibid.*

7. *Ibid.*

8. *Ibid.*

9. Milton Gross, "The Artful O'Malley and the Dodgers," *True*, May 1954, 50.

10. *Ibid.*, 115.

11. *Ibid.*

12. *Ibid.*, 114.

13. *Ibid.*, 113.

14. *Ibid.*, 114.

15. *Ibid.*, 114.

16. *Ibid.*
17. *Ibid.*
18. *Ibid.*
19. *Ibid.*
20. Neil J. Sullivan, preface to *The Dodgers Move West* (New York: Oxford University Press, Inc. 1987; Paperback ed., Oxford University Press, Inc. 1989), viii. Citations refer to the Paperback edition.
21. Michael D'Antonio, *Forever Blue: The True Story of Walter O'Malley, Baseball's Most Controversial Owner, and the Dodgers of Brooklyn and Los Angeles* (New York: Riverhead Books 2009), 185.
22. Fresco Thompson with Cy Rice, *Every Diamond Doesn't Sparkle: Behind the Scenes with the Dodgers* (New York: Van Rees Press 1964), 144.
23. *Ibid.*, 145.
24. Walter F. O'Malley to Emil Prager, 14 October 1946, Folder 1, Brooklyn Dodgers, Office of Counsel and Vice President, Walter O'Malley, Correspondence, 1946–48, Call Number 2004.003. Walter O'Malley Papers, 1946–1957, Brooklyn Historical Society.
25. George J. Pidgeon to Walter O'Malley, 10 October 1947, Folder 1, Walter O'Malley Papers.
26. Joseph L. McVay to Walter O'Malley, 3 December 1947, Folder 1, Walter O'Malley Papers.
27. Walter F. O'Malley to The Norman Bel Geddes Corp., 16 January 1948, Folder 1, Walter O'Malley Papers.
28. S.H. Bingham to Walter F. O'Malley, 16 May 1951, Folder 2, Brooklyn Dodgers, Office of the President, Walter O'Malley, Correspondence, 1951–53, Call Number 2004.003, Walter O'Malley Papers, 1946–1957, Brooklyn Historical Society.
29. John Bellew to Walter O'Malley, 27 October 1952, Folder 2, Walter O'Malley Papers.
30. Walter F. O'Malley to Frank D. Schroth, 17 June 1952, Folder 2, Walter O'Malley Papers.
31. Walter F. O'Malley, 15 September 1952, Folder 2, Walter O'Malley Papers.
32. Walter F. O'Malley to George V. McLaughlin, 18 June 1953, Folder 2, Walter O'Malley Papers.
33. Robert Moses to Frank D. Schroth, Sr., 16 October 1953, Folder 2, Walter O'Malley Papers.
34. Robert Moses to Walter O'Malley, 20 October 1953, Folder 2, Walter O'Malley Papers.

35. *Ibid.*
36. Walter F. O'Malley to Robert Moses, 28 October 1953, Folder 2, Walter O'Malley Papers.
37. *Ibid.*
38. Robert Moses to Walter F. O'Malley, 2 November 1953, Folder 2, Walter O'Malley Papers.
39. Norman Bel Geddes to Walter F. O'Malley, 31 December 1953, Walter O'Malley Papers.
40. Walter F. O'Malley to Frank Schroth, 11 February 1954, Folder 3, Brooklyn Dodgers, Office of the President, Walter O'Malley, Correspondence, 1954, Call Number 2004.003, Walter O'Malley Papers, Brooklyn Historical Society.
41. Raymond A. Schroth, S.J., *The Eagle and Brooklyn: A Community Newspaper, 1841–1955, Contributions in American Studies, Number 13* (Westport, Connecticut: Greenwood Press 1974), 223, citing Hotel Towers Talk, May 5, 1954, pp. 8–9.
42. Frank D. Schroth to Walter F. O'Malley, Folder 3, Walter O'Malley Papers.
43. Robert Moses to Frank D. Schroth, Sr., Folder 3, Walter O'Malley Papers.
44. Robert Grannis, "Brooklyn Must Never Lose Its Team," *Brooklyn Daily Eagle*, May 2, 1954.
45. Mike Lee to Walter O'Malley, Undated, Folder 3, Walter O'Malley Papers.
46. Walter F. O'Malley to Col. Sidney H. Bingham, 7 April 1955, Folder 4, Brooklyn Dodgers, Office of the President, Walter O'Malley, Correspondence, 1955, Call Number 2004.003, Walter O'Malley Papers, Brooklyn Historical Society.
47. S.H. Bingham to Walter F. O'Malley, 21 April 1955, Folder 4, Walter O'Malley Papers.
48. Walter F. O'Malley to Eero Saarinen, 18 April 1955, Folder 4, Walter O'Malley Papers.
49. Walter F. O'Malley to Harold Boeschenstein, 18 April 1955, Folder 4, Walter O'Malley Papers.
50. Robert J. Quinn to Walter O'Malley, 4 May 1955, Folder 4, Walter O'Malley Papers.
51. Walter F. O'Malley to Robert J. Quinn, 25 May 1955, Folder 4, Walter O'Malley Papers.
52. Walter F. O'Malley to Buckminster Fuller, 26 May 1955, Folder 4, Walter O'Malley Papers.
53. "Fans Are Frantic Over Game Shifts," *New York Times*, August 18, 1955.

54. *Ibid.*

55. *Ibid.*

56. *Ibid.*

57. Sydney Gruson, "Giants Get the Pitch, Seek New Park, Too," *New York Times*, August 19, 1955.

58. Robert Moses, Remarks at Commencement of Pratt Institute, Brooklyn, New York, June 3, 1955, Folder 4, Walter O'Malley Papers.

59. Robert Moses to Walter F. O'Malley, 15 August 1955, Folder 4, Walter O'Malley Papers.

60. Joseph M. Sheehan, "Dodgers to Play in Jersey City on Seven Home Dates Next Year," *New York Times*, August 17, 1955.

61. Robert Moses to Charles M. Richardson, 1 September 1955, Folder 4, Walter O'Malley Papers.

62. *Ibid.*

63. Robert Wagner to Averill Harriman, 30 March 1956, Folder 5, Brooklyn Dodgers, Office of the President, Walter O'Malley, Correspondence, Jan-Apr 1956, Call Number 2004.003, Walter O'Malley Papers, Brooklyn Historical Society.

64. Brooklyn Sports Authority, *Interim Report*, November 15, 1956, Folder 7, Brooklyn Dodgers, Office of the President, Walter O'Malley, Correspondence, November 1956–March 1957, Call Number 2004.003, Walter O'Malley Papers, Brooklyn Historical Society.

65. Walter F. O'Malley to J.G. Taylor Spink, 5 January 1956, Folder 5, Walter O'Malley Papers.

66. J.G. Taylor Spink, *Municipally-Owned Stadia Used by Organized Baseball (Class AA and Higher)*, Addendum to letter, J.G. Taylor Spink to Walter O'Malley, 7 January 1956, Folder 5, Walter O'Malley Papers.

67. Chester A. Allen to Walter F. O'Malley, 6 February 1956, Folder 5, Walter O'Malley Papers.

68. Memorandum by Robert Moses to Robert Wagner, 7 December 1956, Folder 7, Walter O'Malley Papers.

69. Walter F. O'Malley to Frank D. Schroth, 27 December 1956, Folder 7, Walter O'Malley Papers.

70. Memorandum by Walter O'Malley to File, 6 February 1957, Folder 7, Walter O'Malley Papers.

71. Roscoe McGowen, "Dodgers Buy Los Angeles Club, Stirring Talk of Shift to Coast," *New York Times*, February 22, 1957.

72. *Ibid.*

73. Dick Young, "Dodger Franchise May Be Moved Here," *Los Angeles Times*, February 12, 1957.

74. Frank Finch, "Sale of Angels Spurs L.A. Big League Hopes: Wrigley Field Plus Franchise Rights Bought by Dodgers," *Los Angeles Times*, February 22, 1957.

75. *Ibid.*

76. Charles Vanacore to Walter O'Malley, 21 January 1957, Folder 7, Walter O'Malley Papers.

77. Ed Sullivan, "Little Old New York," *New York Daily News*, April 15, 1957.

78. City Fusion Party, "Brooklyn Sports Center Should Be at the Queens Border," news release, April 18, 1957, Folder 8, Brooklyn Dodgers, Office of the President, Walter O'Malley, Correspondence, April–July 1957, Call Number 2004.003, Walter O'Malley Papers, Brooklyn Historical Society.

79. Memorandum by the Corporation Counsel to Dr. John J. Theobald, 9 September 1957, Folder 3, Walter O'Malley Papers.

80. Telegram, John Cashmore to Walter O'Malley, 8 September 1957, Folder 9, Brooklyn Dodgers, Office of the President, Walter O'Malley, Correspondence, August–October 1957, Call Number 2004.003. Walter O'Malley Papers, Brooklyn Historical Society.

81. Walter F. O'Malley to John Cashmore, 9 September 1957, Folder 9, Walter O'Malley Papers.

82. Robert M. Baldwin to Walter O'Malley, 11 September 1957, Folder 9, Walter O'Malley Papers.

83. Telegram from Samuel J. Lefrak to Robert F. Wagner, 12 September 1957, Folder 9, Walter O'Malley Papers.

84. Emanuel Perlmutter, "Dodgers Accept Los Angeles Bid to Move to Coast," *New York Times*, October 9, 1957.

85. Gus Steiger, "Brooks Go! City Seeks N.L. Team," *New York Mirror*, October 9, 1957.

86. Tommy Holmes, "Baseball in Brooklyn: A Colorful Cavalcade—1876 to 1957, *New York Herald Tribune*.

87. Paul Zimmerman, "Happy Fans Flock to Dodger Fete," *Los Angeles Times*, October 29, 1957.

88. Duke Snider, *The Duke of Flatbush*, 197–198.

89. Gladwin Hill, "Los Angeles Pipes Dodgers Aboard," *New York Times*, October 29, 1957.

Buhite, Russell D. *The Continental League: A Personal History.* Lincoln: University of Nebraska Press, 2014.

Bryant, Howard. *Shut Out: A Story of Race and Baseball in Boston.* New York: Routledge, 2002.

Campanella, Roy. *It's Good to Be Alive.* Boston: Little, Brown, 1959.

Campanis, Al. *The Dodgers' Way to Play Baseball.* New York: E. P. Dutton, 1954.

Chadwick, Bruce. *The Dodgers: Memories and Memorabilia from Brooklyn to L. A.* New York: Abbeville Press, 1993.

Chalberg, John C. *Rickey & Robinson: The Preacher, the Player, and America's Game.* Wheeling, IL: Harlan Davidson, 2000.

Clavin, Tom, and Danny Peary. *Gil Hodges: The Brooklyn Bums, the Miracle Mets, and the Extraordinary Life of a Baseball Legend.* New York: New American Library, 2012.

Cohen, Marvin A. *The Dodgers-Giants Rivalry 1900–1957: A Year by Year Retrospective.* Kearny, NE: Morris Publishing, 1999.

Cohen, Stanley. *Dodgers! The First 100 Years.* New York: Birch Lane Press, 1990.

Cooke, Bob, ed. *Wake Up the Echoes: From the Sports Pages of the New York Herald Tribune.* Garden City, NY: Hanover House, 1956.

Cottrell, Robert C. *Two Pioneers: How Hank Greenberg and Jackie Robinson Transformed Baseball—And America.* Washington, D.C.: Potomac, 2012.

Creamer, Robert. *Stengel: His Life and Times.* New York: Simon & Schuster, 1984.

D'Agostino, Dennis, and Bonnie Crosby. *Through a Blue Lens: The Brooklyn Dodgers Photographs of Barney Stein, 1937–1957.* Chicago: Triumph, 2007.

Daley, Arthur. *Inside Baseball: A Half Century of the National Pastime.* New York: Grosset & Dunlap, 1950.

Daly, Steve. *Dem Little Bums: The Nashua Dodgers.* Concord, NH: Plaidswede Publishing, 2002.

D'Antonio, Michael. *Forever Blue: The True Story of Walter O'Malley, Baseball's Most Controversial Owner, and the Dodgers of Brooklyn and Los Angeles.* New York: Riverhead, 2009.

Davis, Tommy, with Paul Gutierrez. *Tales from the Dodger Dugout.* Champaign, IL: Sports Publishing, 2005.

DeLillo, Don. *Pafko at the Wall.* New York: Scribner, 1997 (originally published as the Prologue to *Underworld.* New York: Scribner, 1997).

Delsohn, Steve. *True Blue: The Dramatic History of the Los Angeles Dodgers, Told by the Men Who Lived It.* New York: William Morrow, 2001.

DeMotte, Charles. *Bat, Ball & Bible: Baseball and Sunday Observance in New York.* Washington, D.C.: Potomac, 2013.

Dobbins, Dick. *The Grand Minor League: An Oral History of the Old Pacific Coast League.* Emeryville, CA: Woodford Press, 1999.

Dodgers from Coast to Coast: The Official Visual History of the Dodgers. San Diego: Skybox Press, 2012.

Dorinson, Joseph, and Joram Warmund, eds. *Jackie Robinson: Race, Sports, and the American Dream.* Armonk, NY: M. E. Sharpe, 1998.

Drysdale, Don, with Bob Verdi. *Once a Bum, Always a Dodger: My Life in Baseball from Brooklyn to Los Angeles.* New York: St. Martin's Press, 1990.

Durant, John. *The Dodgers.* New York: Hastings House, 1948.

Durocher, Leo. *The Dodgers and Me: The Inside Story.* New York: Ziff-Davis, 1948.

Durocher, Leo, with Ed Linn. *Nice Guys Finish Last.* New York: Simon & Schuster, 1975.

Eig, Jonathan. *Opening Day: The Story of Jackie Robinson's First Season.* New York: Simon & Schuster, 2007.

Eliot, Marc. *Song of Brooklyn: An Oral History of America's Favorite Borough.* New York: Broadway, 2008.

Endsley, Brian M. *Bums No More: The 1959 Los Angeles Dodgers, World Champions of Baseball.* Jefferson, NC: McFarland, 2009.

Epting, Chris. *Los Angeles's Historic Ballparks.* Charleston, SC: Arcadia Publishing, 2010.

Erskine, Carl. *Tales from the Dodger Dugout.* Champaign, IL: Sports Publishing, 2000.

Erskine, Carl, with Burton Rocks. *What I Learned from Jackie Robinson: A Teammate's Reflections On and Off the Field.* New York: McGraw-Hill, 2005.

Eskenazi, Gerald. *The Lip: A Biography of Leo Durocher.* New York: William Morrow and Company, 1993.

Falkner, David. *Great Time Coming: The Life of Jackie Robinson, from Baseball to Birmingham.* New York: Simon & Schuster, 1995.

Falls, Joe. *50 Years of Sports Writing (And I Still Can't Tell the Difference Between a*

Slider and a Curve). Champaign, IL: Sports Publishing, 1997.

Fetter. Henry D. *Taking on the Yankees: Winning and Losing in the Business of Baseball, 1903–2003.* New York: W. W. Norton & Company, 2003.

Fitzgerald, Ed, ed. *Sport Magazine's Book of Major League Baseball Clubs: The National League.* New York: Grosset & Dunlap, 1955.

_____, ed. *The Story of the Brooklyn Dodgers.* New York: Bantam, 1949.

Fleder, Rob. *Sports Illustrated: Fifty Years of Great Writing, 1954–2004.* New York: Sports Illustrated, 2003.

Frommer, Harvey. *It Happened in Brooklyn: An Oral History of Growing Up in the Borough in the 1940s, 1950s, and 1960s.* New York: Harcourt Brace, 1993.

_____. *New York City Baseball: The Last Golden Age, 1947–1957.* New York: Macmillan, 1980.

_____. *Rickey and Robinson: The Men Who Broke Baseball's Color Barrier.* New York: Macmillan, 1982.

Fussman, Cal. *After Jackie: Pride, Prejudice, and Baseball's Forgotten Heroes: An Oral History.* New York: ESPN, 2007

Getz, Mike. *Brooklyn Dodgers and Their Rivals, 1950–1952.* Brooklyn, NY: Montauk Press, 1999.

Gewecke, Cliff. *Day by Day in Dodgers History.* New York: Leisure Press, 1984.

Godin, Roger A. *The Brooklyn Football Dodgers: The Other "Bums."* Haworth, NJ: St. Johann Press, 2003.

Goldblatt, Andrew. *The Giants and the Dodgers: Four Cities, Two Teams, One Rivalry.* Jefferson, NC: McFarland, 2003.

Goldman, Steven. *Forging Genius: The Making of Casey Stengel.* Washington, D.C.: Potomac, 2005.

Goldstein, Richard. *Superstars and Screwballs: 100 Years of Brooklyn Baseball.* New York: Dutton, 1991.

Golenbock, Peter. *Bums: An Oral History of the Brooklyn Dodgers.* New York: G. P. Putnam's Sons, 1984.

Goodwin, Doris Kearns. *Wait Till Next Year: A Memoir.* New York: Simon & Schuster, 1987.

Gough, David. *Burt Shotton, Dodgers Manager: A Baseball Biography.* Jefferson, NC: McFarland, 1994.

Graham, Frank. *The Brooklyn Dodgers: An Informal History.* New York: G. P. Putnam's Sons, 1945.

_____. *The New York Giants: An Informal History.* New York: G. P. Putnam's Sons, 1952.

_____. *A Farewell to Heroes.* New York: The Viking Press, 1981.

Gratz, Alan. *The Brooklyn Nine: A Novel in Nine Innings.* New York: Scholastic, 2009.

Gruver, Edward. *Koufax.* New York: Taylor Trade Publishing, 2000.

Gutman, Dan. *Jackie & Me.* New York: Avon, 1999.

Halberstam, David, ed. *The Best American Sports Writing of the Century.* New York: Houghton Mifflin, 1999.

Heaphy, Leslie A. *The Negro Leagues: 1869–1960.* Jefferson, NC: McFarland, 2003.

_____. *Satchel Paige and Company: Essays on the Kansas City Monarchs, Their Greatest Star and the Negro Leagues.* Jefferson, NC: McFarland, 2007.

Heinz, W. C. *What a Time It Was: The Best of W. C. Heinz on Sports.* New York: Da Capo Press, 2001.

Herman, Gail. *Who Was Jackie Robinson?* New York: Grosset & Dunlap, 2010.

Higbe, Kirby, with Martin Quigley. *The High Hard One.* New York: The Viking Press, 1967.

Hodges, Russ. *Baseball Complete.* New York: Grosset & Dunlap, 1952.

Hogan, Lawrence D. *Shades of Glory: The Negro Leagues and the Story of African-American Baseball.* Washington, D.C.: National Geographic Society, 2006.

Holmes, Tommy. *Dodger Daze and Knights: Enough of a Ballclub's History to Explain Its Reputation.* New York: David McKay, 1953.

_____. *The Dodgers.* New York: Macmillan Publishing Co., 1975.

Holmes, Tot. *Brooklyn's Babe: The Story of Babe Herman.* Gothenburg, NE: Holmes Publishing, 1990.

_____. *1955: This Is Next Year.* Gothenburg, NE: Holmes, 1995.

Honig, Donald. *Baseball America: The Heroes of the Game and the Times of Their Glory.* New York: Barnes & Noble, 1985.

_____. *The Brooklyn Dodgers: An Illustrated Tribute.* New York: St. Martin's Press, 1981.

_____. *Last Man Out.* New York: Signet, 1994.

_____. *The Plot to Kill Jackie Robinson.* New York: Dutton, 1992.

Hynd, Noel. *The Giants of the Polo Grounds:*

The Glorious Times of Baseball's New York Giants. New York: Doubleday, 1988.

Jacobson, Steve. *Carrying Jackie's Torch: The Players Who Integrated Baseball—And America.* Chicago: Lawrence Hill, 2007.

Jennison, Christopher. *Wait 'Til Next Year.* New York: W. W. Norton & Company, 1974.

Jordan, David M. *Closing 'Em Down: Final Games at Thirteen Classic Ballparks.* Jefferson, NC: McFarland, 2010.

Kahn, Roger. *The Boys of Summer.* New York: Harper & Row, 1972.

_____. *The Era, 1947–1957: When the Yankees, the Giants, and the Dodgers Ruled the World.* New York: Houghton Mifflin, 1993.

_____. *Memories of Summer: When Baseball Was an Art, and Writing About It a Game.* New York: Hyperion, 1994. Reprinted Edition. Lincoln: University of Nebraska Press, 2004.

_____. *Rickey & Robinson: The True Untold Story of the Integration of Baseball.* New York: Rodale, 2014.

Kashatus, William C. *Jackie & Campy: The Untold Story of Their Rocky Relationship and the Breaking of Baseball's Color Line.* Lincoln: University of Nebraska Press 2014.

Kavanagh, Jack, and Norman Macht. *Uncle Robbie.* Cleveland: Society for American Baseball Research, 1999.

Keene, Kerry. *1951: When Giants Played the Game.* Champaign, IL: Sports Publishing, 2001.

Kiernan, Thomas, *The Miracle at Coogan's Bluff.* New York: Thomas Y. Crowell, 1975.

Kirwin, Bill, ed. *Out of the Shadows: African American Baseball from the Cuban Giants to Jackie Robinson.* Lincoln: University of Nebraska Press, 2005

King, Kevin. *All the Stars Came Out That Night.* New York: Dutton, 2005.

Klima, John. *Willie's Boys: The 1948 Birmingham Black Barons, the Last Negro League World Series, and the Making of a Baseball Legend.* Hoboken, NJ: John Wiley & Sons, 2009.

Konte, Joe. *The Rivalry Heard 'Round the World: The Dodgers-Giants Feud from Coast to Coast.* New York: Skyhorse Publishing, 2013.

Koufax, Sandy, with Ed Linn. *Koufax.* New York: Viking Press, 1966.

Knutsen, Chris, and Valerie Steiker, eds. *Brooklyn Was Mine.* New York: Riverhead, 2008.

Kroessler, Jeffrey A. *The Greater New York Sports Chronology.* New York: Columbia University Press, 2010.

Lacy, Sam, with Moses J. Newson. *Fighting for Fairness: The Life Story of Hall of Fame Sportswriter Sam Lacy.* Centreville, MD: Tidewater Publishers, 1998.

Lamb, Chris. *Blackout: The Untold Story of Jackie Robinson's First Spring Training.* Lincoln, NE: Bison, 2004.

_____. *Conspiracy of Silence: Sportswriters and the Long Campaign to Desegregate Baseball.* Lincoln: University of Nebraska Press, 2012.

Lanctot, Neil. *Campy: The Two Lives of Roy Campanella.* New York: Simon & Schuster, 2011.

Lasorda, Tommy, and David Fisher. *The Artful Dodger.* New York: Arbor House, 1985.

Leavell, Linda. *Holding on Upside Down: The Life and Work of Marianne Moore.* New York: Farrar, Straus and Giroux, 2013.

Leavy, Jane. *Sandy Koufax: A Lefty's Legacy.* New York: HarperCollins, 2002.

Lelchuk, Alan. *Brooklyn Boy.* New York, McGraw-Hill Publishing, 1990.

_____. *On Home Ground.* San Diego: Gulliver/Harcourt Brace Jovanovich, 1987.

Liscio, Stephanie M. *Integrating Cleveland Baseball: Media Activism, the Integration of the Indians and the Demise of the Negro League Buckeyes.* Jefferson, NC: McFarland, 2010.

Livingston, E. A "Bud." *Brooklyn and the Civil War.* Charleston, SC: The History Press, 2012.

Long, Michael, ed. *Beyond Home Plate: Jackie Robinson on Life After Baseball.* Syracuse: Syracuse University Press, 2013.

_____, ed. *First Class Citizenship: The Civil Rights Letters of Jackie Robinson.* New York: Times, 2007.

Lord, Bette Bao. *In the Year of the Boar and Jackie Robinson.* New York: HarperTrophy, 1986.

Lowenfish, Lee. *Branch Rickey: Baseball's Ferocious Gentleman.* Lincoln: University of Nebraska Press, 2007.

Luke, Bob. *The Baltimore Elite Giants: Sport and Society in the Age of Negro League Baseball.* Baltimore: Johns Hopkins University Press, 2009.

Mann, Arthur. *Baseball Confidential: Secret History of the War Among Chandler, Durocher, MacPhail, and Rickey.* New York: David McKay Company, 1951.

_____. *Branch Rickey: American in Action.* Cambridge, MA: The Riverside Press, 1957.

_____. *The Jackie Robinson Story.* New York: Grosset & Dunlap, 1950.

Marzano, Rudy. *The Brooklyn Dodgers in the 1940s: How Robinson, MacPhail, Reiser and Rickey Changed Baseball.* Jefferson, NC: McFarland, 2005.

_____. *The Last Years of the Brooklyn Dodgers: A History, 1950–1957*, Jefferson, NC: McFarland, 2008.

_____. *New York Baseball in 1951: The Dodgers, the Giants, the Yankees and the Telescope.* Jefferson, NC: McFarland, 2011.

McCauley, Joseph. *Ebbets Field: Brooklyn's Baseball Shrine.* Bloomington, IN: Author House, 2004.

McCue, Andy. *Mover & Shaker: Walter O'Malley, the Dodgers, & Baseball's Westward Expansion.* Lincoln: University of Nebraska Press, 2014.

McGee, Bob. *The Greatest Ballpark Ever: Ebbets Field and the Story of the Brooklyn Dodgers.* New Brunswick, NJ: Rivergate, 2005.

McNeil, William F. *The Dodgers Encyclopedia.* New York: Sports Publishing, 1997.

Meany, Tom. *Baseball's Greatest Players.* New York: Grosset & Dunlap, 1954.

Meany, Tom, and others. *The Artful Dodgers.* New York: Grosset & Dunlap, 1954.

Mele, Andrew Paul. *Tearin' Up the Pea Patch: The Brooklyn Dodgers, 1953.* Jefferson, NC: McFarland, 2015.

_____, ed. *A Brooklyn Dodgers Reader.* Jefferson, NC: McFarland, 2005.

Molesworth, Charles. *Marianne Moore: A Literary Life.* Boston: Northeastern University Press, 1990.

Monteleone, John J., ed. *Branch Rickey's Little Blue Book: Wit and Strategy from Baseball's Last Wise Man.* New York: Macmillan, 1995.

Mullin, Willard, Hal Bock and Michael Powers. *Willard Mullin's Golden Age of Baseball.* Seattle: Fantagraphics, 2013.

Murphy, Robert E. *After Many a Summer: The Passing of the Giants and Dodgers and a Golden Age in New York Baseball.* New York: Union Square Press, 2009.

Newspaper Reports About Big League Baseball in the Big Apple: The New York Giants—From the Beginning to the End, 1901–1957. New York: Historical Briefs, 1995.

Niese, Joe. *Burleigh Grimes: Baseball's Last Legal Spitballer.* Jefferson, NC: McFarland, 2013.

Nordell, John R., Jr. *Brooklyn Dodgers: The Last Great Pennant Drive, 1957.* Eynon, PA: Tribute, 2007.

Okrent, Daniel, ed. *American Pastimes: The Very Best of Red Smith.* New York: Library of America, 2013.

Oliphant, Thomas. *Praying for Gil Hodges: A Memoir of the 1955 World Series and One Family's Love of the Brooklyn Dodgers.* New York: Thomas Dunne, 2005.

O'Neal, Bill. *The Pacific Coast League: 1903–1988*, Austin: Eakin Press, 1990.

Park, Linda Sue. *Keeping Score.* New York: Clarion Books, 2008.

Parker, Robert B. *Double Play.* New York: G. P. Putnam's Sons, 2004.

Parrott, Harold. *The Lords of Baseball: A Wry Look at a Side of the Game the Fan Seldom Sees—The Front Office.* New York: Praeger Publishers, 1976.

Peterson, Robert. *Only the Ball Was White: A History of Legendary Black Players and All-Black Professional Teams.* Old Tappan, NJ: Prentice-Hall, 1970. Reprinted Edition. New York: Oxford University Press, 1992.

Polner, Murray. *Branch Rickey: A Biography.* New York: Atheneum, 1982.

Povich, Lynn, Maury Povich, David Povich, and George Solomon. *All Those Mornings … At the Post: The Twentieth Century in Sports from Famed Washington Post Columnist Shirley Povich.* New York: Public Affairs, 2006.

Prager, Joshua. *The Echoing Green: The Untold Story of Bobby Thomson, Ralph Branca and the Shot Heard Round the World.* New York: Pantheon Books, 2006.

Prince, Carl E. *Brooklyn's Dodgers: The Bums, the Borough, and the Best of Baseball, 1947–1957.* New York: Oxford University Press, 1996.

Rampersad, Arnold. *Jackie Robinson: A Biography.* New York: Alfred A. Knopf, 1997.

Reed, Ted. *Carl Furillo, Brooklyn Dodgers All-Star.* Jefferson, NC: McFarland, 2011.

Rhoden, William C. *Forty Million Dollar Slaves.* New York: Crown Publishers, 2006.

Rickey, Branch. *Branch Rickey's Little Blue Book.* Edited from private papers and public writings by John J. Monteleone. New York: Macmillan, 1995.

Rickey, Branch, with Robert Riger. *The American Diamond: A Documentary of the Game of Baseball*. New York: Simon & Schuster, 1965.

Ritter, Lawrence S. *Lost Ballparks: A Celebration of Baseball's Legendary Fields*. New York: Viking Studio, 1992.

Ritz, David. *The Man Who Brought the Dodgers Back to Brooklyn*. New York: Simon & Schuster, 1981.

Robinson, Jackie. *Baseball Has Done It*. Philadelphia: J. B. Lippincott & Co., 1964.

Robinson, Jackie, and Alfred Duckett. *Breakthrough to the Big League: The Story of Jackie Robinson*. New York: Harper & Row, 1965.

Robinson, Jackie, as told to Alfred Duckett. *I Never Had It Made*. New York: G. P. Putnam's Sons, 1972.

Robinson, Jackie, as told to Wendell Smith. *Jackie Robinson: My Own Story*. New York: Greenberg, 1948.

Robinson, Rachel, with Lee Daniels. *Jackie Robinson: An Intimate Portrait*. New York: Abrams, 1996.

Robinson, Ray. *The Home Run Heard 'Round the World: The Dramatic Story of the 1951 Giants-Dodgers Pennant Race*. New York: HarperCollins, 1991.

Robinson, Sharon. *Jackie's Gift*. New York: Viking, 2010.

_____. *Jackie's Nine: Jackie Robinson's Values to Live By*. New York: Scholastic, 2001.

_____. *Promises to Keep*. New York: Scholastic Press, 2004.

_____. *Stealing Home: An Intimate Family Portrait by the Daughter of Jackie Robinson*. New York: HarperCollins, 1996.

_____. *Testing the Ice*. New York: Scholastic Press, 2009.

Roeder, Bill. *Jackie Robinson*. New York: A. S. Barnes and Company, 1950.

Rosenfeld, Harvey. *The Great Chase: The Dodgers-Giants Pennant Race of 1951*. Jefferson, NC: McFarland, 1992.

Rosengren, John. *The Fight of Their Lives: How Juan Marichal and John Roseboro Turned Baseball's Ugliest Brawl into a Story of Forgiveness and Redemption*. Guilford, CT: Lyons Press, 2014.

Rosenthal, Harold. *The 10 Best Years of Baseball: An Informal History of the Fifties*. Chicago: Contemporary, 1979.

Rowan, Carl T., with Jackie Robinson. *Wait Till Next Year*. New York: Random House, 1960.

Ruck, Rob. *Raceball: How the Major Leagues Colonized the Black and Latin Game*. Boston: Beacon Press, 2011.

Rucker, Mark. *Brooklyn Dodgers*. Charleston, SC: Arcadia Publishing, 2002.

Rudd, Irving, and Stan Fischler. *The Sporting Life: The Duke and Jackie, Pee Wee, Razor Phil, Ali, Mushky Jackson and Me*. New York: St. Martin's Press, 1990.

Rutkoff, Peter M., ed. *The Cooperstown Symposium on Baseball and American Culture, 1997 (Jackie Robinson)*. Jefferson, NC: McFarland, 2000.

Schmidt, Ed. *Mr. Rickey Calls a Meeting*. New York: Samuel French, 1989.

Schoor, Gene. *The Complete Dodgers Record Book: An Authoritative Statistical Record of the First 93 Years of Dodger Baseball*. New York: Facts on File, 1984.

_____. *Jackie Robinson*. New York: G. P. Putnam's Sons, 1958.

_____. *The Leo Durocher Story*. New York: Julian Messner, 1955.

_____. *The Pee Wee Reese Story*. New York: Julian Messner, 1956.

_____. *A Pictorial History of the Dodgers: From Brooklyn to Los Angeles*. New York: Leisure Press, 1984.

_____. *Roy Campanella: Man of Courage*. New York: G. P. Putnam's Sons, 1959.

Schroth, Raymond A. *The Eagle and Brooklyn: A Community Newspaper, 1841–1955*. Westport, CT: Greenwood Press, 1974.

Schulman, Grace, ed. *The Poems of Marianne Moore*. New York: Viking Penguin, 2003.

Selzer, Steven Michael. *Meet the Real Joe Black: An Inspiring Life—Baseball, Teaching, Business, Giving*. Bloomington, IN: iUniverse, 2010.

Shafer, Ronald G. *When the Dodgers Were Bridegrooms: Gunner McGunnigle and Brooklyn's Back-to-Back Pennants of 1889 and 1890*, Jefferson, NC: McFarland, 2011.

Shapiro, Michael. *Bottom of the Ninth: Branch Rickey, Casey Stengel, and the Daring Scheme to Save Baseball from Itself*. New York: Times, 2009.

_____. *The Last Good Season: Brooklyn, the Dodgers, and Their Final Pennant Race Together*. New York: Doubleday, 2003.

Shapiro, Milton J. *Jackie Robinson of the Brooklyn Dodgers*. New York: Julian Messner, 1957.

Sheed, Wilfrid. *My Life as a Fan*. New York: Simon & Schuster, 1993.

Shuba, George "Shotgun," as told to Greg Gulas. *My Memories as a Brooklyn Dodger*.

Youngstown, OH: George Shuba Family Enterprises, 2007.

Siegel, Joel, and Martin Charnin. *The First: A Musical*. New York: Samuel French, 1983.

Simon, Scott. *Jackie Robinson and the Integration of Baseball*. Hoboken, NJ: John Wiley & Sons, 2002.

Skipper, John C. *Dazzy Vance: A Biography of the Brooklyn Dodger Hall of Famer*. Jefferson, NC: McFarland, 2007.

Slaughter, Enos, with Kevin Reid. *Country Hardball: The Autobiography of Enos "Country" Slaughter*. Greensboro, NC: Tudor Publishers, 1991.

Smith, H. Allen. *Rhubarb*. Garden City, NY: Doubleday & Co., 1946.

Snider, Duke, with Bill Gilbert. *The Duke of Flatbush*. New York: Kensington Publishing Corp., 1988.

Smith, Curt. *Pull Up a Chair: The Vin Scully Story*. Washington, D.C.: Potomac, 2009.

Smith, Red. *Red Smith on Baseball: The Game's Greatest Writer on the Game's Greatest Years*. Chicago: Ivan R. Dee, 2000.

Snelling, Dennis. *The Pacific Coast League: A Statistical History, 1903–1957*. Jefferson, NC: McFarland, 1995.

Snider, Duke, with Bill Gilbert. *The Duke of Flatbush*. New York: Zebra Books, 1988.

Snider, Duke, with Phil Pepe. *Few and Chosen: Defining Dodgers Greatness Across the Eras*. Chicago: Triumph, 2006.

Snyder, Brad. *Beyond the Shadow of the Senators: The Untold Story of the Homestead Grays and the Integration of Baseball*. New York: Mc-Graw-Hill (Contemporary), 2003.

Soos, Troy. *Murder at Ebbets Field*. New York: Kensington Publishing, 1995.

Sowell, Mike. *The Pitch That Killed: The Story of Carl Mays, Ray Chapman, and the Pennant Race of 1920*. Chicago: Ivan R. Dee, 1989.

Spatz, Lyle. *Bad Bill Dahlen: The Rollicking Life and Times of an Early Baseball Star*. Jefferson, NC: McFarland, 2004.

_____. *Dixie Walker: A Life in Baseball*. Jefferson, NC: McFarland, 2011.

_____, ed. *The Team That Forever Changed Baseball and America: The 1947 Brooklyn Dodgers*. Lincoln: University of Nebraska Press, 2012.

Spoelstra, Jon. *Red Chaser*. CreateSpace Independent Publishing Platform, 2010.

Stevens, "Big" Ed. *The Other Side of the Jackie Robinson Story*. Mustang, OK: Tate Publishing & Enterprises, 2009.

Stout, Glenn. *The Dodgers: 120 Years of Dodgers Baseball*. New York: Houghton Mifflin, 2004.

Stout, Glenn, and Dick Johnson. *Jackie Robinson: Between the Baselines*. San Francisco: Woodford Press, 1997.

Sullivan, Neil J. *The Dodgers Move West*. New York: Oxford University Press, 1987.

Terry, James L. *Long Before the Dodgers: Baseball in Brooklyn, 1855–1884*. Jefferson, NC: McFarland, 2002.

Tiemann, Robert L. *Dodger Classics: Outstanding Games from Each of the Dodgers' 101 Seasons 1883–1983*. St. Louis: Baseball Histories, 1983.

Thomson, Bobby, with Lee Heiman and Bill Gutman. *"The Giants Win the Pennant! The Giants Win the Pennant!" The Amazing 1951 National League Season and the Home Run That Won It All*. New York: Zebra Books, 1991.

Thompson, Fresco, with Cy Rise. *Every Diamond Doesn't Sparkle: Behind the Scenes with the Dodgers*. New York: Van Rees Press, 1964.

Thorn, John, ed. *The Glory Days: New York Baseball 1947–1957*. New York: Collins, 2007.

Thornley, Stew. *New York's Polo Grounds: Land of the Giants*. Philadelphia: Temple University Press, 2000.

Tóibín, Colm. *Brooklyn*. New York: Scribner, 2009.

Travers, Steven. *Dodgers Past & Present*. New York: MVP, 2009.

Trouppe, Quincy. *20 Years Too Soon: Prelude to Major-League Integrated Baseball*. St. Louis: Missouri Historical Society, 1995. First published 1977 by Quincy Trouppe. Reprint has been edited as needed.

Tuite, James. *Sports of the Times: The Arthur Daley Years*. New York: Quadrangle, The New York Times Book, 1975.

Tygiel, Jules. *Baseball's Great Experiment: Jackie Robinson and His Legacy*. New York: Oxford University Press, 1983.

_____. *Extra Bases: Reflections on Jackie Robinson, Race, and Baseball History*. Bison, 2002.

_____, ed. *The Jackie Robinson Reader: Perspectives on an American Hero*. New York: Dutton, 1997.

Uhlberg, Myron. *Dad, Jackie, and Me*. Atlanta: Peachtree Publishers, 2010.

Vandehey, Scott. *Verboort: A Priest & His Peo-*

ple. Forest Grove, OR: Wildwood Publishers, 2010.

Vitti, Jim. *Brooklyn Dodgers in Cuba*. Charleston, SC: Arcadia Publishing, 2011.

Warfield, Don. *The Roaring Redhead: Larry MacPhail—Baseball's Great Innovator*. South Bend, IN: Diamond Communications, 1987.

Weintraub, Robert. *The Victory Season: The End of World War II and the Birth of Baseball's Golden Age*. New York: Little, Brown and Company, 2013.

Whittingham, Richard. *Illustrated History of the Dodgers*. Chicago: Triumph, 2005.

Who's a Bum! The 1955 Brooklyn Dodgers. New York: New York Daily News, 1995.

Willensky, Elliot. *When Brooklyn Was the World: 1920–1957*. New York: Harmony, 1986.

Wilson, John R. M. *Jackie Robinson and the American Dilemma*. New York: Longman, 2010.

Young, Dick. *Roy Campanella*. New York: A. S. Barnes and Company, 1952.

Zachter, Mort. *Gil Hodges: A Hall of Fame Life*. Lincoln and London: University of Nebraska Press, 2015.

Ziegel, Vic. *Summer in the City: New York Baseball 1947–1957*. New York: Harry N. Abrams, 2006.

Zimmerman, Paul. *The Los Angeles Dodgers*. New York: Coward-McCann, 1960.

Zimmerman, Tom. *A Day in the Season of the Los Angeles Dodgers*. New York: Shapolsky Publishers, 1990.

Zimniuch, Fran. *Baseball's New Frontier: A History of Expansion, 1961–1998*. Lincoln: University of Nebraska Press, 2013.

Zingg, Paul J., and Mark D. Medeiros. *Runs, .Hits, and an Era: The Pacific Coast League, 1903–58*. Urbana: University of Illinois Press, 1994.

Zinn, John G., and Paul G. Zinn, eds. *Ebbets Field: Essays and Memories of Brooklyn's Historic Ballpark, 1913–1960*. Jefferson, NC: McFarland, 2013.

Index